A GOOD LIFE
THE PERCEPTION OF **PERFECTION**

A GOOD **LIFE**
THE PERCEPTION OF **PERFECTION**

An Autobiography

(Second Edition)

KARL LORENZ WILLETT

Copyright © Independently Published 2020, 2021, 2022

First edition 2020 Good Life to Perfection Perception: An Autobiography

Second edition 2021 A Good Life: The Perception of Perfection – an Autobiography

Online edition 2022. Reissued revised edition 2025

All rights reserved. This publication must not be reproduced, stored in a retrieval-organised scheme, or used in any way without the prior written permission of Karl Lorenz Willett or his family representative.

Any queries concerning reproduction must be sent to the email address karlwillett@hotmail.com

For complete information, visit the website www.karllorenzwillett.co.uk

No one is to circulate this book in any other binding or cover, and the same must be imposed on any acquirer.

British Library Cataloguing in Publication Data

Data available

ISBN

978-1-80541-710-1 (hardcover)
978-1-80541-711-8 (eBook)

The front cover oil painting and this image represent some of Karl Lorenz Willett's artistic ability.

A GOOD LIFE: THE PERCEPTION OF PERFECTION AN AUTOBIOGRAPHY

Manuscript synopsis.

The relentless belief in a universe with a God and living with a mental illness unbalance Karl Lorenz Willett. A Good Life: The Perception of Perfection is not just a recount of his life's trials and tribulations but a journey of self-discovery and acceptance. It follows from the insightful and intriguing book The Memoir of a Schizophrenia, continuing the tale of his life. Karl had to find the perfect balance and share pivotal stories defining his history. These chronological stories show his life experiences, feelings, thoughts, fears, hopes, and ideas from one year to the next, allowing readers to identify the events that have happened to him. We hear of the authentic stories of his life experiences, thoughts, and philosophies as he moves forward in his quest, leading him to do the right thing and ask himself how not to get it wrong. He invites you to experience his first-person account of a sickness that beset him and how it could serve as a historic guide into the core of our being.

He writes about his health as a schizophrenic patient, the withdrawal attempt from medication, and his mental battles. As his story unfolds, Karl experiences many life challenges and their related psychotic episodes, taking the readers into the dark regions of his mind and compelling them to witness a healing process. While A Good Life primarily focuses on Karl's healing journey, it offers potent insights into theology, psychology, sociology, cosmology, and relationships. He said, "A Good Life lets me better reflect on my moral fibre myself and the world around me." The book explores his unique beliefs on life, truth, and themes of illness, family, friendship, and psychic exploration. He speaks about the mind's eye, shifts in consciousness, and unlocking intuition and psychic ability. He writes with uninhibited discourse. The narrative sometimes elicits negative and disturbing expressions and articulates honesty, and it is poetic in parts, but he does not confuse the story with facts. The core concept is that he constantly struggles with the psychological condition of schizophrenia, resulting in cognitive impairment. Readers will understand the effects of antipsychotic medication on him and how he had to deal with it over the years. He has shared his thoughts and stories, which makes readers think harder, and it is thought-provoking because the account provides mental stimulation. Karl Lorenz Willett's stream of consciousness while writing offers a genuinely unique viewpoint on paranoid schizophrenia, resulting in a hopeful and inspiring message to all who seek strength and insight. It is educational, providing valuable insights into the experience of living with schizophrenia and the challenges of managing the condition. It offers tips or something to think about regarding a place of peace, tranquillity, a utopia, or a world kingdom that has eliminated fights and conflict. It will resonate with readers who want to see another habitable Goldilocks planet in creation.

TABLE OF CONTENTS

Introduction xiii
Author's Notes xvii
1. Family 1
2. Tapering Down the Medication Part 1 5
3. Spring Harvest 28 March–1 April 2016 13
4. The Christian Message 21
5. Tapering Down the Medication Part 2 25
6. Crisis of Feeling 33
7. Keep Pressing On 39
8. Back From the Brink 43
9. Welcome, 2017 47
10. Change From the Bottom Up 51
11. Holiday and Job Loss 55
12. Drug Dose Reduced 59
13. Scary Times 65
14. Optimistic About Saving the Planet 69
15. Continuous Recovery From Schizophrenia 75

16.	Back on Track With Our Finances	81
17.	The Church, Universe, Bible and Me	85
18.	New Year Resolutions 2018	101
19.	Sexual Harassment	105
20.	Research Into Antipsychotic Meeting	113
21.	I Am Getting Irritated by Media News	119
22.	Over Thinking and Feeling Gutted	127
23.	Further Reduction in Medication	133
24.	Schizophrenia Near to Being Deconstructed	139
25.	Final Reduction in Antipsychotic Medication	147
26.	A Letter to the Assessor, GP and Psychiatrist	153
27.	GP's Letter, Pip Claim, DVLA and Memory Lost	157
28.	Schizophrenia Management Without Medication	161
29.	The Placebo Effect and the Void in My Head	165
30.	Nutrient Support and Coping With Stress	175
31.	Writing Needs and Well Without the Pill	183
32.	Change and Uncertainty That Is Coming	193
33.	Referral for CBT or CRT Online	195
34.	Antipsychotic Reduction Programme	201
35.	Medication Withdrawal Effects Charted	205
36.	Discontinued the Treatment for Schizophrenia	211
37.	The Future With Untreated Schizophrenia	215
38.	Government Systems and Our Tamed Nature	229
39.	Keeping Schizophrenia Stuck	249

40.	Government Systems Extended Challenges	253
41.	A Kind of Dementia Not Known	257
42.	My Brain 238 Days off Antipsychotic	261
43.	Headache Persisted and Psychiatry Seems Worthless	277
44.	Hospitalisation With Psychic Phenomena	287
45.	Retake Antipsychotic and Retained Suffering	293
46.	Restarted Meds Give Severe Adverse Outcomes	299
47.	Schizophrenia Recovery, Nearly	305
Epilogue		317
1A	Additional Stories	329
2A	Schizophrenia Characteristics in My Elderly Life	331
3A	Overcoming Nihilistic Thoughts	341
4A	My Development and Game – Changes for My Psychosis	345
5A	Over Sixty-Seven With Remission of Schizophrenia	363
6A	A Traumatic Event	367
7A	Over Sixty-Eight With Remission of Schizophrenia	373
8A	Ageing With Remission Schizophrenia	381
About the Author		389

INTRODUCTION

This edition is updated with new material about me, now an older man in continued remission of schizophrenia and battling cognitive impairments.

The risk factor of age-related changes in pharmacokinetic drugs has been a concern. However, I am deeply grateful that my neuropsychological function has remained stable as I approach 2025 and my sixty-ninth birthday. This stability gives hope for the future and a deep sense of appreciation for the present.

I am dedicated to making this book a literary masterpiece to be read and admired like a fine piece of art or a mesmerising acting performance. I have re-edited and rewritten it to ensure it has a professional editorial feel and a literary construct that will resonate with readers.

I have taken great care to preserve the trueness of the sentences. They were checked by a professional copy editor who advised on changing meaning, ensuring the true sense of what my writing wants to convey will be noticed. The spelling, grammar, punctuation, structure, and style variation may have a mix of insignificant clumsy writing and some fallacies, but the truth remains.

With my writing, I have this bright light and evangelistic message to bring to people. Writing with less-than-perfect grammar is the most easily solvable problem. But, more importantly, it is about making myself understood, and poor grammar can undermine my writing quality. So, the writing methodology, initially an authentic true voice, is written from my profound truth.

It's a struggle, especially for the working-class, non-white or non-male, to survive in today's cut-throat information world where the cultured Eurocentric perspective has been hailed as the highest form of education, and we are fed a diet of male Caucasian stories.

Mastery of language and grammar is not anyone's proprietary work, but understandably, a professional editor who makes grammar mistakes may pay more cost in their academic careers. So, readers of this book are sure to find no lousy grammar, but it is a challenging read.

My subjective awareness affects my mind every waking second. So, I was required to step into the darkest abyss to write down conscious perceptions, emotions, memories, intentions and the affairs of creativity with schizophrenia that demand mental endurance.

This non-fiction book is based on my experience with profound textualised teachings related to psychic perception, in which the mind's eye shifts consciousness into higher-level perception and unlocks intuition and psychic perspectives.

I have been tracing the gradual process of my recovery from mental illness and the changes in my religious and spiritual beliefs. Also, I have thoughts on 'big questions' about living our purpose, the world and the cosmos.

Other people's thoughts make a big difference in the message I want you to hear, and I do not believe it is a coincidence that you are reading my words. I want to welcome you to this book and my other communication methods.

Howdy to all people and things. I feel good here, where you will find me, revealed on this formal and dignified writing system, without making a quantum leap to becoming a public speaker, expert, or entrepreneur.

I am bold enough to be here, and I can feel the depths of emotion that touch people's souls in romance and love when expressed in love songs and seen in relationships. There are tears of joy, and from a broken connection, there is sorrow. I shed many tears at miseries and injustice.

My mind's mechanistic emphatic system metamorphoses my character and releases agonies in its mapping of pain associated with personal, national and global tragedy. The manifestation of an illness is pinpointed in areas from the feet to the head. Symptomatic pain for the world and widespread problems cause agony in the waistline and tightness in the neck.

My story begins when my ability to act appropriately breaks down and leads to a weariness that produces a subjective manifestation of the mental disorder schizophrenia. As a result, I was hospitalised involuntarily and under the Mental Health Act Section 2 for the tenth time. Admission was on 9 August 2019, and they planned for my discharge after thirty-four days (12 September 2019). So, I have learnt the hard way to create and paint the most crucial parts of my life in words, as literary art. Consuming depressive doom news was harmful to my mental health, and those painful surprises in psychosis in this changing world told me to look after number one: my soul, my heart and myself. As we all do, I have a story to tell, and I remain curious about where the journey may take me.

I am addicted to doing the right thing, and my conscience always tells me to do the right thing and asks me how not to get it wrong. So, words are understood by everyone at any level of ability, and the truth will affect people, and lies will affect people too.

Also, I can appreciate my feelings more deeply. *A Good Life* lets me better reflect on my moral fibre, myself and the world around me. If the things I write are perfect, and the words resonate with other people but may not sound the same, it is my authoritative wording, which nobody will be able to change but accept and agree with.

AUTHOR'S NOTES

*Karl's voice is unique in the wave frequency the reader
hears and sees as words processed on the page.*

I have something that I want to share because it will help many people. It is a high mental disorder called paranoid schizophrenia, and it's medicine. It is experiencing stories out of practical purpose, a good life and the perception of perfection, most often when I cannot act or reason. This book is a guide to the historic centre of every human being. Some naturally feel something there that is intellectually nourishing and sense something so proper it is impossible to put a name to it. Some readers may gravitate towards an earnest God-fearing religion, challenging it as spooky; by doing so, reaching the historic, spiritualised source of its infinite energy everywhere in all devices and people is a good idea. In the right and godly, a frequency process is perfected, and it is a good and efficient power that computes exceptionally well in the individual consciousness of humans.

This book will profoundly affect your thoughts and conscience, so it is hard to analyse them. A general audience might need help reading this. So, instead, I look at differences to grow perfect and everyday feelings to explore the mind and the brain's diversity.

I feel blessed in spasmodic readings when I express the strength of my godly, divine purpose, which is steadfast. I could have handled the equation that comes with processing a god complex. No actual harm will come to me because I am safe from genuine fears, except psychological ones that have haunted me.

This book has good advice for trained medical practitioners to give their patients about compliance with the maintenance dose of antipsychotics.

But suppose the reader is ill from a disease with a personal cause. In that case, the subjective manifestation person should consult a medical specialist trained in noticing the objective manifestation of the condition to be treated.

All humankind and its things have a keen, focused awareness. Still, in some circles in human relations, very little training allows them to communicate a person's pure, subjective thought waves.

Highbred people, an elitist-educated group equipped with sensor devices that explore emotional interferences and thinking patterns, have authenticity because the technology is already here. They use technology to keep the authorities listening, slowly absorbing information and data from the innocent people they spy on and whom they observe. People with a dark skin tone, a pale skin tone or shades in between who have a low standard of education are domesticated body-servants, fulfilling elite people's purposes in labouring in inefficient, shoddy work for wages.

I am encouraged by solidarity with everyone and that every moment of life fulfils a purpose. The processed thoughts of ordinary people are controlled by others who can task their psyche or unawares with unconscious messages. Those educated groups understand the human condition and can selfishly manipulate the commoner's thinking, persuading their better nature. It is a method of tasking human minds with unknown, controlled inferences, other than repetitively practising to learn something. Sounds fictitious? A little absurd and science fiction? Agreed, but it will all become more transparent and straightforward as you read these pages and hear the sound variances with the frequency that differs with words to express revealed truths.

As the facts become apparent, the words come together and sing. That is because they are joyous; the information is undoubtedly known now to have truth. Everyone can understand authentic details. Turning the page will reveal some of the events on which the elites have an inferential hold. They release their grip over us only because we, the enlightened ones, see the evidence showing their way of perpetuating fears.

When I had voided my mind of schizophrenia's expectations and opened my eyes to the antics of the reality my dream state had made, I lost resilience. When you have mental flexibility beforehand, the change can seem terrifying.

It gave me vivid perceptions and allowed me to witness actual mental events occurring in pitch darkness. Unfortunately, this makes ordinary people afraid of darkness and shadows, even though nothing in the dark can touch them.

In my life, living by my mental experiences, I have debunked the elitists' methods of driving fears, holding ordinary people back from the truth. So, the elite is cosy and comfortable having or being empowered with knowledge and confidence that most people would rather ignore or fear more than something in the darkness. But, when investigated by curious people like myself, there is nothing to fear but false stories told to them to cover up truths and enlightenment. It is this curiosity, this thirst for knowledge, that drives us to uncover the truths that others fear. At its most basic, the universe is good with a maintenance system that occasionally creates havoc and chaos for the cosmos and people. The consequence raises goose pimples on the elitists' skin because of entropy, but most people are mortally scared; they think they are going mad and are fearful that the end of time is nigh. I get the chills when I experience enhanced, intense emotions. The increase in strength can be likened to being shocked with a bolt of electricity.

Writing my autobiography is still ongoing intellectually. I left school with low grades in academic achievement in English grammar and literature tests. I had poor qualities that were not worth the paper on which they were written, rated five and six at CSE (Certificate of Secondary Education). I have had an official document to remind me that I needed to improve. My speech and writing reflect my poor educational background. I get to the point quickly and most effectively and omit needless names as best I can. And I blunder or stumble over words that do not mean what I think they mean.

I aim to communicate effectively about the things whose outcomes I attempt to predict. As a result, I gradually progress from the start of a problem and reasonably overcome obstacles and challenges. Also, as a result, I am relaxed and not as stressed about issues as I used to be.

As an author, I spend my time thinking, which is essential for optimism and seeing life as infinitely complex and meaningful. Science predicts that the world's physical reality will surely die. Still, I sustain an optimistic vision as an older adult who has passed through pessimism and defeatism about the world since biblical times, which gives us gloom and doom and a strong defeatist bias as commoners make their way in life. I had fallen into this apparent pessimism, leading to suicide attempts and a schizophrenic emotional illness.

I, therefore, invite you to read exclusive information about me by visiting my website, created in October 2018 and refreshed from time to time: www.karllorenzwillett.co.uk

1

FAMILY

Wednesday, 20 April 2016

In picking up this book, I assume you know more or less who I am. However, I am keenly aware that you may not know. I wrote the first part of my memoir over thirty-four years ago, about my childhood, or as far back as I can remember. I was born in 1956, and this second book of my life story has a lot to say about the beginning of the year where I left off in February 2016, in which the stories meander, but I hope a chronology of sorts has emerged as I shift from theme to theme.

I have surprised myself and finished writing my first book, *The Memoir of a Schizophrenic*. People shower me with praise and attribute qualities that seem almost to verge on the divine because they feel it was a big deal, a fantastic achievement, to have written a book. On the other hand, it made me feel more like a star artist than an author, and I have sweaty palms just thinking about telling my experiences of living on the planet and how the world will benefit from my books.

As I write my autobiography, there is never any doubt about the loved people in my life. This book is riddled with self-consciousness and includes a mix of people who have encouraged me. One of the essential people in my life is my wife, Euphemia. Most of my earlier writings about our relationship contain deluded ideas, and she has remained steadfastly and lovingly by my side since we started dating in 1979. We married, and she is the mother of my three beautiful grown children, Katrina, Georgina and Jonathan, and granny to our three delightful grandchildren, Iziah, Isaac and Kyven. Our eldest daughter, Katrina, is pregnant and expecting her second child in the autumn.*

Readers who take the time to read this book may seek to understand the mindset of people with schizophrenia, and their niggling questions may be answered. Also, I have charted my use of antipsychotic medication and my eagerness to discontinue their application and remain well. I treasure all my experiences and value everyone. Although I have been unfortunate to have this disorder of the mind, I have made this a blessing and a part of who I am. I have been fortunate to emerge from most of what happened to me, from failures to successes, and this book sets out to chronicle the pride, joy and happiness with which I have been blessed. I am immensely honoured to be the subject of your interest, and I hope I provide entertainment along the way. But my writings are not merely for enjoyment and entertainment, for your reading pleasure or my writing pleasure; they are written for close reading and to improve people's lives. I am excited to write using a computer keyboard, a

---

* Our fourth grandchild, a boy named Jenson Peter Nelson, was born on Saturday, 15 October 2016.

mouse and a screen. I have ditched long handwriting with a pen, which presented difficulties in perfecting drafts or rewrites; I am glad to scribble my notes on paper, write with this relatively new technology and have breaks to go to the loo. There is no discernible plot; the story drama does not involve a villain. Instead, the conflict arises from the emotions within me.

TAPERING DOWN THE MEDICATION PART 1

Monday, 25 April 2016

I last spoke to a psychiatrist in November 2015 about my maintenance dose of 25 mg of aripiprazole: one 10 mg tablet and one 15 mg tablet. He had little doubt that lifetime treatment on antipsychotic medication is worthwhile, helpful and necessary to avoid a relapse of the psychotic illness.

Recently, there has been controversy about the long-term use of antipsychotic drugs. In my experience, because of negative symptoms and rehospitalisations, long-term use of antipsychotic meds has not played a crucial role in maintaining remission, averting relapse or improving the quality of my life. Now, it has my mortality in sight. However, there is no question that when I am suffering from chronic, debilitating symptoms of schizophrenia, antipsychotic medication is a critical component of treatment.

Small studies have shown that long-term use of antipsychotic drugs causes worsening schizophrenia. However, there is so much doubt about their sweeping generalisation that the long-term use of antipsychotic medication harms patients. So, I have to decide to discontinue antipsychotics to see a better outcome.

It so happened that I came to hear about a mental health research charity called the McPin Foundation, which, in collaboration with a broader research team, is doing a six-year research trial into medicine to control psychotic symptoms, the Research into Antipsychotic Discontinuation and Reduction (RADAR) study, led by University College London. I filled in the application form to be on the lived experience advisory panel, and my application was successful. I attended a meeting at the McPin Foundation office in London.

I am considering tapering down from the high dose of aripiprazole over two years with a psychiatrist coordinating my care. First, I spoke to my GP, who sent a referral to get me back into the secondary care system to be monitored periodically by a psychiatrist. Still, my GP had doubts about the risks and did not feel confident that the psychiatrist would support my decision to stop antipsychotic medication gradually over the next two years. So, instead of speaking to a psychiatrist, I had to discuss the issue with a psychiatric nurse.

I debated my intention with the psychiatric nurse on the telephone, and she was attempting to get a psychiatrist to coordinate my care. I had intended to reduce my medication as soon as possible and seek psychiatrist approval, but nothing has come of it since I last talked to the nurse in early April 2016. I have not heard anything.

Clinicians, such as GPs, and some literature point to considerable risk in discontinuing antipsychotic treatment. However, critics still claim it is merely a 'withdrawal effect' that occurs when antipsychotic medication is stopped abruptly. Still, it is a highly speculative hypothesis, including the thought that there is a possibility that the drug can cause structural changes in specific brain regions. Taking the medication to help my body do something it is not doing efficiently was the point of having the medicine. Unfortunately, the drug was designed to modify my brain functions, impacting my memory on some level. It causes forgetfulness and difficulty in concentrating for more than three hours. Losing any of my mental capacity is a big deal, and it indicates that I need to compromise, but it is a harsh and unfair choice that I have to face living with mental illness.

It is excellent that symptoms such as hearing hallucinations, autistic thinking, delusions and paranoid thoughts have gone. The very frightening phenomenon that forces my hands to move unexpectedly to body parts, including my genitalia, has given rise to undesirable actions in those areas. Moving body parts swiftly and involuntarily or stiffening them up seems to have been activated by external inferences.

The negative symptoms have persisted, except for the autistic behaviours and ambivalence, where I am too withdrawn and cannot decide. I urinate a lot more, and my body weight has increased, gaining two inches to my waistline; it is now thirty-eight inches.

I get extreme muscle aches in my neck at night and intolerably painful legs. The psychiatrist typically focuses on considerations related to hallucinations, delusions, disorganised behaviour and hostility, which antipsychotic meds are most helpful in treating. So, I must endure physical pain until the prescribed painkillers ease it slightly.

My problems include motivation, clarity of speech and sleeping for up to sixteen hours a day sometimes. The psychiatrist is unaware of the impact of negative symptoms on me. They result from antipsychotic treatment, which could include the physical pains from which I cannot get relief altogether. I believe the effects of a high dose of antipsychotics on relapse episodes are limited. It should gradually taper once I am stable, with the option to restart promptly only if and when symptoms return later. I progressively believe that I should have steadily tapered off my medication. But I feel like a coward and am afraid without the psychiatrist's support because it will be a painful lesson to learn if I am not okay and have relapsed.

Going off meds would be a risky gamble; imagining the symptoms regulated without medication is a dangerous fantasy. Coming off meds is a risk that is usually not worth taking. Still, I am concerned about weight gain on the meds, increased risk of diabetes and cardiovascular disease, and shortened life expectancy. I have already gained weight and am trying to diet and eat healthily; it is a sufficient warning, and critics generalise that antipsychotics harm everyone.

I have done quite well on antipsychotic meds when I have chronic psychotic symptoms. I have to decide whether to stay on or off antipsychotics, which seems to be a choice between extended healthy living or unhealthy early death. I used discontinuation studies to determine relapse rates, but many variables are in play. It is like comparing bananas and pears. It is valid to say that the case is not close to being proven yet, but I realise the tremendous significance of withdrawal could work better. The real lesson from this is that I need to be humble and not assume that discontinuing an antipsychotic drug is right for me because there are disastrous consequences for getting it wrong. Schizophrenia is unique to me and needs carefully tailored treatment with antipsychotics for a while. I do not have that patient-centred approach to therapy; it is a one-size-fits-all to which mental illness applies.

Also, bigotry continues because there are low expectations for people with schizophrenia. There seem to be profound inequalities in treating me as an ethnic black man with schizophrenia. Getting access to mental health treatment is not helping my aim for a sustainable recovery outcome. I have anecdotal evidence that pursuing recovery using medication kept me in a cycle of suffering. I had my ninth breakdown in 2014 since my schizophrenia diagnosis in 1977. I took the drug religiously, but my origin, as a Caribbean man, was probably targeted. The health professionals did not adequately respond to or energetically support my needs as an individual or anyone who was concerned about me. There has been a disproportionate amount of heavy-handedness in involving the police in my access to mental health treatment over the years.

More than half of all my hospital admissions have Section 2 detentions under the Mental Health Act. Most of the time, with police intervention. It was utterly unnecessary. Still, I became stubborn and resisted because I had expected to go into the hospital voluntarily. The mental health team involved the police before engaging with my family or me in deciding to have them present. I strove to learn from my lived experiences of the system and use the black community's lens to talk about poor skills in mental health services.

I hold the person at the top of the mental health board accountable for their low level of engagement at the grassroots level. Their structural factors engender racism, discrimination, stigmatising, stereotyping and deprivation of black people experiencing mental health problems.

> When schizophrenia is alive in me, my brain makes up a vision of what is real. So, seeing was not always believing because my brain filled in the mindless gaps in my view, and I began to trust this fake vision more than the real thing.

Also, they say real-life perception does not accurately represent the world because the brain trusts its generated information more than it sees outside. When my mind goes into psychosis, it stops observing reality as a passive observer and changes how I see things based partly on my mindset. It seems my mind changes the facts when stressed; it affects my capabilities and performance and depletes my health and vitality.

In all our perceptions of the world, technological change and consciousness are forever present in our attributes, which are the ultimate source of value: moral rationality. Still, my humanity intrinsically connects with the natural world. There is no enormous input for my brain to interpret anymore, for there are no delusions. I am almost free from suffering. My mind has naturally created a historical reality to explain what I experience through the senses. My values will shape my future, and my culture will shape my values and past. My hormones mess with my head and sift fact from fiction, and I want to blame my out-of-control moments on this biochemical signalling. I like to think I am in charge of my behaviour, my thoughts are under my conscious control, and my actions are mostly reasonable, but I blame a surge in hormones for making me feel and act like a different person. My biographical history is dominated by schizophrenia, but I think my character must be my creation.

I can recall a moment –and it was probably my fourth episode of psychosis in the twentieth century – when my wife and the GP were observing me taking the prescribed pill, and I tried to pass it down my neck. I did not attempt to open my mouth. I was about to drop it down the indent where the Adam's apple sits on the throat. I took the pill in my hand and put my hand through the V of my shirt collar. They told me I would have to open my mouth and take it with a glass of water, which my wife had in her hand. I had a distorted view of my existence (body ownership and mind) and the environment. Where the doctor and my wife were, the objects in the room took on a distorted appearance.

As a survivor of over forty years of psychiatric drugging, which is psychiatrically disabling, I am fighting the mental health care system to take a paradigm shift and stop using a high dose of antipsychotic drugs for maintenance treatment. Unfortunately, it is tough for the psychiatry industry to swallow, so they must try harder.

3

SPRING HARVEST 28 MARCH– 1 APRIL 2016

Thursday, 28 April 2016

I went to my first religious festival at Butlin's in Skegness, called Spring Harvest, with my wife and two female friends. We gathered with Christians of all ages and stages of faith from around the UK and beyond. We stayed for five days, using the Butlin's facilities, and we could chill out; I was self-inspired and felt confident from the week's theme: 'The Game Changers'. I felt energised by the Bible's teachings, which have not lost their purchase on my collective imagination, and when one thinks hard to consider the evidence outside of scripture, they say it amounts to "a lack of faith". I enjoyed the celebration, singing and the religious atmosphere. I wanted to understand the Bible and whether we are kidding ourselves about Christianity.

I wanted to strip away the centuries of theological interpretation of the biblical text, like writing narratives, aphorisms and poems.

The thoughts in my mind were the letters that both the Old and New Testament Bible authors used for their purposes and textual anomalies in the book from overzealous interpreters.

Would they tell us the worthy truism about Christianity, which is about the living and not the dead? The strength of ultimate love in a person is more powerful, incredible and expressive than the death of people. Death can go no further, but love lives forever in the hearts of mortals, creatures and vessels, and the things it touches or in its forever existence.

Is Christianity a lie when it says Jesus died for the sins of the world and Jesus rose from the dead?

I attended lectures on the 'big' questions, and they calculated that the equation between humanity and God is incomplete without Jesus Christ. From a lawyer's perspective, the evidence is there to prove the resurrection, the expiration of God, and why suffering blames humankind for interfering with nature, like climate change. Could they not see the fraught relationship between humanity and the one God who first appeared to Moses? Yet, only Christians gave Jesus, God's only son, for our sins; he needed to be crucified and then rose from the dead for us to have atonement. With open contempt, I rejected the idea that an all-powerful, omnipotent, omniscient being would want what I hear is called substitutionary atonement.

I cannot find all good, valid memories of the ancient people's past. Stories from the Bible are stories of wisdom; some speak with no sense at all and are fabricated lies that put fear in the absolute functional good of God. Those determinist elitists have opposed this energy since the beginning of known time; the eye of every human consciousness has invisible, unseeing power linked to the 'Creator God' of the divine absolute's forever functioning good source.

Eventually, people found ways to thank and appreciate the cause that brought them into existence. All people aimed to reach the best human standard of their time on Earth to get closer and closer to what seems to be an impossible, impeccable source of perfection. So, ancient people started the journey they could see in their mind's eye; nothing is impossible, and they got as close to the centre of experiences in truths, to the excellent worthiness of being in the middle ground, as possible.

The opposers deliberately shut down their forward, inner-looking navigation system, resulting in a choice to latch on to a dumb state. So, the foolish and the ridiculous appeared intelligent, and they became more brilliant than the rest of us, but in the truth of advanced knowledge of reality, they are not at all clever but smartly stupid.

The intended purpose of those people bedded in extreme variables loitering in the alley of our good intentions leads to an immortal criminal offence to change our minds, to discredit the very existence of a God. This beginner energy creature is universal forever. It is an unperishable substance in people who are still aware of what made them exist. Those people are warped by their diverse faculty perceptions of the mechanics of eventuality and reality; they lie because they became blind, and the universe is giving them time on Earth to reconnect to the absolute wisdom of truth.

Christianity's awfulness is not a surprising truth. Since the dawn of time, the diverse power that envies the pure love of the good has been a constant throughout history, acting up in untrustworthy people. They untangled themselves from the rigid hold of good causes, fought for the wrong reasons, and flourished in the harms of this cunning environment that had no intention of being good.

People witnessed a public event in Christianity and recorded it in human history. Unfortunately, elitist non-conformists kept meddling with the message and making changes. Differences in interpretation kept popping up to discredit the truth of the news that occurred, which is entirely open to scrutiny and investigation. The noble life of the man Jesus is a story of a godly, mentally focused person who dispersed the negative thoughts that plagued him. Still, he was an ethically sound man with an agenda to abide fully. He practised the complicated and most challenging disciplines that are exemplary and correct and used them to connect and embrace our full humanity. Jesus was one of the best examples of truths and love, portrayed in his thinking, feelings and behaviour towards others.

He asked his followers to practise those same principles in themselves continually. Practise the best control from one human being to another and develop continuous training to become their absolute best. He told them his futurist dreams of himself so the community would see they would be a better place. It resonated with people to imagine peace on earth and a heaven place, for their thought of hell is destructive; the hellishness of their existence was not forever. Change is inevitable, and the vision of heaven will be reached by sticking to ethical, rightful principles. Unfortunately, the authorities killed a good man who went around practising the best in the human condition and relied on his internal sound system to keep the focus on regulating what was wrong with us and was always with us.

I reflected on my thoughts, which were far removed from the lecturer's point of view. I shall continue my inward world journey of non-denominational God-centred merits in living a high-principle life. I have a sensitive, alert conscience not to deliberately break the rules gifted to us that teach us the best in human functioning that we can have, and I would feel the hurt in opposing them. The lecturers' speeches affirmed the full support of the traditional history of Christian doctrine on the humanity and deity of Jesus, faith in Christ's divinity, death and resurrection.

I had a vigorous debate over whether I was correct in wanting to state that I do not believe in the divinity of Jesus as fully God and a perfect man. He lived by high ethical and morally right principles and aimed for the perfection of an entirely godly life. The god of the Old Testament they discussed was sick for playing death games with his people. Destroy humanity and kill innocent men, women and children. That is sick! The god in me that opens up my senses and leads me to the truth, which is good and righteous and of love, cannot see that God's spoken word in the Bible is the true 'God' of creation. You may have been concerned and criticised and argued with me about divinity and God. But under the influence of my sick mind, the divine spiritedness in my cells reaffirmed that God was with me to release the suitable proteins and feel-good hormones for my hellishness to go away.

Jesus was a good-spirited man born into a refugee family fleeing a murderous regime. It was a turbulent time. Jesus, a holy man, lived in a religious part of the Middle East under the occupation of a foreign power. The earliest witness of the Church altered the Jewish faith; the things that they lived and died for were still in their sins and needed to be pitied. Jesus was the very best that he could be.

We all have holiness and divineness, and we cannot claim we are God-like. The disciples believed Jesus was God because he remained holy and pure and lived according to an ethical code. His death caused an ethical dilemma, moral injury and profound psychological consequences. The stories of Good Friday, Easter and the cross are universal. In Jesus' journey, we witness the passage of injustice, persecution, suffering and death that many people experience. We also observe the ultimate example of forgiveness and hope from despair. Jesus spoke to people about forgiveness instead of taking revenge and was unjustly tried and executed. Jesus, a good man proclaiming this way of life, will be no more; believers, we will be in a heavenly place. His day's religious and political powers could not comprehend whom he was talking about or the message about ourselves we must learn. Jesus endured a sham trial by the Sanhedrin, the supreme court of the time, and under pressure, Peter, Jesus' most loyal friend, would claim he did not know him. In my journey to discover the truth about the Christian religion, Jesus' crucifixion was not pretty; it was awful. He was exposed, humiliated and executed ruthlessly, and little has changed in two millennia.

I am worried that future generations will still inherit a world fractured by divisions and wars. Does humanity know what they are doing to let religious and political pressures rule the world again? Humankind compromises justice by sometimes putting people into 'deserving' and 'undeserving' categories. The consequences for those considered unworthy can be terrible as they are consigned to places where fundamental human rights and justice are denied. Thank God for Jesus for speaking of a different kingdom with a different set of values. In his physical and mental torment on the cross, Jesus faced the terror racing in his heart and eroding essential trust in God's energy, a permeating system of eternal love, the vital power in the good that exists forever, but he feared it was the ultimate end of his life; his existence ended here. Jesus silenced his doubts and trusted that love is more durable than any other force, even though such love makes kindness seem unrealistic, even irresponsible. Jesus' final word placed his consciousness in a god we trusted and committed his knowing spirit to it, confident he'd be back, but not, in reality, to a place known in our earthly life. The rhetorical abstraction about how he had risen from the dead could be a faux pas, an embarrassing social blunder that generation after generation of people do not want to think about fixing, which includes the bizarre claim of a virgin birth.

Christians can be confident that there is plenty of archaeological evidence for the many events, people and places described in the Bible. When the truth of the Bible gets tested, there are reasonable grounds to trust it. The Bible presents us with the message of the kingdom of God but seems coded with words that look and sound familiar but have differing meanings, which irritates me. There are things in the Bible that have no archaeological evidence. The stories are told in parables or are metaphors to teach us something about the human spirit of God within our souls, and they are hard to understand. Despite all the debates, the Bible remains a trustworthy source for the history of ancient people and places. Still, the messages have been tampered with, and it appears European people have changed the origin to suit an agenda that is not spiritual.

Admittedly, we should look inwardly to meditation, our dream state, and our conscious and subconscious birth to navigate this first earthly reality of 'time'. There are probably three different realities that our human, unseen, spiritual waves must reach to have the conscious eternal life our creator made for us in a different kind of realism. Even if we cannot prove that a miracle happened, the Bible deals with real people of their time and in real places. Biblical characters left their ideas in writings on stones; their handprints and footprints are all over the planet. Foreign people without spiritual insight ravaged the land, abused the original people's knowledge and manipulated the facts for their culture to have super supremacy and authority over all people.

Good theology can justify some nasty things. Jesus was constantly teaching his Jewish compatriots to unlearn the untruths of Judaism, and many people needed more time to be ready for the tangible evidence that made Christology entirely rational. We need a spiritual science that will show the masses that the elite wrote religion to have control over them. I discovered that before Christianity, most religions did not place a high value on morality. Almost all people who have ever lived, I think, believed in a god or, more likely, gods. The gods our ancestors found were unlike what most people believe today. They do not seem to need great religion or the intuitive mental tool of morality today, and moralising faiths like Christianity are doomed because more affluent parts of the world see its decline. The Church's control of earthly life has waned, but I do not think religion will disappear altogether because it contains God. Moralising looks less relevant than ever, and some people are worried that anarchy will ensue without moral guidance. If religion continues to preach about God, poverty, chastity and obedience, we will do well without moralising. And it seems any set of beliefs about God are being used to justify selfishness and cruelty.

4

THE CHRISTIAN MESSAGE

The Christianity that is selling is not the truth in a man and God. It has a poor interpretation of a good man's vision and God.

Jesus was a good, gifted, disciplined and realistic man who went to places to share and to fill people's hearts with God's rigid principles. That promise was guaranteed to bring their lives to a level of perfection and discipline they would enjoy and develop the best control of negativity in their thoughts. In you, there are godly, saintly, ethical codes and soundings of positivity to practise; anchor your guide to them. So, it makes sense for these to be teachings. They will lead you firmly into a good life and the absolute afterlife. You will not have a thing to fear, for you are in the fields of the ultimate good 'God'. It is not a reward, but just how good things can be when you opt to work to change your life around for the better, and the good 'God' will bless you into living eternity.

Those who choose to continue to do wrong or stay negatively charged with harm are dead for eternity. They will not get to live in eternity, as the road they have taken in life on Earth does not go there. It has to lead them to die the absolute death of the dead. So, you will not return. It is not moral punishment or something to hurt; it is the universal law of fairness for the afterlife.

Some people fear religions because they often do not practise the more loving parts of what they have heard preached, and preachers do not do what they have said.

Christianity and traditional religions are not just growing; they are experiencing a global phenomenon. This growth, however, is not as pronounced in the West. These religions are built on the belief in a personal, moralistic God who oversees sexual practices, cares about human actions, and metes out appropriate rewards and punishments. Some argue that the reason for this flourishing is rooted in ignorance.

It is true that, in today's world, people who are part of evolving religious beliefs are rethinking the religion given to us, and I am one of them. This fits twenty-first-century experiences of working faith and knowledge of the world. Moral condemnation will decrease with religious belief as our environment in this wealthier part of the world improves even more. Maybe they started the idea that a good God created an ordered universe and that this God demands moral behaviour from his paramount creation, humankind. The critical success of Western faith is a belief in civilisation moving forward, giving a reason to rethink moralising religions so they can eventually disappear and be replaced with a new ideology.

My mind seems extremely receptive to supernatural explanations for the world around me, and religiosity is a default setting when there are personal and societal upheavals. Unbelief in God does not seem to entail unbelief in other supernatural phenomena. That seems weird, and I guess people who do not believe in God still have a moral compass and live with similar values to those who accept religion or spirituality. But it must be that atheists can be religious too, as Buddhists technically are. Non-religious people are humanists, and moral virtue or tolerance is not guaranteed. But habits of kindness, empathy, decency and patience come from practice rather than belief.

I hope that Western societies and the rest of the world's ruthless rogues do not use evil ideology and undo the outstanding achievements of the human race to make their honest and moral evaluations from saintly personality traits of empathic people. I hope, even though some people do not ascribe ultimate meaning to the universe, nature and themselves. Instead, they endorse objective values and human dignity to religious and solely spiritual people. Unfortunately, the diversity of people's views and ideas which do not acknowledge supernatural phenomena seems to be increasing and is set at extremes of opinion. It is not suitable for humanity and the planet. They directly threaten other human lives, harm other species and separate living things, which encourages significant divides.

5

TAPERING DOWN THE MEDICATION PART 2

Sunday, 12 June 2016

On Friday, 3 June 2016, I received a response letter from the primary care liaison team apologising for taking so long to write back. However, in my request to reduce my antipsychotic medication, one of the psychiatrists needed more information about the RADAR study and what I wanted. Therefore, before it could be agreed upon, I had to write about the research details and the support I required. Consequently, I wrote the following letter to the psychiatrist on 7 June 2016:

> Howdy do, Doctor,
> I thank you for your involvement and the clinician's support in helping to stop my antipsychotic medication; I already have family support.

There has been controversy regarding the use of antipsychotic maintenance treatment. The Research into Antipsychotic Discontinuation and Reduction (RADAR) trial aims to try and reduce slowly and, if possible, stop prescribing our antipsychotic medication. I am interested in the study, but only service users in the London area can apply. I am on the RADAR LEAP group, the lived experience advisory panel, and the mental health research charity McPin Foundation's research team doing the six-year study.

How does the study work?

Service users are divided into groups A and B. Their psychiatrist is told that their patient has either gone into the drug reduction group (A) or the treatment group (B), which involves participants continuing on their dose of antipsychotic medication. The computer will randomly decide to which group participants are assigned.

I am not in the geographical area to take part in the study. However, I am keen to bring to your attention my need to have my high drug dose discontinued within two years at a constant reduction until I am entirely off antipsychotics.

Why I want to come off antipsychotic meds and how you can help

In trying to control averting relapses, antipsychotics were not maintaining remission, and now my mortality is in sight. The drug's use has reduced my life expectancy by twenty years less than the rest of the population.

There is no question that when I am suffering from chronic, debilitating symptoms of schizophrenia, antipsychotic medication is a critical component of treatment. Unfortunately, small studies have recently shown that long-term use of antipsychotic drugs causes worsening schizophrenia.

I want to taper down from the high dose of 25 mg of aripiprazole over two years with a psychiatrist coordinating my care. I heard it said antipsychotic drugs could cause structural changes in specific brain regions and shrinkage of brain tissues. The medication was given to me to modify how my brain functions, which has impacted my memory somehow.

It is excellent that the positive symptoms (hearing hallucinations, delusions and paranoid thoughts) have gone, but the negative symptoms have persisted. I now believe I should only be given medication in an episode of relapse, get gradually tapered once stabilised, and promptly restart if and when symptoms return.

Coming off meds would be a risky gamble that is usually not worth taking. Still, I am concerned about the meds increasing cardiovascular disease and diabetes risks. My late mother was diabetic; my aunt lost sight because of it. In addition, my father died of a degenerative illness, PSP, and I have schizophrenia, with the seeds of destruction sown very early during my brain development. So, I am anxious that using antipsychotic medication will shorten life expectancy even further.

I'll be sixty years old on my next birthday, 14 September 2016, and the decision to stay on or off my antipsychotics has tremendous significance in my life because it seems a matter of mortality. Of course, it is valid to say that the case is not close to proven yet about antipsychotic drugs, but I have learnt the truth that smaller doses for shorter periods could work better.

Schizophrenia is unique to me, and I do not feel I am getting adequate treatment; it's a one-size-fits-all approach in which mental illness is applicable. Furthermore, I have anecdotal evidence that pursuing recovery using antipsychotic medication stuck me in a cycle of suffering.

Support required

I will meet with the psychiatrist to discuss the best way to start reducing my antipsychotics and the reduction schedule. Finally, I will decide with the psychiatrist to lower the dose after this appointment.

We will also discuss making a relapse prevention plan to identify early signs of relapse.

Follow-up schedule

During the rest of the two years, I will reduce my antipsychotic meds every six months; I might want to cut down slowly or more quickly, and I must discuss the reduction schedule with the psychiatrist if I want to change it.

I will see the psychiatrist once every three months. When I see the psychiatrist, he should find out how I am on the lower dose and whether or not I am happy to reduce it more.

I aim to go on to the lowest dose of antipsychotics eventually. Then, if I feel okay about the treatment, I can stop taking my antipsychotics.

I suggest the schedule be discussed with the psychiatrist, who can advise me.

Month 1: 25 mg of aripiprazole

Month 3: 20 mg of aripiprazole

Month 9: 15 mg of aripiprazole

Month 18: 5 mg of aripiprazole

Month 24: stop if possible

I believe that once I am stable and the symptoms of schizophrenia have disappeared, my brain may be able to mend itself and reverse schizophrenia symptoms. It is fortunate that I now want to use this last cycle of my life to come off antipsychotics because they severely damage brain tissue and cause early death.

Summary of what I want

- To start a programme of reduction of my 25 mg aripiprazole to nil. After that, stop meds, if possible, within two years, or aim to go onto the lowest dose of aripiprazole eventually.
- To be able to decide that I no longer wish to reduce my antipsychotic medication and have follow-ups according to the follow-up schedule.
- The reduction schedule should be frequently discussed to complete the reduction and discontinuation process within two years.
- Make a relapse prevention plan to identify early signs of relapse.
- If I feel unwell, inform the psychiatrist immediately or contact the crisis support service or my GP. They might ask to see me more to check my progress. The psychiatrist is to adjust the dose of antipsychotics, and provide additional medication to help with any side effects or offer therapy advice.

I trust that the information was informative and shows my readiness to start reducing aripiprazole to 25 mg on the anniversary month of coming off 30 mg to 25 mg, which, if I recall accurately, was July 2015. I want your support and do not have to do it alone.

Within a week of posting the letter, I received a reply to confirm that an outpatient appointment to see the psychiatrist at the community mental health hospital had been made for Monday, 18 July 2016, at 11 am.

I am telling you my story as a patient, which is an act of empowerment, for it takes power back from the system of psychiatry, and my perspective of coping with my reality is empowerment. Schizophrenia symptoms can cause an illness that does not discriminate in severity. Thank God I no longer have sensory malfunctions and am finally learning to heal myself. I believe a stupidity trait exists in psychiatrists who lack imagination and have unthinkingly adhered to giving me costly biomedical treatment for years. There was no complete clinical remission or unimpaired functioning. They must have been using a failed or faulty theory about medicating the emotional state of people's minds and the physical conditions in their bodies.

So far, the psychiatrists I have dealt with are zealous in defending their practice. Still, there is a growing chorus of voices of evidence from many of my psychotic breakdowns proclaiming the naked truth that there is a bigger picture, and the toxic social, environmental and economic factors of a modern industrial society traumatised me. Medication has been non-healing for me because I am a conscientious objector to these systems in contemporary life, which is unfair.

My brain needed to talk to me; CBT or CRT may help me learn the truth and change my mindset to survive in toxic environments, but they are telling me it is not on offer, and Freudian psychoanalysis is not practised in the NHS. My beliefs and faith may need to be altered to fit in with how the world is. It may prevent me from leaving behind the problems of reality and getting schizophrenia and recurring psychosis as the way to exist in these toxic environments and living my life with a daily dose of realism that involves suffering, gore, hate and violence that have sensitised and hypersensitised me. I must learn to activate the desensitisation probe that lives in my 'real' existence.

My physical body has recognisable traits that are being adopted and healed. But for my brain to improve, the movement of my purpose-led force to the universal spirit, the divine, the universe energy and

Mother Nature, known best as God, are sources to which my mind is automated. And my conscience thinks it knows what is going on. The injectable dashes of realism can polarise life events positively or negatively. They can disconnect me from the stream of life's abundance, or I can try to build an active and more robust circuitry that comes from the source of harmonious balance, a transcendent agent. When the circuit overload or unbalanced networks are sparked, realistic fiction and non-fiction are indistinguishable, and my organic brain's two minds are out of sync.

6

CRISIS OF FEELING

Friday, 8 July 2016

It is rare to come across honesty in people unknown to us.

I lost my wallet in a black taxi in London on Friday, 29 January 2016, while returning from a RADAR LEAP meeting. It was returned to me via a London branch of my bank.

The good Samaritan, I suspected, was the taxi driver or one of his passengers who went into the branch and handed in the entire contents of the wallet: debit cards, bus pass, driver's licence, personal documents with photos and £50 in notes and a few loose coins. Of course, I was devastated to have lost it, but the next day, I had a phone call from the Swish Cottage bank branch manager, eight miles from my drop-off point, St Pancreas International Station, to let me know the wallet got handed in at the branch.

When I go to London, I see homeless people on the streets, and some are begging. Knowing I am prone to empathic distress, I dodge eye contact. My responses to human misery recently malfunctioned because of an emotive media cover-up on 8 July 2016. The press had saturated us with reports in April of Japan and Ecuador's powerful earthquakes and terrorists detonating bomb-laden luggage and bombing a subway that month in Belgium. There were substantial wildfires in Canada in May, forcing Canadians to leave their homes in the most massive evacuation in their history. A young female MP named Jo Cox lost her life campaigning for the rights of immigrants in this country, and there were many race hate shootings in America in June. Today, snipers shot five police officers dead at a rally protesting against police brutality against black people.

I am trying to blunt my ability to feel what others are suffering because I am on an empathy overload. Empathy may be a healthy and robust emotion, but can it be that I have too much of a good thing? With my capacity to share others' feelings and take their perspective, I am overdosing on their misfortune. I am vulnerable to catching the pain of others, making me build up anger and unhappiness.

My wife tells me, "Don't let others' emotions affect you. You can care without letting it consume you, but you are prone to empathic distress. Seeing or hearing of suffering people distresses you. Try not to let it."

I am trying to avoid retaining the ability to understand another person's feelings, which is emotionally draining. I cannot shift my motivation to stop engaging, even though much of my mental capacity is used up; it feels right. Why don't my selfish instincts overwhelm them? It is good news that society must encourage people who stifle feelings to think about the sad, frightened person's feelings.

It is said and often viewed that empathy is a virtue that enables helping behaviours, but it primarily affects me; it irritates me. I must be robust and less efficient to feel empathic to reach out and want to help needy people such as victims of natural disasters, immigrants, refugees, and the other examples in this writing. Doing this will stabilise me emotionally and take away the quick snap, the immediate keen mental effort, to pick up empathy directly. I would still practically share others' feelings by putting my hand in my pocket to give money. If I could work, I would labour with my skills and talents without having a wage from charity organisations.

I do not know what might be responsible for sustaining such extraordinarily high levels of a morally excellent and worthy perspective. It is seen as a 'good' feeling to act altruistically towards others with empathic, unselfish behaviour that could give me a good reputation, but it is considered harmful to me. So, I need to do something because too much developed empathic perspective is terrible for me.

I am still trying to modify and better regulate this incredibly built-in capacity to take another person's depression, trauma and sad perspective. I am feeling their hurt, their pain, and the experiences of the moral emotions of guilt and shame because I want it to stop. I struggle to control an invisible ruler in myself that guides social behaviour and promotes cooperation.

I keep trying to live my life in a saintly way. I want to get others to see from the perspective of my inner personal worldview, which reaches all people and encourages them to socially bond with cantankerous people to win over their selfish attitudes, and so, pick up on their distinctive traits of an empathic, generous and godly personality or observe and copy the personality traits of kind people. There will be a change in the harsh reality of the external world when spreading my yearning for humankind to love and be loved. Justice, peace, and harmony will lessen the suffering on Earth.

The natural juicing of my brain with dopamine chemicals is getting interfered with by antipsychotic medicine; could that be why my emotions are going haywire? I feel that dopamine should be left alone to do its job naturally. The drug is artificially meddling by regulating my dopamine brain and is not helping me cope well with emotional responses; maybe that is messing me up. It feels bizarre to have stimulus boosted in such an intensely empathic, intensely spiritual way and profoundly believe in literal textual fundamentalist writings.

It is not only that I empathise, but I am getting scared for the world, the planet we all share. It is well-known internationally that we need to tackle climate change. We all share the same atmosphere, which is in a severe state. Still, the Zika virus, carried by mosquitoes and causing congenital disabilities, was declared a global health emergency earlier this year and not taken seriously. Governments are saying that the Olympic Games, which will be held in Brazil on 5 August 2016, the heartland of the Zika virus outbreak, must go ahead.

Ebola, which has affected West African countries, refuses to die, and they are saying that fresh episodes repeatedly appear, seemingly out of nowhere. Yellow fever, which typically lives in forest monkeys, is an epidemic in Congo. It is another piece of bad news that tilts my axis; I am not so stable. The information worries me even though the problem is not near home. More so than the upheaval of Thursday, 23 June 2016, when the country decided to leave the European Union in an EU referendum.

I had put X in the 'remain' box, uncertain of the consequences of leaving. The younger generation's future would seem brighter, safer, and better if we had remained. But in the long run, I will become more confident; things will work out for the best for leaving the EU, known as Brexit.

Brexit is a heartbreaking outcome for the general public because they were misinformed, and I was frustrated at this turn of events.

However, I have got over my disbelief and hope the country comes together, for no one knows what the future of Brexit will do to social values if the impact is recession.

We must keep watching the government strictly to ensure that the introduced measures will not harm the economy. The referendum showed how few people understood how the EU worked. I discovered that the EU has an apparent success story in technology, sciences, farming, fishing and defence, but it has yet to be debated. People needed more insightful information. The only issues discussed in the referendum were immigration, democracy, sovereignty and money.

Theoretically, leaving the EU gives the UK government much more power, and its future depends on the UK's deal with Europe. We hear that parliament is to elect the next prime minister because David Cameron will be stepping down in September 2016. Two female MPs are the candidates to battle it out to be the Conservative Party's leader, and the winner will also be named prime minister of this country.

Since the early hours of Friday morning, 24 June, when I heard that voters voted to leave the European Union, I have seen a range of emotions on TV, including a swell of extreme pronouncements and verbal attacks filled with hate directed at the most disadvantaged and vulnerable groups. In addition, scaremongering campaign tactics around immigration make such people feel even more threatened and unsafe.

However, one thing I hope reasonable people must not allow to become normalised is the growing tide of unashamed racism that has sprung like a poisonous well, including hate crimes and poor behaviour. The government sought to navigate this new Brexit path, and there is no more critical time for people to stand proud of our shared values: champion dignity, respect, fairness, diversity and justice at a time when the two main political parties are in turmoil over leadership.

I cannot understand it all, and Brexit has caused national divisions. Things are now as changeable and unpredictable as the weather has been since Brexit, but there is no way of preparing for every eventuality.

After attending the RADAR LEAP meeting, I encountered a homeless woman crying and begging at the side of the street in London last Tuesday, 5 July. I walked by without caring about a fellow human, and it hurt. So, I came home and told Euphemia that I did not do a simple act of kindness to make a difference, and I needed to rebalance the stupid choice I had made to stare at the crying, begging woman and walk away.

It so happened that I won £15 in last Saturday's Thunderball lottery and had a PIP benefit entered into our bank account this week. Yesterday, more than most days, I felt compelled to show compassion and respect to a young Roma woman vendor selling the *Big Issue* newspaper at her usual pitch in the town centre in Kettering. A copy sells for £2.50, but I gave £5. It was an opportunity for her, blighted by poverty, to earn a legitimate income, and it was a good read. And I will be her customer again.

It does not matter where she comes from, what she looks like, what her religion is or what language she speaks. With dignity, compassion, love and respect, I know how to look out for her, talk to her and offer words that support her. I have become a *Big Issue* reader who actively wants to help and give a donation of £2.50 more than the sale price next time and provide a simple kind word each time because I have strong morals, an ethical code about things and a remarkable ability to sense kindness and trust.

7

KEEP PRESSING ON

Saturday, 22 October 2016

> *"I have not already attained or perfected a good life; I press towards my goals."*

My strength is growing out of my struggles; I am enthusiastic and think I will become rich. The blessings I received at birth from the creator to have the capacity to believe have led my mind to conceive it can do it. It takes faith to find power in oneself and rely on something other than a secure belief system. Have I gained possession of my mind, and my mental attitude limits my capacity to believe it?

My life is what I make it; whatever the mind conceives, it can do it. So, I tell myself that I believe it and can do it. I can grow rich; I tried this method of thinking before and quit. I will not stop this time because I realise faith is the antidote for failure. The motives that drive my emotions of love, sex and the desire for financial gain are burning desires that are not satisfied without achieving wins. The feeling of being impoverished and improvised, having fears, having poor literacy skills and getting rid of superstitious ideas all seem to need the enthusiasm to reach the heights I set myself to rise above those negative feelings.

We have all seen bridges, lifts, hoists, and elevators display warning signs that they should not exceed the structural maximum load limit. Severe damage or complete collapse can occur from overstraining. Some people can sustain the pressure of stressful challenges and woes better than others, but everybody can get to a breaking point, and the problem becomes too much. They may get warning feelings from people, and the circumstances push them beyond what they can bear. Money problems mainly press down on me, but I take courage, knowing that I have learnt the limit of my ability under life's pressures, standing up to them and fixing them.

My brain has an uncanny knack for working stuff out, and it seems not to need conscious involvement. For many years, I have been taking life's pressures with an alert eye, but the thought that I did not know I was having (the unconscious ones) has been running my life. I used to think about a problem until I was stuck, decisive emotions broke out, and something helpful bubbled up in my unconscious mind to ease the pressures. Regarding life's stresses, I am not out of the forest yet, but I can see the wood for the trees because I know that my subconscious will better deal with decisions than conscious deliberation.

Thanks to unconscious processing and invisible 'forcefields' around the conversation between my body and mind, I instinctively know where my limbs are and what they are doing. Also, nerves, muscles and the senses detect what is happening outside my body. I cannot work out how to pass myself off as a winner without changing my mindset from quitting to never giving up. Then, I predict economic success, which feels like intuition when it is the result of my unconsciously held biases. I make hypotheses about external information and make predictions from emotional signals coming from my body. So much of what I do in my daily life happens without conscious thought, whether driving, making tea or balancing when I take steps to walk. Unlike many of my other unconscious talents, I have had to learn these skills before my brain can automate them. How it does this might allow me to think my way out of bad habits. Circuitry enables us to carry out a behaviour without thinking about it and involves turning all kinds of practice into habits.

The psychiatrist asked me to be cautious while we work together to reduce the medication to a dose of 5 mg by the year 2018, as my aim is for complete discontinuation. I have been taking two 10 mg of aripiprazole once daily since July 2016, a reduction of 5 mg from the previous dose. I am confident that my tendency for psychotic experiences has nothing to do with chemical imbalances but psychosocial stressors, which result in me having severe acute relapses. Taking antipsychotic drugs needs to be discontinued when my full consciousness returns; the initially healthy unconscious was regulating it. Psychosis results from my unmet expectations sending me over the edge. I need to wait patiently, but ideas of expectation run through my mind, which turns into jumping to conclusions faster than evidence from the senses, and I begin to flip. Although I know why I get converted into psychosis, I usefully recognise the dangers and take my decision to phase out antipsychotic meds very cautiously.

Making predictions has downsides when an incorrect inference, reinforced by the repetition of habits, makes it hard to reverse a projection, like when the wrong lyrics of a song we hear get learnt. It can be challenging to stop listening to them. Just before psychosis, I have the feeling of being at my maximum level of stress and being overwhelmed. My head is spinning. It is a figurative saying for most 'normal' people, but it reflects a tangible reality in my schizophrenic mind, and more weirdness follows. The weird thoughts and perceptions I have experienced in psychosis are difficult to distinguish as awakening consciousness because I neither know if I am asleep (dreaming) nor awake. Then, they vanish over time like a dream upon waking. I discovered I had again revealed parts of my inner life that can be scary if the process is not fully understood.

I am in a desperate search to manage, in a different way, schizophrenia, and I am embarking on a healing journey to treat the underlying trauma that gives me repeated attacks of psychotic episodes to cope with my reality.

I do not think I can eliminate my schizophrenic traits because my thoughts are not as sound and structured as most people's straightforward and sensible ones. This obscures and challenges the views most people would say are the correct way to look at things. My wife gets frustrated with me and says, "Karl, you aren't thinking straight again and aren't making any sense."

8

BACK FROM THE BRINK

Sunday, 23 October 2016

I recently wrote, "Psychosis results from my expectations not being met." It may have sounded unpalatable, but let us face the facts. When my expectations are unmet, I emerge out of psychosis without memories and exist in a zombie-like state, impulses moving me around, and I have no conscious awareness for days. The family used to try to jog a memory from when I could not remember my existence, and they asked hospital staff to tell them of my bizarre thoughts. The family continued to ask me, "Do you remember them?"

No, but I will inevitably keep doing that, pushing me towards my goals. Is it possible to give my psychosis a suicide switch that automatically flicks once I stray outside boundaries that define good mental health?

Although my brain can repair and heal itself, it needs to be impregnated with feel-good hormones. Not toxic chemicals that switch on and wash into the brain like a climate change ecosystem reaching a catastrophic tipping point. As I attempt to manage the systems in my mind that are too complex to control, alarm bells ring in my head and give a horror film effect because I am again experiencing the steady worsening of my circumstances. We need help with mortgage payments, including council tax and utility bills. There is a food shortage officially. My wife's work insecurities are a worry, and I am cautious about these recurring circumstances, for I remember how high the stakes are. I have already experienced massive financial hardship when I was without money.

We have been in a better position for months because a substantial amount of inheritance cash came from my deceased parents' house sale, and I took retirement: a tax-free lump sum from my pension plans. I hired a contractor to have our paths paved, landscaped the front and rear garden and had my sixtieth birthday party in the modern, easy-to-maintain rear garden. I invited members from the URC, friends, and family to celebrate with me. My children treated me to my first Royal Albert Hall classical concert and presented me with an Armani watch. We were comfortable for a while, but now we must escape the tipping point, and the basic premise is to treat this current shortage with an injection of optimism and faith.

The chassis of my circumstances gets busted; new things come into existence as I wait patiently for the creator and our prayers to shift us to prosperity again while maintaining good health and happy relationships. A gradual shift rapidly accelerates like the pull of gravity on an object. Playing the Thunderball lottery is accelerating a big win for us because I only asked for the entire whooping £500,000 from the jackpot to be financially satisfied. So far this year, from January to October 2016, I have won the lottery fifteen times and pocketed a total sum of £88.60. I do not think the suffocating of our cash flow state is permanent. Things can get tipped back, but what is impressive about the shortfall is that it crept up on me again. Shortage reached a tipping point within months as the algae of demands on the cash spread and entered the surplus money's crystal-clear water. Then, the carpet of capital stock was suffocated by its share demands. I have a radical way to ravage the cycle of shortages, win the lottery, and beyond that, who knows?

9

WELCOME, 2017

Thursday, 16 February 2017

I traditionally greet the new year with rash promises of financial improvement and self-improvement by exercising to keep fit, but I struggle to keep my promises. Instead, I try to prepare for the worst because my willpower is too weak to resist eating that second biscuit. I am no different now. Over the years, I have set myself New Year resolutions with mixed results. My oath to keep on top of my spending was partially successful, and taking moderate exercise was not. As a result, we are in the middle of the second month of the new year, and I feel lousy and worried for the people and planet Earth.

Every year has a turbulent uproar, and 2017 has been no different from the previous year's war, bloodshed and chaos. The persistence of ISIS, the Taliban, North Korea, Russia and Brexit seems to put the world in a dangerous, crazy place. But unfortunately, the Americans elected Donald Trump as their president, and he does not follow the conventional rules of politics. The rival of 2017 had moments of triumph, with victories from violent outbursts in January. Still, terror shook me because when I expected peace, the nations remained at loggerheads with each other.

Western nations have handled most places on the planet. The exception is North Korea, with many mysteries, oppressive rituals, military-style code words and bizarre restrictions the media say create an apocalyptic belief that Armageddon is coming to me and the free world.

It is hard for me; I cannot shake off the idea that our existence must have significance beyond the here and now. Indeed, there is a greater meaning to life, beginning and end, to shape daily personal, national and international behaviour. As far as the universe is concerned, we all are nothing but spirited dust when the randomly assembled collections of energy and matter are rare and transient. But I have a greater purpose set around one of my core values, a mission statement, "to spread peace, love and happiness, to encourage people to live life to the full and help others to do the same". The acts of terrorism the North Koreans and Russians are bringing us are the real stuff of wicked, evil people who put the world in crisis. Anxious people are worried, scared and very nervous. The term evil can be harmful or destructive, but most people would not apply it to their relationships, nor would I to myself with my mental illness. We do not see the actions of someone like me, with mental illness, to be 'evil'. Rightly so, many of us characterise evil as a term only relevant to movies, but it is somewhat controversial. Some people are evil in their intentions, especially if diagnosed with a personality disorder such as sociopathy, and may derive gratification from their acts towards others.

Parts of the world have engaged in bluffing or 'call my bluff'. The Brexit outcome will shape our future, our children's futures, and their children's futures, and other things will present themselves in ways that shock. I am trying hard not to be affected by uncomfortable feelings. However, I find it hard to escape the persuasive power of the media engaging me in depressing news; even with the volume down, the sense is always hurting. I can see no end to this. Every day, there are reports of human suffering, animal cruelty, environmental disasters and crime, and the charities pull at my heartstrings to donate to help the afflicted. I have persuaded myself to pay attention to them, but I cannot stand it. I am trying hard to put up with it. I avoid looking at the pictures and turn the volume down.

There are widespread doubts about news and information-gathering services giving us fake news and propaganda. My pen is poised; 1 April (April Fools' Day) is a couple of months away, the only day when a phoney story has some people hysterical and is known to be a hoax. Virtual reality, computer simulation, airbrushing imperfection and street drugs confuse the general sense that it is the fundamental truth.

Red Nose Day, also known as Comic Relief Day, is coming on Friday, 24 March, when people take on a challenge to raise cash for charity. I look at all the things that have gone wrong and cannot laugh even at poor performance; I do not often get to laugh because things that were seemingly going right were going exceptionally severely. In life, including in my personal experience, I wish it was not like that. Drawing a line through history and geography, I find it perplexing that people hate people and cannot stop suffering. I feel sorrow for not accepting it as an absolute, unchanging fact.

Walking in a straight line of love and joy is easy for me. I cannot imagine; my imagination cannot take it. It will become sick, wearing the shoes of the person who hates so severely, a racist, and consciously knows it is inhumane to do wrong to somebody. Why can't they transform from despising to trying to love? Can't they imagine it first and take steps to like and love instead of hating? It has been insightful; we were not equipped to reverse roles, and people stay pig-ignorant to racism and a wild world. Some people enjoy doing wrong and like the very foolishness of it; that is an inhumane mad way, an inhumane mad thrill that does not consider consequences. Do we all have to go through life as we know it? It plays on the theme of insanity, crazy people whose sanity has disappeared.

Therefore, our existence must have significance beyond the here and now. I am full of questions about the struggle to penetrate and change the current world's madness. My best days are when I know I do not have a clue, and it is funny in the post-truth age; everything I try to say with sincerity is poo-pooed. I have a web of ideas but need more than one string of thoughts to follow through and change the social, economic and political systems. They are all well above my grade.

How does one transform the social, economic and political systems that make people face emptiness, rejection and suffering? Mirror, mirror on the wall, who can...?

In science, social networks and civilisations throughout history, I have learnt that we are surrounded by evolving notions about God and the second coming, which gives us a doom-laden scenario. Is it the universal truth that suppressive systems will only fall by cosmic intervention when the beliefs in God are shifting rapidly and radically?

The world is trying to convince me that I want more and need more, but people should realise that genuine happiness is with those who give.

10

CHANGE FROM THE BOTTOM UP

Tuesday, 25 April 2017

The news about how we manage our finances has gone crazy, and it seems to be a current craze to have experienced a mental illness. It deflects from the people who genuinely have a psychological condition. There is no end to our trauma, and it is impossible to figure out the worst that can happen financially because I no longer plan for the worst of the worst but to change from the bottom up and emerge to better myself.

I am feeling the pinch because the county council, on 1 April 2017, took over the company my wife was working for. Euphemia's salary calculation was inaccurate. We live daily by budgeting the Employment and Support Allowance (ESA) government benefit, and my wife's salary pays the mortgage. The shortfall in salary will cause the mortgage payment for this month to be in arrears. No amount of analysis can swing this bewildering error in wages to be able to pay this critical bill. Although the failure is getting sorted, it may come too late. There is a distant feeling that the new employer has cut her salary. The one reality we face is that life is getting harder and tighter again.

Our economic, social and environmental problems, such as the planned trip to Singapore to see our family on 20 May 2017 and the car's yearly service and MOT test, will use up our reserve cash. Ignoring that we may experience economic failure due to one salary default is challenging. Not getting the expected salary has thrown us and put embedded debts under our noses again. The key to our inability to make a difference is also under our noses. The constant competitive pursuit of money drives nearly all our problems, which is the route to prosperity. The healing power of belief in God is all around us, and it can make me feel inexplicably better.

I only know how to surf this wave of wage loss by thriving to win this week's Thunderball lottery. I take it for granted, like fish that do not identify water because they are immersed in it. Thunderball represents the new game-changer, and everything will begin to add up. From January to April 2017, I won nine small cash prizes from Thunderball. This process of playing the Thunderball lottery shifts my perspective because small wins are the closest I think I will get to extra money. I no longer feel apathy, vainly disempowered, hoping to be able to afford the essentials. By playing the lottery, it is visionary but pragmatic to have a big win because it reveals an evolutionary pathway to change.

I am sixty years and seven months old, and we have got into more and more danger in that time. It is as if we are about to be gobbled up like a hungry trout that has swallowed a fishing fly. Standing over me like the Norse gods of old are more mental health problems and a gap between becoming more productive and more miserable. My worn-out protest of striving for more money has not worked over the decades and is not working now. Instead, there are new threats, new poverties bigger than the previous ones. Although there has been an enormous advance in my buying power, with little disposable income, I exist to this day just getting by.

Anxieties have exacerbated our challenges. The county council is cutting jobs, and Euphemia's child support worker role is getting slashed. During consultations, they said that some of the workforce would be made redundant to make efficiency savings, and the organisation would undergo restructuring. As a result, they only need child practitioners.

They said child support workers and others would be made redundant at one of the consultation meetings. They had eight weeks' notice before employment with the organisation would cease. So, Euphemia will be divorced from the job she loves two weeks after we return from our holiday to see our daughter, son-in-law and grandchildren overseas in Singapore.

Given the unique circumstances that Euphemia will be losing her job, flexible and imaginative solutions are needed, which include avoiding a hard fall back to the brink. On the ground-floor level, the first thing you may notice about Euphemia being made redundant is that we cannot pay our mortgage. I have been in touch with our mortgage provider, and they asked me to get legal advice because the debt may go into arrears for a long time. The house will have to be sold to clear the debt. We owe £45,818.49, the monthly mortgage payments are £888.35 until 2021, and our non-priority liabilities with eight creditors amount to £51,582.73.

I reject any notion that changing from the bottom up to better ourselves is too optimistic.

The great temple of Apollo in Delphi had the inscription "Know thyself". Socrates' idea that the unexamined life is not worth living is that Roman philosophers promoted the virtue of self-knowledge. Although I am in a period of possible disappointment again, I am happy to be able to understand myself and temper life's regrets.

In this journal, where I write down things that strengthen my mental health, I try to make better sense of the jumble and stress of everyday life. The rationale is to count our blessings, be grateful, appreciate our good fortune, and not get stressed by writing daily memoranda about life's difficulties. Life's challenges are sucking the marrow out of my bones. The obstacles give me minor life fractures – nothing that cannot be fixed by a shared strength of purpose and determination to get healed and live a fulfilled life.

As I write, I am confident that my thoughts are friends because the act of writing does not judge me, and the journal is a good friend who will always listen to me. I sleep better after life-loggings because I have decided to self-improve and tackle the challenges in my life. I hope that recording helps our lives have a platform to share moments and update occasionally. Although I sometimes wake up at night and write, my nightly behaviour goes out of sequence when an idea wakes me. I am glad I can spill my heart onto the pages because I want to pack them with truth, authenticity, substance and soul. It gives me a buzz.

Writing frees me and allows me to express myself, but my health is becoming more strongly linked to my financial status. Income matters more than it has in the recent past, and I know that a good salary cannot buy good health, but poor pay has always disadvantaged us.

11

HOLIDAY AND JOB LOSS

Thursday, 15 June 2017

We had a beautiful three-week holiday in Singapore, from 20 May to 9 June 2017, visiting our daughter, son-in-law and two grandchildren.

Unfortunately, time sped up when we wished it would slow, and vice versa, before, during and after the holiday. We experienced fast hours and marathon minutes over there; time just ran away from us. We enjoyed the time with them so much that we could not sense the perception manufactured by our minds until the pace changed. Something shifted in how I paid attention, and the activity made time seem slower. Paradoxically, although the happy times dashed by, they looked long in retrospect because the joy enriched our memories and bathed our dopamine brain, leaving us plenty to remember.

The final consultation that decides the new structuring of the organisation Euphemia works for has postponed the decision to make redundancies across the department that supports childcare. On Euphemia's return to work after the holiday, on 12 June, a new proposal was discussed, and a decision will finally be made about redundancies a week on Monday. It is a present worry, not a future worry for us. It might pull the comfort blanket out from under our feet. I am bracing myself for a knockdown that Euphemia may lose her job, so we must get back up and fight to keep our house. I may have to tag someone to jump in and take over the mortgage as an investment for them, or I will have to find out if we are old enough for our house to be suitable for the equity release scheme.

Since our return from Singapore, every day, a war between good and evil has come to me in my head. It is maybe because of the bombing attack at a concert in Manchester in May while we were away that is still talked about. And then, on Saturday, 3 June, three men driving a van ploughed into pedestrians on London Bridge. One got out and attacked a passer-by with a knife in the Borough Market neighbourhood, and all three were shot dead by police. It has made me feel unusually low to be back in the UK. There was a terrorist attack on Westminster Bridge in March 2017 before we went on holiday too, and the third such attack in Britain has been raising a big question these last three months. Is there a global solution to these types of assaults on ordinary people? I submitted a similar question to myself when extremist groups in 1982 kept killing innocent people. I wrote that I hoped moderate people would stop the slide of extremist groups alongside environmental changes.

The ideological battlefield has mainly shifted to cyberspace; this ideology has a safe space to breed extremist planning. I suppose that most Western countries have reckoned that ISIS attacks would continue, but this country showed resilience and dignity as it mourned.

On Thursday, 8 June, the prime minister, Theresa May, and her Conservative Party had a disastrous night in the general election, called to boost her majority and win a mandate for Brexit. They now have to form a coalition because the election resulted in a hung parliament. We did not vote; we were still out of the country and did not set up a vote by proxy.

After the dark events that have shaken this country over the last three months, I would like to think hope, not hate, is inspired. I feel sympathy and grief at the loss of innocent people's lives, and I have no deep understanding; I do not understand the callous cruelty that caused their deaths. Everyone has to be actively vigilant and not be scared of terrorism because the essential things in life are love, optimism and openness. I have been sad again in the last twenty-four hours because, on Wednesday morning, 14 June 2017, firefighters battled to rescue people caught inside a twenty-four-storey tower block in West London. Unfortunately, the fire engulfed the tower block, causing many fatalities.

Today, Sunday, 23 July 2017, eighty people are known to have died in the accident; still, people are missing.

The meeting that confirmed voluntary redundancies gave the date their employment is anticipated to end: 30 September 2017. A required action from the meeting was for all staff to have a one-to-one session with the manager a few weeks later to start working out their notice. Euphemia knows that her last day of employment will be Thursday, 24 August 2017, and the new structure will be operational on 1 September.

12

DRUG DOSE REDUCED

Monday, 31 July 2017

On 21 July 2017, I reduced the dose of my antipsychotic drug, Abilify, from 10 mg to approximately 7 mg. Before taking steps to slash the medication, two appointments were cancelled with a psychiatrist at short notice. Although I am supposed to be under medical supervision, my meeting was postponed because of cutbacks in the health service. My next arranged appointment with a psychiatrist is on 21 August 2017.

Although I am reducing the dose slowly, I have safety concerns that this may trigger withdrawal symptoms. So, I have personalised my tapering of the medication, but the level of the drug in my body fluctuates because it is not an exact science to snap the pill into smaller pieces to give a 7 mg dose.

While it is true that antipsychotic medication can help control the symptoms of psychosis, I carefully weighed the risks and benefits of discontinuing and having a psychiatric illness relapse. I have been clinically stable since 2014, and dose reduction may theoretically be helpful because, despite adherence to the medication, I have relapsed in the past. However, I am paranoid about being paranoid, claiming to be no longer psychologically disabled. Based on my stress vulnerability and biological, personal and environmental factors, I am not out of the woods yet. A supportive family is the best psychosocial treatment for preventing psychotic relapse and rehospitalisation. Their seamless approach to restoring my functioning and quality of life has me focus less on the condition and more on being me. Aripiprazole, also known as Abilify, was approved in 2002 and was heaven-sent to me in 2004, my first use of it, as I struggled with bouts of psychosis and depression.

My diagnosis of paranoid schizophrenia has been life-changing and has almost become life-defining. Living with me with schizophrenia and its symptoms has been tough on my wife and family, and the forward step towards getting back to myself is to stay symptom-free. The most effective way to be a well-stabilised schizophrenic and reduce the risk of future psychotic episodes is to reduce medication. That will allow my cognitive functioning to be corrected and my social functioning to get better, and I will also manage stress better.

I have concluded that antipsychotic drugs increase the risk of relapse because decades' worth of personal evidence suggests that the medicine given was a contributing factor in most of my nine regressions between 1977 and 2014.

I am cautious about coming off my medication. Staying on medication following the compliance medication regimen is a significant problem because I feel now I am running out of biological time, which drives life expectancy. However, my 'norm' is becoming so typical of ordinary people that digital technology is thus not too scary, nor is the future so frightening. My cognitive and motivational impairments seem to be gradually improving. I am getting rewarding experiences and achievements because I have more control over my future.

I have no extensive network of paranoid thoughts and ideas, resulting in a disproportionate amount of time spent thinking about things other than taking time out to think up solutions to problems in my standard orbit. I have noticed cognitive deficits and challenges of short-term memory and decision-making to plan adequately, and maintaining constant focus and attention was not addressed by giving the antipsychotic drug. Remembering information has a significant impact on my day-to-day life. Knowing that I am tapering the medication, my brain function has some slight improvement, but not enough to put me back in the real-world setting, such as work and building other mutual relationships. Thank God my brain is trying to heal itself, and for me, schizophrenia has not been cured but is just disconnected.

I had looked to psychiatry to roll up its sleeves to help me with safe and effective treatment to normalise things in my mind that acted up. However, I had no idea how to explain to 'myself' what I had been through, and my conscious brain was no good at all at helping me understand what the hell happened when my mind had acted up.

The aripiprazole drug worked perfectly on positive symptoms when I needed it. It has allowed me to heal, but I believe my body is telling me it no longer needs this regulation, and my sixty-one-year-old brain will think of a way to thank me for giving it a chance to heal itself while it can. However, the drug's long-term alteration of my mind scares me; a change in brain chemistry is indeed scary.

I know schizophrenia is debilitating. I have done that and will wear the T-shirt. However, this disease is not curable, and there are methods to suppress the symptoms by working with tools that will allow the body and mind to heal after a period of antipsychotic drugging.

Evidence shows that compared with white British patients, black Caribbean patients experience worse clinical outcomes and are socially disadvantaged. For example, it is known that people with psychotic disorders in my ethnic group, black Caribbean and African in the UK, experience more negative pathways to and through care.

Black people who receive the labels of mental illness and psychiatric diagnoses have the criteria for entry to NHS mental health services. Still, it seems irrelevant that white British patients can use facilities like the NHS, like a hostel, and nurses are their wardens. Diagnoses do not appear as inclusion criteria for them, and I wonder if they are sick at all.

My family thinks I got deluded again for saying what I observed as my mental health improved.

I recognised that instinctive non-adherence to the medication dose, which I aim to discontinue, is better for my full recovery from mental ill health because it is a good act of human resistance. I am also urged to reassert autonomy, fight for self-determination and not adhere to medication best tapered to improve my recovery. My effort is driving me to regain my self-belief that discontinuing the drug is best for me. I am learning to listen and trust my inner voice to ultimately come off medication eventually.

I cannot help but feel that following doctors' orders and sticking to the prescribed treatment regimen would end in severe brain damage caused by the long-term use of antipsychotics.

In my teens, my sense of self began to disintegrate. I moved slowly, then rapidly accelerated until gravity could no longer hold me. Tectonic plates were shifting, and universal truths were being revealed to me throughout the decades. As a result, I have had treatments with antipsychotic drugs in psychiatric wards when the psychotic episodes were acute.

I have an antipsychiatry fire flaring in my veins because I fear progressive diseases or movement disorders caused by long-term use of antipsychotics. They cause brain circuitry malfunction and do not allow my brain to heal itself. I have not forgotten that my mind used to skip in seconds, like a scratch on a gramophone record, and then it returned to me. In next month's visit to the psychiatrist, I hope he will support my decision to reduce the dose again, so it becomes 5 mg daily.

13

SCARY TIMES

Sunday, 20 August 2017

The world is more dangerous today than in a generation because of the sheer number of converging threats, making it increasingly perilous and unsafe. I have never seen so many unpredictable challenges at this age, and I was born in 1956.

Terrorist violence horrifies and bewilders me; it seems intentional to confound all of us. Extremist militants and others out to harm others wherever they are on Earth are just plain evil people. It appears Western capitals are under threat from foreign ones. London, New York and Paris have experienced danger from extremist groups said to come from the East, and some extremists are homegrown. They are citizens of the country they are terrorising.

There is a rise in support for radical right-wing neo-Nazi organisations. Religious bigotry and brainwashing ideology are exacerbating the threats rather than defusing them.

These days, there are more terrorist groups than I have ever known, and bad news stories tell us that weapons of mass destruction are proliferating in North Korea. Russia and North Korea are more assertive and are nations likely to bring war, causing instability in the world. I am nervous because North Korea is threatening the US Pacific territory, and US military power has threatened to unleash war on North Korea with the best military equipment in the world. It is scary if they cannot find a politically negotiated solution to the crisis. Today was the last day of August 2017, and North Korea has rattled nerves worldwide with a massive underground nuclear test that caused a 6.3 magnitude earthquake. It is not enough to think that climate change is the great challenge of this generation when weapons of mass destruction are in the hands of a ruthless rogue. Future suffering only seems to worsen because of climate.

Natural disasters in September 2017 ripped the Earth's fabric, coating it with superstorms, a strong earthquake and devastating floods in various places around the globe.

A superstorm called Harvey hit across America; another hit the Caribbean and headed for Cuba and Florida. First, the storm was classified as a five, then a four, and Hurricane Irma destroyed island after island. I am concerned about my relatives due to the hurricane heading towards the Leeward Islands, where they live, on Saturday, 9 September. I have heard nothing about how they are because all communication with the commoner in mind is down, and I am anxious to know they are safe.

On 7 September 2017, the strongest earthquake to hit Mexico in a century collapsed some houses like playing cards, and others moved like they were sliding off a heap of wet bath soaps.

I cannot forget Bangladesh's monsoon rains have caused colossal water dumps this month. The floods have killed some 50,000 people and flattened villages and there are bodies, bodies everywhere, and the full horror of that deluge is not even in Western minds. Awful destruction came from that monsoon, and it was not even on the front pages of the newspapers, only the tiny print inside them, and it got a discreet mention on TV. I saw how quickly people in developed countries forget such horrors to humanity and cling to gossip about celebrities and fashion, and people's interests go separate ways.

Floods have blighted the lives of Bangladeshis, and there has been no outpouring of sorrow or grief for those killed. However, the rainfall caused by Harvey in the US, which resulted in 40,000 people living in shelters, was strewn across the media. It is hard for me to accept that it will keep happening that way, and it is a shame that diversity issues in poor communities do not get littered across the news.

Another horror on humanity is ethnic cleansing, which is happening again in this millennium, like in the past. An insurgency has sparked violence in Myanmar, and Erdoğan accuses Myanmar of genocide. Thousands of Rohingya have fled to Bangladesh, where monsoon rains are wreaking havoc. After a few months of extreme tension on the world stage of missile launches, military exercises, troop movements and natural disasters, it seems time to take cover in the bomb shelters, panic on a hillside or take what comes to us. But no. The UN has used sanctions on North Korea. The diplomatic tit-for-tat seems to have backfired, and millions of people's lives are at stake if the nuclear arsenal is deployed; these are 'scary times'.

Since 1945, the world has been peaceful, and I thought this was a new conflict-free era. But is it a blip? A major war could be around the corner. The Second World War probably resulted in the worst military casualties in history. On the other hand, this present time in history is said to be the most exciting time to be alive because discovery and innovation are reshaping the world around us. Still, minor conflicts have not stopped, even though it may come to be seen that they are departing from a major war.

14

OPTIMISTIC ABOUT SAVING THE PLANET

Thursday, 2 November 2017

In late August 2017, I was gripped by society's deadly ignorance and world leaders burning into our minds that it was a dangerous time. We risked being plunged into World War III, having put into our minds the fear of the wicked, bad, and evil god. Yet, the catastrophic conflicts and natural disasters have somehow taught us something new about how the Earth works, and we (humans) are being beefed up to inspire shock and awe to end the world.

Dosh! My brain may have lost the plot, but I am right to worry about nuclear war because it will eliminate the human race.

The fallout from North Korea's latest nuclear weapons test is only political for now, but it continues to provoke its enemies. It is an age when more authoritarian forms of rule seduce many people, and it is good to be in a democratic process that encourages engagement, debate and broader understanding. But I cannot pretend, for it seems it needs an upgrade. A democratic system of government is the best solution for poorly governed countries, but it is not all-wise and requires updates to fit the purpose it was designed to serve.

The arms race seems to be back on because the States are getting more and more likely to settle their differences with violence. Climate extremes and local wars have become numerous, and 2017 is the second warmest year on record. Global warming is increasing, meaning that storms are becoming even more significant than Irma and Harvey; my mind senses that a nuclear accident is a more likely danger that will lead to atomic tragedy. The likelihood of atomic war may appear as high as it was during periods of peak crisis in the past. Still, the threat of a fluke accident due to instability in the storage of nuclear substances wrecks my nerves.

A month ago, on 2 October 2017, the US witnessed its worst-ever mass shooting when at least fifty people were gunned down at a concert in Las Vegas. Two days ago, on 31 October 2017, a truck-driving terrorist carved a long path of carnage as he ploughed through helpless victims down a cycle path in Lower Manhattan, New York City, killing eight people. Screams must have filled the Halloween air, blood spilt on the pavement, and my writing instantly gave me the horrible horror scene chills on that Halloween night. I am having a break! I have to stop writing about this tragedy. I had an impactful vision of how it may have been, which drained me as I thought about how awful it was. I'll be back soon when I feel restored. Hail, razzamatazz.

Turning to the mind that has been self-rested, I have wondered if religion is why a group or individual acts violently. Are religious groups more violent than their secular counterparts? The discussion on religion, politics and world crises, mainly the apparent terrorist attacks, currently brands Islam as a robust, intense, extreme faith. I believe that violence is demonstrably found in groups and individuals, regardless of whether they are religious or secular, and rejection of violence cuts across religious and secular lines. Some groups reject violence and are deeply spiritual, and other groups who oppose violence do not present themselves as religiously motivated.

Why do some people commit violence and horrifying acts against others? There must be a profound, essential reason, whether secular or religious. What spurs people to do something beyond the humane themselves? Violent acts have their most ambitious action to carve society in a way nobody cares about, but I do not know; I really do not know.

I had the ambition to do something beyond myself as an extremist does, and I am not an extremist. I stay in the humane bracket of human good. Thank God acting well feels better for most people who are doing poorly. It can sound grand to say that my doing good in the world is bragging about my achievements, but it can feel terrible. Still, it will be a world-changer if I can have an impact as an author. I will feel good as a connector because my messages move between different worlds through translation and distribution, and my written words connect people. My experiences are unique to me, but readers may be able to relate to them, and we will all feel good.

Worries and fear have affected much of my life. In retrospect, I realise that I would have had a much fuller and happier life if I had let these feelings go and continued to build on openness. I had clung to negative emotions as a crutch, but writing is an excellent medicine for my anxiety and working out strategies. Writing down my thoughts and feelings will be more tangible and less scattered and scary in my head. I am developing a broader perspective on what is happening in my life and the planet. My brain can produce a cosmic flash that is not based on real earthly experiences. It could be said that schizophrenia has come back and then goes away quickly, like a dream one cannot remember when waking from a deep sleep. I am okay; I have awareness skills. I am not ill. It is usual for me to have and live with schizophrenia unless my experiences become troublesome, and it is a narrow line: wellness to disease.

The world bombards me with sensory information, and my brain's attention system is at total capacity. Then, I find it difficult to process everything, so I make educated guesses because my mind goes blank in parts, and words turn nonsense. Spelling seems impossible, and the letters begin to lose meaning. My PIN occasionally flies out of my head, and my memory can get messed up. The phenomenon of faces in inanimate objects scared me until I blamed my frame of mind for slipping. Sometimes, an entirely inappropriate word, not a swear word, pops out in conversations, and I say things I did not mean to say. I correct myself immediately, but sometimes I am asked, "What are you saying? Where is this conversation going?" On the face of it, this makes no sense because the phenomenon looks so much like a schizophrenic episode. However, the higher dimensional structures of my conscious mind remind me that it is common to have memory loss and suggest that negative thoughts are not always linked to illness all the time.

I have plenty of concerns about the planet, but there are reasons to be hopeful about the world's fate for the first time in a long time. Excellent stuff is happening worldwide, and people are working out solutions. The death of carbon fuel is closer, and renewables and conservation are increasing the ripple effect of new technologies where they are most needed first.

David Attenborough's stunning documentaries about planet Earth remind me of the world's incredible beauty and how species are in danger. Aside from the threat of cosmic catastrophes, climate change and pollution now threaten the Earth as we know it. Stephen Hawking has even argued that we need to consider abandoning the planet. There is a strong case for optimism and determination to save the Earth; this Earth is home to all known species on planetary world systems.

Innovators and scientists are devising new ways to tackle our planet's problems and penetrate its mysteries. Despite what many conspiracy theorists say, the Earth is not flat. It is still a sure thing that it is a globe.

Science has decoded some of God's handiwork. I look for God's laws of creation and humankind with diminished moral, cognitive and sensory capacities to have a religious duty and an obligation to understand the world God has made. Ethical and holy people who deny evolution and the Earth Age are in a peculiarly modern delusion.

As a species, we may be able to develop a future super-intelligent machine that would be god-like to satisfy our soul's desire to pray to a principal god's head and see it. Humankind will promote the realisation of God's authority based on artificial intelligence or lab life, the live mechanical organisms giving birth to themselves. The thought that future super-intelligent machines would be god-like is neither a science fiction concept nor a metaphor. It is arguably so because it is rational to believe in gods even if they might not exist. If super-intelligent machines are possible, they will reward us for bringing them about. The emergence of super-advanced computer machines programmed by groups of people with sincerity, ethics, faith-orientated goals and peace-making skills that implicit responsibility would not take part in violent struggle or war. A fight between mortal gods does not work out in mythology. Super-intelligent machines would not compute to consider being an enemy of other digital deities.

I have spent more time than I realise running future scenarios through my mind because I think about being watchful for danger, but this has turned out to be fruitless and exhausting because I have found myself worrying. Finally, I have come to a place of balance, realising I have no idea what is next in our lives or what will happen globally. 'Life' has a way of happening to us, and chewing over decisions as if one outcome is more important than another is fruitless. In reality, I am not very good at predicting what will happen. I have worried about future consequences, and the sooner I let go, the more in the present I can be, and the less time I need to worry about things well beyond my grade. We live in a thought-created reality; I mean that we do not experience the same thing in our minds or see the rich mental world similarly. All our experiences pass, which means we all have natural resilience. Over the years, I have learnt that life sometimes confuses my plans and that things work out better if I follow them.

For there are things that lie beyond the joy and anguish of this life. While suffering is unavoidable, death is not final when hope is eternal in my planning.

On Thursday, 19 October 2017, our solar system received an alien visitor, and luckily (or sadly), it was not a spaceship passing through, or so was the thinking. What if the interstellar object's true nature was to explore the universe and us? What if alien visitors from another star flight path reached Earth, where our type of humanity of the human species lives? But the interstellar spacecraft was just a giant, rocky, iced asteroid exposed for millions or billions of years through the solar system.

The universe may be closer and more accessible than previously thought. The most complex ideas entertain me and seem credible because science and revolutionary technology can forecast the future.

15

CONTINUOUS RECOVERY FROM SCHIZOPHRENIA

Saturday, 4 November 2017

I have always identified myself by my diagnosis as a paranoid schizophrenic and titled my first published book *The Memoir of a Schizophrenic*, which tells the first part of my life story of living a paranoid, delusional life, getting married and bringing up our children. My wife has become an expert in helping me manage instances of delusion, fatigue and paranoia that lead to psychotic behaviours. It is terrible for anyone to experience their loved one not being in their right mind. Sometimes, I think I have burdened my spouse, and she is automatically unique because of the uniqueness of what life has thrown at me, and she has taken it on for better or worse. Of course, life happens to all of us, but mental illness is not like cancer or diabetes; it is arguably an abusive emotional illness, and in my house, it was so much worse before it was better.

Every day we are together, I feel like I have won the lottery because my schizophrenia has not been easy on my spouse and me, and she has stayed with me. We have just celebrated our thirty-sixth wedding anniversary abroad in Italy. I am my wife's biggest fan; she is a great, fantastic, unique and god-sent person in my life. She is an angel and a saint in the actual use of the word. My wife's existence is a gift from God because she is perfect for me, yet I have got into relationship problems of straying.

My love loves me with an intimate bond that involves empathy. My love can understand me, share and care about my experiences with her and continually accept my ups and downs and quirky behaviours. I do not want to disappoint her, but another unique relationship is pulling at me from within my mind. I am falling romantically in love with a friendly woman.

I am glad we have a marriage, two people in a caregiving arrangement with love, and it is not an act of charity. At the core of me, I do not change when I function poorly with mental illness because my heart is full of kindness, love and honesty, and I wish to stay faithful. My darling has recognised this, and she married me. We fight problems together instead of fighting each other because we are firm allies on the same team, tackling conflicts, and they strengthen us. Laughter has been rare in our relationship, not comical; life has been challenging. However, over time, I have improved at making her laugh, putting her first, and putting the world on the back burner. After thirty-six years together, we laugh a lot more and enjoy each other's company. We are in sync with each other and share hopes and dreams. The marriage feels perfect, although we can find things irritating about each other. However, we have eventually worked through things, communicating and not letting little things become extreme.

I am an enduring sufferer of schizophrenia in a totally non-clinical paranoid and non-audio hallucination way. Still, I get deprived of thinking straight sometimes because the condition causes my mind to be confused, and my words sometimes aren't understood. At times, my thought process feels like it is permanently damaged. Things are not so coherent, and this might be the best it will get with the recovery from schizophrenia. My mind thoughtfully and respectfully refrains more from characterising myself as a 'schizophrenic' because I am more than a diagnostic label. The diagnostic name perpetuates ignorance and misunderstandings. A mental disorder in shorthand is 'mad' or 'crazy'. It has no functional purpose. The term devalues people, and my mental disorder will not be accepted as another health condition until I think my diagnosis deserves the same dignity and respect that people apply to cancers and other medical diagnoses.

I have been tracing my gradual recovery process, which comprises several small achievements in medication reduction. In following the story of my life, you have shared my initial positive signs and symptoms. I have had continued support from my family and strength from within myself to reach this stage of recovery. Although I was first affected by many stressors as I jumped blindly into the unknown about medication reduction, for there were no robust data on the effort of coming off medication, a small clinical trial has shown significant improvement in patients. So, I chose to be a guinea pig in my lab and self-analyse the effects to improve my quality of life. Through numerous leaps of faith, I have learnt a few steps that have eventually made reducing medication not so overwhelming and not so scary.

On Monday, 21 August 2017, my psychiatrist okayed and reduced my antipsychotic medication, aripiprazole, to 7.5 mg a day, and I am pushing for another reduction in the new year. I think he understood my determination to free myself from the poison of the medicine and only resort back to it when I am ill. In my experience, the medication does not prevent relapses, but it is good at stabilising the positive symptoms of schizophrenia. The positive psychotic symptoms of schizophrenia and the disruption they can have on my daily life have not affected me since 2014. I put it down to my determination to allow my brain the time to heal itself.

Recovery started by easing up on being stressed about world affairs and life generally. Good physical health and social support reduced the associated risks of relapse, lifestyle changes made me less nervous and anxious, and I enjoyed life. I have recovered significantly from the worst aspects of schizophrenia. However, the dysconnectivity of my brain and impaired cognition, which stop me from thinking straight, are still affecting me, as mentioned before.

Despite having access to costly biomedical treatment, essential recovery still needs to be included. There must be something wrong! There is no complete clinical remission or unimpaired functioning, even on a much lower dose of medication. Being on antipsychotic medication is non-healing for me because it is trying to treat my conscientious objections about life's unfairness; the world does not fit my expectations. There must be a better distinction between my internal perception and externally generated changes. I attempted to predict the outcome from my perspective of always striving to be fair and ethically reasonable. I thought that one day, my practice of being 'good' would erase what was terrible and flawed in me. The externally generated sense data blurred my belief because my model of living in the world was pure, erasing all errors as I became better and better at being 'good', but how I perceived the world was wrong. Nobody is always all good or all bad, for we all are a mixture of both. What I learnt automatically modified what I perceived, and what I observed automatically adjusted what I knew. Still, when I think, my lively subconscious always sees the error. Persistent and unusual experiences arise due to confusion between perceptions and stored representations. Things seem different. The world does not fit together as uncertainty rises about what harms and punishes me, and I should head to what will reward me. However, my sensations and precepts do not have direct access to those things, which causes an error in my disruption of prediction and perception.

Trying to medicate my mind like an illness in the physical body will not heal it. What I call the moving of the character in the Holy Spirit (or the divine, the universe, Mother Nature) is in our minds, and it can acknowledge belief and faith to motivate a drive in me to update my inferences. New meanings get sought, things feel novel, and some form of marker perceives the noise for distinguishing internally from externally generated sense. It may very well explain the emergence of my delusions.

If I tell myself the cognitive explanations and interpretations or other people tell me them, it does not change the problem in my active schizophrenia gene to deactivate itself. What seems to help me most is talking about (verbalising) the thoughts or writing them down, allowing me to gain control of the terrible impulses my willpower cannot control. The right words at the correct time are enormously influential, like when one gets tickled. It is an excellent stimulus to help make my senses know something obvious; it is a unique external thing, and I laugh. But I do not respond if I stroke myself, trying to understand what was happening in my psychotic state. I can predict the tickle. It cancels the sensory feelings and consequences of the action. Still, I am much more accurate at judging internally generated forces in that state, which are terrifying, scary, and petrify me.

I required symptom relief when my brain scrambled itself into toxic experiences, and antipsychotics helped the biologically flawed to be stable. Still, it became an episodic disorder, repeatedly putting me in and out of hospital. Antipsychotics have not worked for me as a permanent solution to symptomatic remissions. There is no sense of a cure. I have recently been gutsy in wanting better control and to fix the underlying biochemical abnormality to improve the symptoms caused by the umbrella term schizophrenia.

I have a brain chemistry problem like dew evaporating on grass, which will disappear when I get relief from stressors. The medication should eventually stop it. It has not. My brain is a biochemical factory with biochemistry imbalance challenges, and the treatment I receive is not making me as well as I can be.

The psychiatrist is not attempting to discover my biochemical individuality to remove the agent causing my stress intolerance. On the contrary, the drug worsens my condition over time. Another stressful environmental event may break me back into a challenging state because of my incapacity to eliminate toxins.

16

BACK ON TRACK WITH OUR FINANCES

Saturday, 4 November 2017

I have worked hard to prevent another crisis in our financial management during the past few months. Good, sound ideas flooded my mind, moment by moment, during the long struggle with economic challenges, and I had less of the personal pain that could come from my choices. So many times, life has moved too fast, and then I burn out with schizophrenia relapses. My life is paced appropriately now, with what I have done and the value I shall leave behind. It is easy to get swept away with day-to-day things and not take a moment to reflect.

Thank God we are inching our way towards the coming year, 2018. We have already forged and secured our financial future, which was a big wow moment. We had unsecured debts before and after the 2007–08 financial crisis hit the world banks and collapsed one of the central banks. So, the pressures we faced being behind on our household bills and struggling to make ends meet were resolved satisfactorily. However, the zombie spectre of not being debt-free in our lifetime can now be seen as a spoof fallacy. I searched for fixed investments and pension plans and cashed them early, including those on which I had struggled to maintain monthly payments.

Hip, hip, hurray! Cashing in the plans raised enough money to pay all our creditors, who have accepted part of the payment and recorded it as the final settlement.

This autumn, November 2017, the days are getting shorter, the mornings are darker, and it is the last weekend before the children return to school. Finally, the leaves on the trees have turned brown, and our burden of huge, unsecured debts has been lifted. Hurray! I have been rescued thanks to dormant investment policies and pension plan growth over forty-two years.

The mortgage was rescued too. It is no longer part of our financial priority outgoings because it was redeemed through an equity release scheme by Legal & General Home Finance, which provided us with a cash lump sum. As a result, we do not have to make any payments during the life of this new mortgage, known as a Flexible Max Plus Lifetime Mortgage. The amount owed included all of the interest fixed at 5.74%, and charges will be repaid from selling our property when both of us have died or if we move into long-term care. A substantial early repayment charge is applied if we choose to repay the loan at any time. We have an illustration of an estimated twenty-six-year term for this lifetime mortgage, but if we are still living in our home at the end of twenty-six years, the lifetime mortgage will continue to run.

We had been trying for a long time to deal with repaying our debts and making the mortgage payments. I kept motivated by writing down goals I wanted to achieve when debt-free and focusing on the crucial work of wanting nothing more than for our children to be okay, happy and protected from pain and suffering in whatever form. I did not wait for 'one day' to live my dreams, but I am living my goal now: to buy a modern, automatic, used car. The car would be no more than three years old. True to my spirit, I researched the pros and cons of car purchase and durability, with Euphemia liking my choice. I bought with cash a reliable Arctic white Mazda 3 2.0 SE-L Navigation 5dr automatic car on a 15 plate and registered Euphemia as owner and keeper of the vehicle.

Managing a tight budget still exists; I promise to avoid falling into money poverty again, to use our resources sparingly, to stretch the money, to save some cash, and to budget the money well. I always pledged to control my money and avoid debt coming back into my life by living within my means and avoiding credit. I had been in so much of a cash flow crisis when cash in our current account was dwindling at an alarming rate that I have completely changed my approach to shopping and will stick to spending budgets. I have an electronic virtual jam jar budget, which means splitting the income into various electronic jars for each budget area. Jam jar budgeting to track my finances is flexible, but no matter how clever I get at following my money, there will be no more anywhere for the spending plan. It has made me feel better off. As the household bills get covered, I know how much I have left to spend on other costs, and savings go into an emergency savings account. Despite reduced returns on savings, I set aside what I can.

If you have followed my stories year after year, you may sense that we are a cash-strapped family, spending more on overdue bills than food. Spiralling debts and hardship have caused stress. Thank God! We are debt-free! Hurray. Alleluia.

Most of our unsecured debts were passed to the debt collection agency because the original creditors could not get arrears repaid. My original creditor sold or assigned our debt obligations to the collection agency because the amount I paid to them was not enough for them after our account had defaulted. For a long time, the debts got suspended, and every three to six months, they contacted me to produce income and expenditure sheets or discuss if my circumstances were likely to change in the coming months. Most debt collection agencies were friendly and understanding about my plight, but it did not prevent me from feeling intimidated by others.

17

THE CHURCH, UNIVERSE, BIBLE AND ME

Sunday, 5 November 2017

What I am about to write about is excellent news about the Church, the universe, the Bible, and me that I cannot and will not retract because it is neither safe nor proper to go against my conscience. I cannot do otherwise. So, here I sit, pressing the lettered keys on the keyboard after making a few notes on paper; may the one 'being' God help me as I pray to the one higher 'being' in all human beings to help them use their unbiased clever wit to understand my message.

I have religious urges, and I cannot think they are justified because church and worship are no longer part of my 'to-do list'. Those converted 'born again' believers have a significantly damaged atrophy of brain cells by their religious practice compared to losing faith and shifting towards atheism.

I have not lost my belief in God and recognise the social benefits of gathering with people of similar belief systems. The Church today has not developed the concept that the God of creation is just the abstract belief in a higher power. My intellectual enquiries suggest that people accept that the universe and God are the same yesterday, today and forever. Changes are ongoing, and our brains change things. Our thought processes, which are messy and complicated, can change our minds. Belief in God, the higher power, is independent of any aspect of a neurological shift that initiated a change in my thinking over time. A valuable part of my brain function turned out an activity that is naturalistic to be less analytical, ceasing to pick up on an atheist mentality. I have a more intuitive thought process that gives me a keen, sharp sense of empathic interpersonal bonds with relevant people, and I hope the outsiders work on their biases to start the change in themselves.

The founding theorist of Christianity came from the mind of the apostle Paul; he had some crazy visionary rhetoric embodied in his letters. I get the sense that Paul had in his mind that there would be a timeless, gorgeous place where human society would live forever. It is such a wonderfully inclusive place that all of humanity must repent to be there. It incorporated the passionate idea of Jesus Christ as a cosmic figure who would transform history, establishing this new heaven and earth, and this latest creation would be the kingdom of God.

I believe Paul had this fiery image in his head, a radical vision of a new heaven and new earth that he could not let go of as his vivid imagination was loopy in parts. He also had a vision of what it meant to take on the entire mindset of Christ, which involved taking up the cross. Probably for him, it meant following the path of self-abandonment, uniting with the philosophy of Christ, where every type of person – Jew, enslaved people, male and female – would find reconciliation in unity with God.

Paul's faith seems to mean many things, giving rise to tricky theological suggestions and fragments of his letters getting pulled out of context. So, a thousand years after Jesus died, those fraudster theologians authored complete substitution theology into the history books. God became man, and humanity could be saved by salvation or imitating Christ, the anointed one. Therefore, it showed us a pathway to reconciliation or atonement with God.

My research and analysis of my experiences suggested that my functional biology systems have become too extreme and sensitive. I worked my conscience to be too finely tuned, and all the good in me can drain out, and I grow tired. The central part of me responsible for developing intelligence slips too low, and my mind and body functions fail to respond to the senses—senses of excellent stuff—to replenish it from the right source. So, my brain stepped back to my primary education.

When it comes to many of its diverse experiences, I reach the truth, and all my words are inspired, but not all of my writing is. My book impacts the reader's senses by providing a touch with that source most of us call Almighty God, and it stretches the reader's imagination to an understanding of this thing, God. Nobody knows of quantified factual evidence of that 'being' God, who knows all about us and all environments. It remains a human experience, as well as a mystery and story. Some readers will find my words talk; personally, others get emotional chills or excitement because of senses or a great insight that is natural to experience as you follow where the spirit of God takes you.

Education and emotions at any level make readers make a hard choice about which side of the fence they stake their lives on. My earthly reality of the world is mutually middle-grounded.

I cannot determine that dosing on faulty compounds in antipsychotic drugs over many years is the prime factor that, I think, damaged the language centre in my brain and the area that flashes with thoughts and makes its ideas.

According to autobiographical memory, I had begun living my life before my first prescription for antipsychotics. Nevertheless, I had a few noble thoughts in my infant life about developing the character trait I wanted to have when I grew to maturity.

I want to feel good about myself, be of good character, be mature, and be the best person I can be, like Jesus Christ.

I practise being good and learning to better myself from my mistakes. Unfortunately, I kept up throughout life, tried to lightly trim off flaws from life's challenges, became too good at it, and damaged my good self.

So, I cannot say that the compound ingredient used to make antipsychotics caused me to decline because the medicine had been used for far too long; was it the cause or just a considering factor? It needs to be looked at differently for something else to take the blame, or I was entirely responsible for everything that happened to me.

After reaching so far, the truth has grown about the theorising to us from the twelfth century. Those theological fraudsters wrote that all people, including Jesus, had to suffer at the primary level. The hellish agony of an excellent ethical, principal characteristic of a godly man's death is necessary to pay for the sins and failings of the human race on the world. "Jesus suffered and died for us sinful creatures. He paid the price for sin." It is a kind of transaction; without that deed, humankind will get punished in hell. It is a capsulated wrong idea that a good God Almighty could not love his human creation without a horrific atonement and is a vengeful father figure who did a bad thing to create humankind. A great deal of harm has been done; it has damaged and traumatised people down the centuries and in these modern times. I had reluctantly accepted this view for a long time and couldn't stomach it, but I put up with it, and eventually, I felt sick imagining it and fell ill with the practices of it, the fake Christian messages.

In my teens and young adult life, I preached to my peers that the world was doomed and that we all were sinners whom the blood of Jesus must save. I looked to find ways to bring people to be saved from the eternal flames of hell and not perish. As I grew in wisdom and better understood the New Testament messages, this was a constantly unhappy notion for me. It is ridiculous that the true God of creation would require a blood sacrifice to 'satisfy' himself. We, just poor creatures, must say "I believe", and we shall be saved from hell damnation. That is what the theorists made up for us.

I understand Jesus in strictly human terms as a religious reformer, a politician or social revolutionary, an apocalyptic prophet, a mystic or even a Jewish jihadist. Unfortunately, the debate continues about Jesus' mix of political and spiritual messages, and his awful suffering has remained essential. Being of good character and knowing that God is love is at the tip of Jesus' message and is still misunderstood today.

Jesus built a minor and eccentric community around mutual affection, multiple sharing and love; people reflect on him and God. They idolised him and fell at his feet in devotion.

I have found that the mean-spirited and transactional idea of Christianity is still told and retold; it stinks. It is awful, disgusting and an abomination, and I turned away from the stench of religion. As a child, I was uncomfortable with this fundamentalist belief in my household and the broader community. Blood sacrifice was ridiculous to swallow. It cannot be so, and I have always felt the 'chill' and the horror of it all. But I went for years peddling to other people the terrible Christian theology and violent murder, which I found repellent: the heart of Christianity's message I had struggled with horrifying troubles to accept.

The practice of having red wine symbolising the drinking of holy human blood and taking bread to eat it to be holy human flesh was appalling. I had to change the interpretation to receive the sacrament, including the practising of rituals that symbolise the belief that death is the prerequisite for resurrection through death and dismemberment. All must come except what the apostle Paul says: God forgives humanity 'through faith' in this process. I had psychological locking and fought to hold what was dear in me, saying the proper understanding of the transformation of the spirit was what Jesus modelled. Understanding faith, as trust in God and God's universe, is a cosmic spiritual energy. The worthiness of looking deep into the root truth is freeing and is a unique power of the energy network information given to inform the world.

I am one guy filled with Jesus' teachings that are not imposed on others because I have seen people do whatever they want; they do not think twice about ethical teaching. We can change ourselves; no education is necessary, so the teachings of Jesus may go the way of the dinosaurs. Jesus denounced the rich and powerful and pronounced blessings on the poor and marginalised. The teachings of Jesus are pivotal to turning the other cheek, loving one's enemies, giving over one's cloak and giving no resistance to an evil-doer. Christians must heed, but in this earthly reality, that will wipe them off the face of the Earth. The whole truth is about the future now and calculating the probabilities of how personal life and the secular human systems are going. 'The truth' in the experience works with you to have life forever and works with secular material systems to support the people who want that life. Everything else is dead and stays dead forever.

Jesus embraced politics and religion to change his society, but in the end, he was too political, and they executed him.

The Bible tells us about people of the ancient past and how they interpreted God's intervention in their lives and communities. However, the interpretation in the modern world is significantly different.

I consider the kind of universe I would expect the true Christian God to have created and view the world in which we live. The traditional Christian God ideas need reform to consider discoveries that seem to show the cosmos is not human-oriented. We are all put on a guilt trip by the Bible's authors if we still cannot fathom the reality of our earthly life.

Jesus came out of unconsciousness, was hungry, and ate; Jesus was alive, not dead. Jesus eventually died like every mortal and is not coming back. Jesus is not returning people to this reality; understand this reality of our world. Jesus is not coming back, and he is not perfect. He is like all of us, with flaws, imperfections and problems, but he is as good as is possible.

Biblical texts tell us God is human-oriented because God created humankind in his image, is deeply concerned with human beings, and highly values us.

We know the universe is vast, and humans occupy a tiny space, the tiniest fraction of it, and we have been around in the blink of an eye. Earth is a drop in the ocean of space, and there is an apparent discrepancy between the universe we live in and what we would expect God to create. Should not there be plenty of human life on planetary systems if the God we say we know loves the creation of humankind so madly? Oh gosh. Am I to lose my correct belief because of it? I will not fail to understand; I cannot forget the experience of godly, truthful insights and turn atheist or take on an in-humanist mentality because of this discrepancy. Godliness is directly in existence and part of my functioning; after all, the divine is mysterious.

I can hint at reasons why good stuff and crazy stuff exist, and tiny humans and other creatures are in a prominent place, and it seems to sweep towards atheism. If the fact is, atheism is the simplest explanation for the unknowable, perhaps the gullible will get sucked into it because their creator may seem to have valued cosmic dust and rocks more highly than humans. The mental energy that creates the heavenly universe is mentally created by God's doing. Our minds produce a reality; the first in existence (God) is the solid, self-made consciousness energy known through our brain's mental force, giving us minds we can never seem to measure. Although we do not know if God exists in a physical entity, we should keep asking about our mental capacity factor because the delights of paradise await.

I believe in correct belief, collecting positive feelings, maintaining thoughts that are good for you, and loving a good idea. It remains a good idea that can improve as it 'goes beyond' as 'metaphysics' uses the mind to go beyond the boundaries of its consciousness. The thought of the self is God-centred, and it opens up the little memory of the self of the ego that is frank to communicate what self-taught can teach others about the cosmic Jesus or authentic practices of good faith in us lay. It could be that the soul's spiritual cell has rebirth. We experience the resurrection from the death of the mortal body into a new life. New cells cluster that take form for endless possibilities to take up life in different environments again and settle on what the universe has out there.

Opening up to the cosmic God spirit puts you beyond triviality and focuses on improving things you do to them as you do to yourself, the godly mind in us.

In the infinite God spirit, all people find a name that utters God, or the unknowing mind has educated itself. It is known that even the most elite, highly trained in education, meet this puzzle and the problem will forever be so that it is impossible to name. Hence, 'it' is the infinite God spirit that all human minds eventually find but object to putting a name to, and there is nothing spooky about the thing 'it'.

At this moment, we utter the name of God or Christ. Jesus Christ, in the language, is recognised and gives the soul powerful energy – 'the Almighty God'.

It feels useful for a practical purpose. It is positively good for the body and the mind, and one day, spirit cells can retake a quantum leap into biological systems and dwell on other worlds and other kinds of realities out there. Places and worlds exist in harmony and equality, with peace throughout.

I am optimistic that it is a radical human vision of justice, equality and peace. I yearn to sink into the physical and mental geography of myself that works and plays on the five senses, which inspire me. I embrace them like a mental exercise. I discover ideas and phrases sunken into my unconscious, the concept of the eternal soul I had to erase and unlearn, and the wrong impression I picked up to keep my mind at peace.

In my first book, I had been wrestling with the ridiculous parts Christianity taught me. I had to draw on my wild, visionary sense of reality. I invented my theology to get peace of mind and enter entirely into my cosmic spirit so that the soul spirit guided my spiritual journey and did not let the textual one learn to rule. Knowing the goal towards which I strive as best I can with my time here is the earthly duty to love and to live the best I can. I am using my built-in godly, holy, divine, good spirit, personality and character to make a difference in this harsh, competitive reality, which is just one fact that exists on planet Earth to evolve the species.

Biblical texts used to explain the universe are also used in the most horrific practices and policies to justify slavery, genocide and colonialism. Although we cannot afford to ignore the Bible, it is a tool for confronting injustice when we see it. In modern times, people's excellent characteristics have evolved very slowly. Events in the Bible have been described graphically for adults and children to read or speak in oral storytelling. Slavery, sexual abuse, assault, genocide, torture, false imprisonment and the death penalty have not disappeared for decades. Real-life violence is still present in today's society too.

One part of the biblical story that has been overlooked is the stripping of Jesus before his crucifixion. Christians and the Church should recognise Jesus as a victim of violence and abuse.

They reflect on the disturbing story of the torture and crucifixion in the season of Lent, which must be one of human history's most widely known and often-retold stories. Yet, despite being read and remembered, the stripping of Jesus receives minimal attention and little discussion. I think most present-day Christians consider abuse as an exclusively female experience.

There is a tendency to deny, dismiss or minimise the dominant display of humiliation by the stripping and exposure of Jesus. It was a devastating emotional and psychological punishment – more than just physical discomforting – and should be acknowledged as an act of abuse and gender-based violence.

I identified Jesus' stripping as violence or abuse because the purpose was to humiliate him and expose him to mockery by others.

The stripping was done against his will and was a way to shame him publicly. I assumed the Romans used humiliating actions to degrade those they wished to punish.

Recognising historical reality is necessary because Jesus' gender is central to understanding this abuse. Male and female nakedness has always been viewed differently. Naked women are immediately noticed and identified as sexual objects. More so than the stripping of Jesus in the gospel. If Jesus were a female, I suppose most people would not hesitate to say the ordeal was sexual abuse. The scriptures seem okay with treating sexual assaults as punishment for disobedience and that annihilating a significant number of groups of people can have justification within religion. A horrible thought that has just buzzed in between my thinking is that in the Bible, God could be compared to an enslaver who dehumanises people they own into shreds. Some Bible writers' ideas are plain enough for me to say they are wrong about a good God, and I, too, can get interference in thinking straight that puts me off track from the point I make.

Biblical texts give us tools to confront violence in many communities where society is not peaceful. Why are Old Testament gods more devilish, and why does the devil in Satanism do less harm? Finally, I grappled with the issue of injustice, and the laws from God seem to write off black and mahogany people as foolish, inadequate people because of active melanin in their skin and have them as enslaved people.

I see churches not flinch at showing images of extreme torture through the crucifixion of Jesus Christ and photos of starving Africans. The horrific crucifixion of Jesus is often glossed over, but pain, the death penalty, false imprisonment and colourism (prejudice based on skin tone) are still present in society.

Theology or ideas about God affect civilisation and beyond, and the Christian dispute over divine justification in the past has affected many fundamental aspects of contemporary society and culture. Still, these days, it seems far from its religious origins.

I have found the language of mathematics to help me understand the kind of Earth God made. Of course, I still add up sums using my fingers, but the discovery of mathematics was one of the human mind's great discoveries.

All people, children and adults, need attractive qualities that are godly and have an awareness in mind to always want to do the right thing. It opens the mind to understanding the scriptures and whether the inspired word was changed or new terms later added in the text to fit a regime's corrupt agenda.

Most ordinary people are susceptible to losing their minds because the pastors and preachers of paramount principles are not mindful when teaching ordinary people not to close down the account on the rigidly fixed principles of godliness but open their thoughts to extend them. Those knowing better about them, the educated preachers, have yet to expound the people. All seeming carriers of truths and godly principles preach corrupt ideology, and people continue to fear the unknown and the things of it and not be able to explain the idea of reformation about God and what is next after mortal life finishes. Where will life go? And human dead shall stay dead forever; God knows and is personal to each of us. The truth of the thing, 'God', is that we have an awareness experience that there is nothing but our human mind sense, something humankind can't name and has no name to say. All people, especially the most ordinary, familiar people with closed minds, call 'it' – the thing, God – spooky. All people who finally reach enlightenment know that the chill experience is not frightening. When we are enlightened, we understand the process.

The churches that are flourishing today are flourishing because of ignorance.

It has been said that in the early centuries, forward-thinking intellectual Protestantism challenged long-held beliefs that salvation was contingent on the capricious authority of the priest before being admitted to heaven. Protestantism opened the way for forward-thinking against conservative, anti-science, Catholic dogma. When the world's major religions began, the universe was not known to be a mind-boggling, enormous, prominent place with trillions of galaxies.

In our times, some people move through a journey of faith, including an early time of certainty, often expressed as fundamentalism. But then, in the middle of the belief, doubts take hold, and the stage of agnosticism arrives. In that challenge of believing that nothing is known about the existence of God comes liberal views, which I cherish.

Seven weeks before Christmas 2017, it is time to get geared up for this festive celebration. Of course, by now, nativity scenes will all be in place in churches, complete with shepherds, oxen, sheep, donkeys, and a baby. However, I learned this week that, according to leading European Bible experts, none of those creatures were there.

There were no animals in the Bible nativity scene. There is some misunderstanding, of course. Although for many, Christmas is a traditional celebration grabbed from the pagans' main festival of the calendar year, the so-called experts have no clue.

As I continue to write the thoughts of my mind, it feels like, if I try hard enough, it is possible to override my deep-seated religious tendencies with rational deliberation, but it takes great mental effort. My evolved cognitive skills used to underpin my beliefs, and the roles of culture and society also shaped my mind. Having been told that a supernatural entity watches over us, intervenes in our lives and passes moral judgement, I had already thinkingly accepted it. It pays to assume that agents cause all events, but religion piggybacks on feelings of existential insecurity. The randomness of some things, loss of control and knowledge of death are soothing when the idea is that somebody is watching over us and that death is not the end of existence. It feels right, and none of my senses sense that my evolutional gene pool brainwashed my mind. The same entity directs events and everything that happens for a reason. I argue that God has made this implant in the aperture of the skull to maintain her physical presence in our heads.

If we are to be like God, a perfectionist being, or likened to the things that self-righteous must be, which are perfect, we can change our imperfections. Also, God is physical in design with skin tones, and the existence of the human brain came from a person like us. God did a lousy job because there are flaws in the brain's functioning mind, which gets dogged by bias and requires eight hours of routine shutdown for daily maintenance. The brain is highly susceptible to severe malfunction. God, the actual supernatural forever-living creator God, has not blundered in the design area that gives us a deity in our mind, the non-feeling brain, and the deity in our heart we can feel.

Any person who has considered some deity and God has to confront that our brain is perfect to believe in it. The religious belief appears intuitive because it requires hard intellectual graft to shift to atheism, even in today's world of enlightenment and materialism. Coaxing more of my analytic thought may lead to decreased belief because neural functioning begins to change. Still, could I have different circuits connected with analytical thinking activate while others become deactivated? I cannot shift to atheism; it first takes guts to deny there is a God in creation. I haven't the guts or that kind of courage.

According to neurologists, my unwavering belief and atheists have the same architecture and process information similarly. But I accepted higher inner power convictions of God that give life meaning, security and experience of transcendental states. They are more associated with intuitive, empathic ideas and a sense of mysticism. God in the brain does something to my mind and provides positive benefits like a brain on recreational drugs gets. It gives us a rush of euphoria, and contemplating withdrawal has damaging side effects. The altering perceptions and changing beliefs damage the creation of 'self' between self and the rest of the world. My hypersensitive God detection device would struggle with confusion trying to figure out the belief change to anchor 'the self' and how to maintain the conceptual structure in mind. I am sensitive to the subtle realms of experience, and because God has to mean an existing creator, God is neurologically real to me.

There isn't a pathway or spiritual part in my mind that facilitates God; it is natural. The whole brain has inescapable certainty properties of the mind to reason for thinking about thinking. It is like understanding ideas, an approach to the self, the cosmos and the 'thing' God. The nature of the creative agent reality and the conception of truth are universal in our human existence. The seeds of this regulate my behaviour and religious sensibilities, which have deep historical roots in the evolutionary lineage. We know we only occupy a narrow space and time in the great cosmic story of the universe on planet Earth. Practitioners of religion, science, rationality, atheists and agnostics cause horrible atrocities worldwide because their perspective is short-sighted. None are natural and reasonable; they fight to forge our human species way ahead, but science and rationality have facilitated some of the worst modern phenomena, including eugenics, the atomic bomb and drone warfare. The other types of people with educated consciences argue and declare war none subjective or are a personal commitment to one's values of connection to self, others, nature and the transcendent with both eyes open trekking on towards the future that is opening up before us or in front of us.

Whatever that future ends up being, if we humans are to be there, I do not think that it is a realistic option for the human species to exist if the trait of God disappears from them. Their horror and horrible atrocities will kill them like a lethal virus that infects people to bump off the species.

18

NEW YEAR RESOLUTIONS 2018

Friday, 5 January 2018

Happy New Year, folks!

At this time of year, it is all about resolutions.

My New Year's resolution for 2018 will be to make us healthier and happier, but sadly, most of these promises of self-improvement will quickly be a memory for most people and me. "This year will be different," I say to myself. Nevertheless, I feel committed to it, and it is a significant change that I won't have to make precisely the exact resolution for next year. Using the month of January is a sufficient motivator to be intrinsically motivated to work on goals. My wife warns me not to be obsessed with money.

It is January 2018. I have evaluated what transpired in 2017 and what I would like to experience in 2018. I have constructively and compassionately considered where some unexpected and unhelpful detours occurred. By listening to my intuition and feelings, I could connect to the current truth and develop creative solutions. I gave myself credit for that and our positive direction to bring about change.

I look back on 2017 and want to say how we lived for that entire year provided helpful frameworks for getting out of a mental rut, working through thorny problems, and reacting to internal and external expectations. The experiences and insights improved my personal development, which is utterly refreshing. So, I would like to approach and navigate this year with a shared vision with my wife. I talk to my darling Euphemia and our children, who are most important to me. They make me feel happy, fulfilled and relaxed. We have built meaningful, satisfying lives by being intentional, thoughtful and proactive.

I have again had to determine or reaffirm my true desires to take appropriate action for wishes that stem from me regarding establishing priorities. I must adhere to my spouse's wishes and feelings to be what we should be, ourselves, and what we want. My darling tells me to consider when we have been most content with our lives: "Remember what was going on in our experience at the time. Our belief in God, togetherness, excellent family support, friends and a unique social support system helped us pull through. Stop working yourself up over money. A loving family is the most essential commodity; do not have worrying concerns about money this year and beyond."

I get up in the morning, and sure, there is a plan to look forward to because I will focus better on our most basic intention. I find at least one moment of enjoyment every day of waking up this year and beyond. I have learnt to be flexible when obstacles present themselves and to continue pursuing my goal. I break down my approach to problems into manageable small steps and give myself a timetable. I may slip; slips are inevitable because slip-ups are part of human nature. I recognise there is always the next day, and I will not need to give up in despair. Even within the next hour I can get back on track, which makes slips learning opportunities, not certifications of failure.

If I reflect on why my slip-ups occur and then return to working on the goal, I tell myself they are less likely to happen again. I tell myself these things to prepare my conscience and gear myself up for whatever 2018 has in store for us. I ask myself why the ideas that come most effortlessly often need to be revised and lead to slip-ups, which appear on reflection as sloppy thinking.

As I write this chapter, time has moved on, and it seems to get faster and faster the older I get, so I am dedicated to this year's resolution to enjoy myself and engage my imagination in some of the processes. I also immerse myself in subjects I usually would not gravitate towards, which invites my curiosity. I hope 2018 will be an incredible year that inspires, uplifts or surprises me. So, I paint my dreams or day thoughts or feelings on the pages and continue to doodle my self-portrait as a memoir.

Life moves so quickly that my day is crowded out before I know it. I am busy, and time moves fast. So, time must be spent doing satisfying things.

Another hope for this year is that I get armed with plenty of tactics to generate great ideas and creative epiphanies, even when tired. I shall connect with what makes me feel alive and resolve to prioritise items that align with my values. In each moment, I intend to live to the fullest by having a positive attitude, a smile and genuine enjoyment of life. I want to conduct myself in the world with a final mission to love the people and the environment around me and establish things that matter. And thrive with passion, compassion, humour, and style.

I don't know about you, but it is tempting to believe there is an easy solution to all our problems if only I could magic the answer out of my head. But it is true that life is hard, and to get what we want, we need to do the work and dive into changes instead of fantasising about them. The compass will guide me when life gets in the way, when I am too busy, tired or hindered by my limiting belief in myself, which begets doubt and frightens me to plan. The power of planning and understanding gives purpose, and time and effort put into a cause position me for a life of happiness and success on my terms.

I am planning for my most fulfilling year, reflecting upon last year and reminiscing about times when I have been happiest, down, and in moments of peace and distress. The times I have found great inspiration have already helped make 2018 a good year because I contemplate where I have been and where I want to go.

My decisions enormously impact my happiness, ambivalence or disappointment more than the decisions of external decision-makers. My thoughts lead to my life experiences, more so than obvious inferences, and those experiences I share with others.

These thoughts provoked an analytical evaluation and inspired me to make positive changes to our advantage in the future. During millions or billions of thoughts, impulses have likely flashed through my mind in years past and will continue throughout my life. I either act upon those thought impulses, leave them in the recesses of my subconscious mind, or ignore them.

I am determined to have greater clarity of thought in 2018 and a great passion for living to begin living my future destiny.

19

SEXUAL HARASSMENT

Tuesday, 23 January 2018

Since July 2016, I have been a good friend to a young Roma woman who sells the *Big Issue*. You might remember that I befriended this woman to show my compassion, kindness and respect and offer simple words of support. I buy a paper from her to help her support herself legitimately. I invited her to my sixtieth birthday party in September 2016, but she could not attend. She could not make it with two young children to look after, as their father is absent from their upbringing.

The *Big Issue* newspaper is marketed to help homeless people earn a living. I have been a regular customer of this young woman, and the friendship has grown. We regularly chat over lunch at a favourite cafe in the town centre for no other reason than to show kindness and goodwill to a woman who sometimes goes without food, as the food she buys feeds her children and her mother.

We showed that we were just terrific friends for weeks and weeks, and my wife Euphemia saw this friendship develop into casual hugs and a kiss on the cheek. My darling warned me that streetwise young women could manipulate vulnerable mature men to get money, and how I looked at this woman and seemed excited to hug her was a sure sign that I was falling in love with her. My darling told me that my principles and morals of good value were slipping.

I said, "No, I just like her as a good friend, and I look like I could be her father or even her grandfather, for I am old enough, but I also look at her as a daughter."

The relationship was mutual, but I had been kidding myself because, after months and months of hanging out with this young woman at the cafe and buying the *Big Issue* from her, something sinister clicked in me. It urged me to have the nerve to try to develop this relationship into one of romance and sexual expectations, and it changed my mood.

After the thought became persistent and I had constant butterflies in my stomach, clumsy in her midst and sensing a romantic connection, she informed me that she would be going away. However, I would see her again on the occasional weekend when she came into town on the train. I gave her my business card, which promotes my published book, *The Memoir of a Schizophrenic*. It has all my contact details on it.

I missed her so much that I thought of her for the three months she had not made contact between October and December 2017. My feelings were becoming more potent, and I craved to glimpse her or hear her voice on the phone. I was strained with feelings of fond affection and not knowing how such a nice woman on the streets was worrying me.

I met her again on Thursday, 11 January 2018, and oh my God. It was like a celebration party in my body, especially in my heart and head, and none at all were sexual feelings. I was just exceedingly filled with joy on her return. We hugged more than once momentarily and kissed on the cheek on the busy town centre street, and the contact did not stir any sexual desires.

We had a meal at the usual cafe, and she said she had missed me and had lost my contact details. She had looked for them again at Christmas to wish me Merry Christmas and to find out how I was doing during her absence, but she could not find my card. She reminded me it would be her birthday on 20 January; I remembered her age was twenty-three in 2016, and this would be her twenty-fifth birthday celebration.

Just over a week later, and a day before her birthday, we met again and greeted each other in the usual way in a public place. I asked her to come to my parked car to escape the rain and the cold. I had something to say and something to give her for her birthday. She came and sat in the car, and I gave her a birthday card. She was about to open it in the vehicle, and I said, "Don't open it until your actual birthday, and I would like to take you to the cinema."

She looked so excited. She hugged me, kissed me on the cheek, and hurried to get out of the vehicle to open it, I suspected, then left, saying, "See you later."

I had written a romantic message on the blank leaf of the birthday card and concealed £30 cash for her as a gift to help support her living. The writing on the card expressed just a glimpse of what I was thinking about her. It excited me to see her, and I thought I was falling in love with her. It may be a sin, and sins can be forgiven, but I could not forgive myself if I did not tell her I was falling in love with her. The message included a hug, kiss, and happiness to her and God's blessings xx.

The next day, her birthday, remained wet and cold and rained intermittently. Euphemia usually goes to her mum's but changed her mind. She said she felt lousy and would stay in bed late. I ensured she was comfortably resting and asked her to phone me on my mobile if she needed anything because I was going to the local library for a while. I muttered in my head, "God, please forgive me for lying," as I leaned over the bed to kiss her. I instantly saw that Euphemia's intuition suspected I would not be visiting the library. She looked at me and froze as I kissed her. She swiftly sighed and shook her head. "I don't know why I keep putting up with this. Do you know it's all in your head? It's not reality," she said.

I played stupid by pretending I did not know what or to whom she was referring. I felt the adverse side effect of guilt and was deeply saddened to leave my wife tucked up in bed, but the thrill of meeting a potential second lover again was a greater incentive. My rational mind suppressed the natural urges to kindle love with my soulmate, who is deeply tied to my moral fibre and dislikes being alone. I was in the presence of my wife, and yet, as my most dominant sense told me, I was missing an opportunity to affectionately love my dearest friend, my right-loving partner, my wife. I love her dearly, but I still walked out the door in the pouring rain to chase the chance of meeting my sweet friend, who may be part of my fantasy of having two lovers rather than the reality that she was just a good friend.

I met my sweet friend, who smiled broadly and hugged me, and we kissed on the cheek in public. Then, we took the bus to the cinema, and she lit a cigarette at the bus stop. I had just learnt that she smokes. After the cinema, we returned on the bus and arrived at the train station just in time for her to catch the 4:25 pm train home. I spent an entire afternoon with her, and she wondered what my wife might think about my deceitful absence and our friendship. I tried to laugh it off as nothing, temporary collateral damage, but my massive intake of breath as I grinned and bit my lips was my body language's way of squealing at me.

It was not right to temporarily suspend the love in my soul for my wife, but I did manage to verbally tell this woman in the train station waiting room that I was falling in love with her. She seemed shocked, like I had suddenly startled her, and then was a bit annoyed that it had spoilt our friendship.

"I only love you like a daughter's love for her father and as a good friend. It's a crush," she said.

Oops, oh my, I had humiliated and shamed myself before her. She had not read my message on the birthday card. I risked challenging her feelings because I was disappointed and attempted to force them to change. You will be shocked to learn that I sexually harassed my good friend. I tried to kiss her on the lips after we had hugged goodbye as the train approached the platform. She resisted, pushed me away, said goodbye, walked to the train carriage, and gently waved. I was humiliated and shamed in full view of the CCTV camera and the public, but one consolation was that she waved from the train, which restored some of my dignity.

Recently, the media has exposed men misbehaving, which has shattered their credibility and respectability because they dropped their inhabitations and sexually harassed, exploited and groped women. Allegations spread from Hollywood's most beautiful female film stars and female parliamentarians to men-only charity functions with female servers.

I believe in gender equality and respect for women, but I misbehaved. I am very sorry. With a loving wife, I initially sought to see a young woman as a good friend, but when she became absent for three months, I felt crazy about her. My critical faculties became dulled when I told her I was falling in love with her. Still, this giant leap temporarily affected my happiness because she rejected my advances as a crush on a young woman. I felt ashamed and foolish in openly declaring my passion for her, which I should have kept secret. However, she did make it quite understandable that her love for me was only a love that a daughter holds for her father or a sister for her brother, which would not be romantic or sexual. She was shocked to learn this was where our friendship was leading. Hell's bells. She did not want our relationship to develop beyond good companions and the close love of a friend of the same gender. It dragged me into a depressive spiral for a couple of days because the real sadness was that it had frazzled my brain, and I had to tread water. I may not be able to talk to her at all. I avoided being where she might be; I felt like a fool, a dirty older adult, and a constant embarrassment.

I was as mad as hell at myself, and my pride was hurt. Right now, I am unhappy with my philosophical slip and feel dysfunctional; it is pathetic. I look like an idiot because it is absurd to be a mature, married man sensing a strong emotional tie to a young woman who only wants a good role model of a father in her life, and I let her and myself down. Everyone who knows me is let down because I committed sexual harassment. It was her right to shove me away, and to accept the rejection was painful. It is a terrible feeling, but she was right because the attitude towards women must be respectful and consensual.

Euphemia asked why I avoided answering her questions about my female friend. "You left me in bed and went out in the pouring rain to meet her. What happened? You were not thinking about me, and you fell in love again with another woman."

"Yes, I was with her, but I don't love her like that anymore, in that way, but only how I rightly should have continued doing. I found out that she smokes cigarettes, lit up one before me, and said she was stressed; it relaxed her nerves. I can't go to see her anymore, ever."

Euphemia probed and probed, but I told her no more than this, and I asked her to drop the subject and allow me to focus on her needs and our love life.

Two weeks later, on 2 February 2018, when I was out shopping earlier than usual in the town centre, my friend appeared as I emerged from a shop where she usually stood. When I went into the shop, I did not see her, but as I came out, she was getting ready to sell the magazines, and our eyes met. She timidly smiled as I walked up to her. I swallowed, anticipating the awkward feeling that may erupt in my stomach. However, I was okay and did not attempt to touch her physically. We stood in our safe personal spaces, and I exchanged money for the magazine and talked. I asked her how she was, and she expressed shock at my behaviour and her honest feelings for me again. She added that she needed time.

She said, "I still love you like a daughter who loves her father and as a friend, but I couldn't believe you would think of me in any other way."

"I am sorry," I said.

She asked how my wife was and how she was feeling.

"Okay, but she has a few aches and pains." I do not think she understood that I was referring to the physical aspects of aches, pains and emotions.

The conversation ended as she repeated almost these exact words to me. "Look after yourself, take care, and I hope to see you around next time. Bye, and God bless!"

And I walked away.

20

RESEARCH INTO ANTIPSYCHOTIC MEETING

Saturday, 3 February 2018

I had prepared a printed piece of writing about my experience with antipsychotics for the RADAR meeting agenda number 7. I have added some more details to the script today:

Meeting date: Wednesday, 31 January 2018
Agenda number 7: Experience with antipsychotics

I had over forty years of antipsychotic drugging, nine times hospitalised between 1977 and 2014. Unfortunately, I believe that lifetime treatment on antipsychotic medication has not played a crucial role in maintaining remission, averting relapse or improving the quality of my life, and now my mortality is in sight.

There is no question that when I am suffering from chronic, debilitating symptoms of schizophrenia, antipsychotic medication is a critical component of treatment.

The medication was designed to modify how my brain functions and impact my memory. It causes forgetfulness and difficulty concentrating. It sedates and causes cognitive impairment, slowing the speed at which I can take information in and understand it. It affects my working memory.

The medication was very good at managing psychosis, which consists of hallucinations, delusions and thought disorders – the positive symptoms I had. Still, it could not treat my apathy and social withdrawal symptoms.

I came to believe that antipsychotic medication should be limited to relapse episodes and gradually get tapered once I am stabilised and restart promptly only if and when symptoms return.

After bouts with psychosis and depression and being given a high dose of antipsychotic and antidepressant medication to treat it, I was stable again. Antipsychotic remedies for remission had a long-term detrimental effect on my brain chemistry, and it began to scare me. The trial on antipsychotics and reduction was well overdue, and I was pleased to be accepted to the RADAR panel.

I gradually believed that I should have progressively tapered off my 30 mg of Abilify, but I found myself being a coward without the support of a psychiatrist. It will be a painful lesson if I am not okay and have relapsed.

Trying to come off medication was a risky gamble that is usually not worth taking, but I was concerned about the risk of heart attack and shortened life expectancy. I humbly assumed that discontinuing the antipsychotic drug was right for me; there would be disastrous consequences for getting it wrong. Although I was reducing the dose slowly, I had safety concerns that lowering the dose regimen may trigger withdrawal symptoms and increase the relapse risk. The reduction in dose time and time again was scary. Still, through many leaps of hopefulness, I learnt a few steps that eventually made reducing my antipsychotic medication less frightening and overwhelming.

Over three and a half years, I have come out of the hospital on 30 mg of aripiprazole and 10 mg of haloperidol. From June/July 2014 to February 2018, I have reduced it to only 5 mg of aripiprazole daily.

I feel like I am in the process of detoxing, and I have just begun to allow my brain to heal by slowly getting rid of the pharmaceutical chemicals in my mind and body.

I used to have sixteen hours of sedated sleep and am now experiencing sleeplessness and persistent biting of my lips to keep them moist. I experience out-of-control chewing actions; sometimes, my teeth nip the flesh at the sides of my jaw as I eat. I feel quick, tiny, uncontrollable twitches in my hand as I write. I have light headaches that feel like a tight-fitting hat, adding pressure around my head and making the pain unpleasant. It feels like my brain is a sticky treacle forming inside my skull, pouring like a running stream of volcanic lava down my forehead, around my head, to settle around my eyes and ears. I also have all-over body aches and low energy, which I am attempting to reduce by discontinuing antipsychotics in the long term, for they are the most troublesome symptoms.

On Monday, 15 January 2018, I had a home visit from a GP because I had severe pain in my neck, lower back and right leg; I could not move. I was immobile, could not shift my body and could not straighten up. Five hours later, the pain had eased, and I had some mobility. The GP said I had a tightening of the muscles in my back that had caused the pain and mobility problem. He prescribed ibuprofen gel to rub into the affected areas and paracetamol and ibuprofen tablets for pain relief. He advised me not to use the gel and ibuprofen tablets together.

"Return to the doctor's surgery after four days if things have not improved by then so that an investigation with X-ray or scans can be carried out. What I can do here is limited," the doctor said.

The worst part is the rigidity of my neck, back and legs, which have spasms, weakness and tightness. There is also that constant tightness in my skull, like the pressure that has built up, squeezing nerves to feel like goose pimples raised through my scalp. The hairs on my head feel like they are standing on end, and my forehead is much more wrinkled. My limbs and joints are in pain, causing decreased mobility.

I had two thirty-minute back massages booked at a beauty treatment centre three weeks apart. I went to the first appointment on 18 January, and the therapist used the lymphatic drainage technique to relax the muscles. Still, within a short time after the treatment was complete, the pain returned with higher intensity.

Paracetamol and ibuprofen tablets moderately control the pain, and on a scale of one to ten, one being the least intense, the pain is at a threshold of seven or eight and sometimes even worse during the night.

My cognitive functions and motivational impairment are gradually improving. I am getting rewarding experiences and achievements because I have more control over my future.

I have concluded that my brain function has improved in tapering the drug, but not enough to put me back in a real-world setting, such as work or high social functioning.

I made an appointment to see my GP. The earliest was for 30 January. I cancelled it because a letter from the Planned Care and Recovery Clinic (formally known as the Community Mental

Health Team) came through the post asking me to attend a physical check-up review on the same day. They reviewed the data collected in August 2017 to identify any changes. My height and weight, which had increased from 92 kg to 95 kg, were recorded. The nurse asked questions about diet, alcohol consumption and exercise and noted the answers. The nurse also traced my heart rate (ECG) and sent me to have my blood taken for testing for various possible ailments that taking antipsychotics has on my health.

If there are concerns about the results of the blood tests, the GP will contact me. My next due appointment with the psychiatrist is 6 March 2018, and according to the letter, it is an outpatient caseload review. The new clinic aims to deliver personal, responsive, focused care, including nurse-led clinics and pharmacy support sessions. However, I may have to go back to primary care to continue my reduction in antipsychotic medication under an already strained GP service, which also undertakes medication reviews.

Today, Tuesday, 6 March 2018, the psychiatrist agreed I could take 5 mg of aripiprazole daily. He thinks it is the lowest possible chemical protection I will be getting, so I must not attempt to reduce it any further. I reminded him of the schedule I worked out and wrote down, seen by the previous psychiatrist, of my intention to have another medication reduction in six months, August/September 2018.

The psychiatrist could not be sure that I would see him in the clinic for my next appointment in September, but he would like me to remain on the 5 mg dose until something can get worked out at my next meeting on monitoring my future care.

21

I AM GETTING IRRITATED BY MEDIA NEWS

Tuesday, 17 April 2018

I want to know the basics of what is happening in my community and the world, so I watch regional and world news and listen to radio bulletins, mostly when on the move. I am careful not to get depressed by one troubling story after another. I cannot play ball with harrowing human stories because I am too sensitive. I will be the odd one, like a square peg in a round hole. My behaviour is unreformed and is like a flat, cold-water ocean that washes to the surface of my mind to temper and calm my sensitive feelings. Stress has seemingly irreplaceable power.

My darling wife finds the news interesting and entertaining rather than distressing. Although the reports are timely and frequently tell tragic stories, the news readers can detach themselves from being oversaturated.

"I feel empathy with the news, and I don't think deeper when it's repeated and repeated. I get on with doing things, and my mind is elsewhere," my darling said. She is not paralysed or besieged by the astonishing amount of distressing news every hour of every day and with no satisfactory conclusions.

On the other hand, I get irritated and angry, for the stories should be followed up. The current political and social climate is a source of stress, and to keep my balance when fierce goings-on buffet me, I must avoid exposing myself to too much television news. So, I leave the room, for I know too well that the stresses of chronic exposure to troubling events release a stress response in my body, triggering a schizophrenic attack in my mind. I have continually reduced my stress-related activities, not increased them. I have joined a writers' club and am taking up drawing again, doing things I enjoy. I also enjoy music, and I am a keen gardener. The writers' club will guide me professionally as I continue my authorship. I am now at the computer keyboard and typing the stories forged from thoughts that woke me early at 4:30 am.

At that time, dawn was breaking, but it was still dark. I could not see my hand or the pad and pen. I outlined the shape of every letter using my imagination in the darkness to make a word and completely form sentences. I did not put the bedroom side light on because I was trying not to wake my darling Euphemia.

I am on a low dose of medication, and my aim is for total remission without the drug to prop me up. Stories in orbit this month are testing my resilience to stressors. My body and mind are not resilient enough to deal with them, for I am a hypersensitive person; chronic exposure to TV news unleashes symptoms from a dormant mental illness. Bad news releases a stress response in my body and mind that can damage me. The long-term effect of continuously exposing myself to stress, bringing about emotional sickness, is chronically worrying. If the nature of the chronic stress does not revert, I am stuck in either flight or fight mode, or other bodily processes increase.

I know what I can handle to keep me functioning well without feeling overwhelmed, traumatised or debilitated. However, I do not want to be ignorant of my sensitivity, lurking in the danger that staying glued to troubling news will bring to my well-being.

Martin Luther King was assassinated half a century ago and was remembered on 4 April, and Enoch Powell's 'River of Blood' speech was fifty years ago. Both were in the year 1968. Today, Britain is multicultural, which works quite well most of the time because British laws outlaw all discrimination, whatever form it takes. But America remains an odd place to live because class divides are replacing openly shown racism. I might need a sedative as I have to weigh up the risk of my emotions not being able to cope well with historical events that happened and upset me as a child in England: racial tensions, skinhead violence, offensive name-calling, patronising comments and the mono television showing violence against black people directly in our home, mainly on the daily news programmes. The sitcoms *Love Thy Neighbour* and *Till Death Us Do Part*, *The Black and White Minstrel Show* and Golliwog images were for our entertainment. Yeah, oh boy! Oh boy. It was an insult.

I am irritated by the headline story today: there has been news about the use of a nerve agent on English soil in the attempted assassination of a Russian ex-spy in Britain and his daughter.

On 7 April 2018, the Syrian government used chemical weapons to attack its people. Russia denied Syria was behind the attack, and international tension rocketed. The USA, France and Britain aimed missile strikes into the region where Syria's chemical weapons were being made or stored and bombed them to smithereens. There were murders in London, mainly through stabbing, the tally in April a little higher than New York's in February and March, the news media said.

This weekend marks twenty-five years since the tragic death of an unprovoked racist attack in London on eighteen-year-old Stephen Lawrence, who had aspirations to become an architect. He was attacked while waiting at a bus stop with a friend. A bungled investigation followed and exposed institutionalised prejudices in British policing.

His death became one of the highest-profile racial killings and a watershed moment in British history, which changed society's attitude towards race relations and positively impacted UK law and police practices.

This and other stories fuel my anger and dismay, and it is possible to get depressed by them too. So, I shifted to listening to the radio and selectively reading news captions and articles online to stop myself from overloading my body and cognitive system. If I am not careful with my exposure to horrible news stories on TV, radio, and the internet, as well as in newspapers, magazines, and general gossip, my well-being will be at risk.

Our experiences dealing with the police in 2000 revealed foul play in their investigations. For example, we felt they were not impartial or unbiased in our domestic dispute with a racist neighbour, who caused criminal damage, bodily harm and emotional distress and got off scot-free.

We felt that the police were themselves racist and discriminatory and could not be trusted, and we believe it to this day. (The whole story is in my first book, *The Memoir of a Schizophrenic*.) Today, eighteen years on, some black citizens still do not trust the police.

Catastrophic loss of confidence in the police shows they do not serve all sections of society, and trust is lost. However, there were campaigns after Stephen's death, and his family pushed for justice and reform, and there have been some profound changes in the justice system. However, like Stop and Search, they have scaled back. His death caused people to come together across the country to celebrate the positive contributions of diverse communities to British society.

To do my bit in crime prevention in the area where I live, I am a part of the neighbourhood watch scheme. I aim to coordinate and encourage people to have a community spirit, respect their neighbours and property, and be vigilant. I distribute newsletters to members' houses where I live.

The legacy of Stephen Lawrence will ensure that caring adults give advice and help support, inspiring and encouraging the young to fulfil their dreams. Stephen never had the opportunity to achieve his vision at the time of his murder. He was studying for his A-levels. The young should live their best life while they are young and not be afraid to dream so that they achieve their best and they will feel good and noble about themself. From a young age, they can create or contribute to a society where everyone lives and strives for a specific change in an inspired role away from crime and wrongdoing. As they grow, they will see growth in people and themselves, taking a holy, divine and positive attitude into their adult years. They will also learn to look after themselves and better care for the environment and our planet.

The young need to have a more substantial life purpose. This will steer a decisional conflict mechanism that is mundane and straightforward between committing a crime, continuing to execute it or going straight. A more persuasive guiding purpose statement is, "I have a sense of direction and use it in my life." It can help transform young people susceptible to crime into more socially sensitive people who contribute to society with skills learnt or talents in their gene pool. I had a humble beginning, and I started finding out why I must try to avoid wrongdoing at a young age. My higher sense of purpose did not equate to getting a job to support me financially as the essential purpose in my life. When leaving secondary school, I said, "I don't know what career I can do!" I asked the history teacher, "Was there a real historical man named Jesus, and was his father a carpenter?"

I wrote 'A Character Study of Jesus Christ' in my CSE portfolio. The English language teacher gave me twenty-one points out of twenty-five. I kept up my efficiency grades intuitively, knowing that my consistent ideas about God had maintained their conceptual structure since I was a baby. I actively considered my beliefs in God and continuously transformed my undesirable behaviours.

I learned from Jesus to be good, do good, and be kind, and I did the activity and practiced what I learned. I had become addicted the same way as a drug addict, and my concept of fate and destiny was genetics-driven and shaped my outcomes. I became socially incompetent, experienced multiple episodes of psychosis, and wanted to achieve functional recovery between bouts. Unfortunately, getting treatment early and consistently by taking antipsychotic medication did not improve my chances of recovery. I had said, "I am addicted to Christ. I don't know who I am. Is Karl a copycat of Jesus?" at the start of the prodromal period. It could not have been hard to pin down the disruptions to my human mind's functioning and quickly get a working diagnosis of schizophrenia. Serious crime can result in a life sentence as punishment or a reform programme in prison, which professional, legally trained people say is proper. The medical profession appears to say schizophrenia is like a life sentence: there is no cure, and it is only suitable and appropriate to stay on antipsychotic medication. Eventually, they might get lucky, and probation may come.

In evaluating my emotional response to hard news, it has become apparent that emphasis placed on words inappropriately brings attention. Dramatising keywords in the human stories hit a raw nerve and broke my resistance to absorbing information, especially tragic and shocking facts, affecting my well-being. Clear visuals of gory images of suffering, torture, violence, killings and cruel acts will likely upset most people. It is not well known that critical words in broadcasting cause maximum discomfort and upset sensitive viewers when they dramatise and emphasise strong words such as 'kill' and 'dead'. They are sharp and cut through me, etch deep and hurt.

Hypersensitive people prefer 'killed', 'death', 'die', 'died', or 'dying'; they are more acceptable words for mortal loss. These words do not provoke immediate attention or urgency, and they give a feeling of sympathy and absolute respect to a life cut short, be it by the hands of criminals, disasters, intentional killing or natural causes.

Strong words can hurt, and dramatic emphasis on words only makes the pain more intense, damaging us psychologically.

Words known to damage the psyche should be restricted in real-life human stories, where negative emotions should be watered down so that they stir positive feelings instead. Proper sentences should be balanced with emphasis to capture attention.

22

OVER THINKING AND FEELING GUTTED

Sunday, 3 June 2018

Theirs seems to be an inner world, a conscious experience of waves of thought that gives the feeling of overproductive thinking. I am at a roadblock with no obvious diversionary route, which bothers me. I have come tantalisingly close to writer's block, and what a difference a couple of months makes.

Today, 3 June 2018, I pressed the keypad and connected the thoughts of my mind that were reluctant to flow on the page. I am writing catch-up stories and reminiscences.

Two months ago, on Thursday, 12 April 2018, I submitted three pieces of my earliest artwork to the local borough council's open contemporary art exhibition. So, naturally, I priced them high, even though I had omitted my best works.

I asked the family to choose the pictures they would like to hang proudly in their homes when my and their mother's lives have ended. Some of their choices were my best pieces of artwork, which are priceless. I found pricing and selecting my artwork for exhibition hard because I considered almost all my artwork invaluable and not for sale. I sought professional recognition and public appreciation of my paintings, not sales. I wanted them back. There was no guarantee I would win a place in the competition because of many things beyond my control. I have had failed attempts with my best artwork in the past, and being unsuccessful then had me overthinking. However, it reflected the quality of my work, and it felt the same again.

My self-belief allowed me to recognise that my work has the potential to be shortlisted, and it was refreshing to chat about it with friends and family who could see something evident and invigorating about the art pieces.

On 17 April 2018, I was notified by phone that the panel of three judges had rejected my artwork without any feedback. I felt gutted, bravely collected them and took home the booby prize. So, I am back to the drawing board and keep trying to reinvent or push my ideas in abstract art that translates into my voice and forms the heart of my artistic practices. Eventually, the art world will recognise my ability, like my handwriting, as my writing has a unique style.

Following Euphemia's redundancy over six months ago, her Job Seeker's Allowance ended at the beginning of March 2018. Euphemia still had to sign on at the job centre to continue to show that she was seeking employment and having her National Insurance contributions credited. All fortnightly payments stopped, and she is not entitled to any other benefits. The newly introduced Universal Credit benefit will be in our area in October 2018, and we are using up our cash reserves to get by.

I applied for Euphemia to be added to my ESA, which will increase until Universal Credit becomes effective.

I received the extra allowance on 4 May 2018, almost nine weeks after sending the form to the relevant government department. Luckily, on Monday, 16 April 2018, Euphemia found employment on a zero-hours contract at a local private day nursery. Unfortunately, her first monthly wage was in arrears on 1 June.

I have been ruminating about past mistakes, those uncomfortable shades of grey that hurt, and I have explored them in writing to put them to rest.

I had mulled over, for the umpteenth time, losing my mobility. I regret my wife's suffering due to me purposely colliding with a thirty-nine-ton articulated lorry on 3 March 2003 on the busy double carriageway A14. I am annoyed at the way the passage of time has undoubtedly sped up. I am ageing more quickly and missing out on things taken for granted. I am incredibly sorry that my wife missed out on ordinary stuff because of me. My whirling thoughts are focused on the things I cannot do. Writing gives me relief, a sense of freeing the mind from regrets and disappointments that lurk at the back of my mind, which I mull over repeatedly.

I have accepted that I cannot change the past. I thank God that I cannot because if I could, world history and, in most cases, my personal history would have changed.

While self-reflection brings attention to the past, it has been helpful to be in the present moment again. We have experienced more than our fair share of tough times. My personality and emotional makeup interpret events in my life with thoughts that run through my mind like clockwork. I have hurt myself and others I love, and I had to forgive myself and ask for forgiveness to let go of my wrongness, which allowed me to move on from my mistakes.

I feel no more moral than anyone else and believe I am less harmful than others. Still, there is an ambiguity when unethical behaviour shows up in my self-righteousness. My moral norms of kindness and respect for others are the same as everybody else's, but my inside perspective on myself is saint-like. I always try hard to act ethically, but I feel gutted, less valuable, and least accurate when unethical. Even though my intentions and motives were to do the right thing, look after myself, treat people fairly and be generous, I have the fatal flaw of making terrible mistakes. Also, I was not born with the physical disabilities that make me immobile, having to use a pair of crutches for support. It is due to the multiple injuries I sustained in the road collision. I cannot run, jump, jog, skip or dance properly, and I miss not being able-bodied to do those physical activities most people take for granted.

I cannot let go of the fact that I did it to myself by attempting suicide in 2003. Life was tough; money, relationships, the environment and religion were all stressors. The home appliances broke down, the car malfunctioned, Euphemia lost her job, a loved one died, and rain spoilt a pleasant walk on a summer's day. There is no protection from daily annoyances or tragedy; the only exception is belief in a loving existing creator, God, who sustains. However, accepting the mysterious workings of faith gives me inner confidence, peace, and favourable external vibes that allow me to sense the protection of the supernatural. It can be overwhelming without the subconscious mind regulating or limiting my conscious life beliefs. I had an inner war beating myself up at the funeral on Friday, 20 April 2018, of a departed soul known to the family. The thanksgiving funeral service for the life of a brethren saw me mourn his death and simultaneously feel a range of feelings. Sadness, guilt, anxiety, sorrow, sympathy and regret had tears cascading down my cheeks for my own life that I deliberately nearly cut short. I had self-pity.

In the prayers for the departed, the shortcut of self-bashing and crying ceased because I was caught up in the positive effects of prayer: blessings, optimism, peace, worthiness, confidence, trust, security, positive affirmation, and the mental empowerment of ourselves to change.

The time in prayer was a temporary fix from dwelling on my toxic negative emotions. Certain hymns whitewashed my insecurities, and 'The Lord's My Shepherd' and 'O Lord My God When I in Awesome Wonder' brought back the weeping. At that moment, I felt the emotional toughness that my wife endures when we act like lovers wanting to hold hands as we walk down the street and at parties wishing to embrace and dance. Giving up on biological activities that feel good and generate endorphins in us is tough for her.

Fortunately, despite my life's twists and turns, I have attained blessed bliss, and I am thankful that it has led to happiness through a shift in my state of mind. Unfortunately, my joy was derailed when I suffered from illness and bad things happened, and I am grateful to all who heightened my hopefulness from the negative impact on my mood.

The first weekend of spring, 21 April 2018, the temperature outside was above mild; it was hot. It was fantastic by mid-afternoon when a sprinkle of rain fell in our region. In the evening, after a hearty supper, my darling Euphemia was anxious to work off the calories and exercise by dancing in the middle of the living room floor. I watched her adoringly sexy dancing.

"Would you be able to walk this fine evening?" my darling asked as pop and R&B music played on the radio.

"I want to attempt to walk with a single crutch around the block. I think I can do it. Stroll on flat ground," I said. My mobility had deteriorated because of the ageing process, which has caused wear and tear on my joints, which are often painful, so I use painkillers to moderate the pain.

Going on the walk was iffy. I had to stop periodically to feel comfortable and physically rested. But emotionally, the trail was like creating pearls in an oyster. It was a beautiful feeling, such a positive way to draw my attention to my spouse.

The walk, which would be twenty minutes for a non-disabled person, took us one hour. It seemed as if time had slowed down. The trail looked comfortable, and we took it slowly, like a low gear that allows one to cruise but does not accelerate the vehicle. We both felt great. I held her hand during the stroll, and it released trapped energy, the tension in our bodies.

My darling and I connected in this moment of more quality time together. Just the subtleness of holding hands, the sweet conversation that brought laughter, and the pauses to look into my lover's eyes made me very happy as we savoured the person we loved moment by moment.

"That was nice, Karl, perfect, but I didn't burn off any calories," my darling Euphemia said.

So, we took a moment to kiss on the doorstep as we entered our house.

I felt blessed for all eternity to have Euphemia in my life, and I hope that going for a walk together can become a ritual, like a religious ceremony.

23

FURTHER REDUCTION IN MEDICATION

Monday, 2 July 2018

I have associated my body's aches and mental fatigue with antipsychotic medication reduction. The physical pain had worsened, and I had rebooked an appointment to see my GP for a complete physical check-up in February/March 2018.

My complaints ranged from pain in the sole of my deformed left foot, muscle sprains in the thighs, a very stiff neck, lower back pain, bilateral knee pain and a painful sore on my left Achilles. A surgeon had removed a surgical pin. Unfortunately, that area suffered trauma in the road collision in 2003, and it appears it has not healed.

My GP sent me to have an X-ray of both knees, a blood test, and hospital referrals to physiotherapists and orthopaedics. According to the GP over the phone, the X-ray results were abnormal but expected because of natural wear and tear in bilateral knee osteoarthritis. Knee arthritis is a degenerative condition. However, the X-ray also discovered osteochondroma in both knees. This is a benign, non-cancerous tumour on the surface of the bones. Since childhood, I have been aware of them as a painless bump that causes deformity and pain with activity.

The blood count showed a percentage fall of white blood cells, and I was to repeat the test, but I have not done so yet. I had my first physio appointment on 1 June, and I still have follow-up sessions. I am encouraged to keep doing the set exercises at home, and the therapist says I am progressing well. I am still waiting to hear from the orthopaedic department. The physiotherapist and a podiatrist examined my posture and movements and measured each leg length. The collected information suggested that my left leg is 20 mm shorter than the right leg due to a total left hip replacement operation following the trauma in 2003.

I am taking 5 mg of aripiprazole, and on my birthday, 14 September 2018, I aim to discontinue and observe how I get on with no milligrams of medicine in my body.

Antipsychotic drugs are usually considered to be one of the twentieth century's major medical breakthroughs. They were often believed to be so compelling that they brought about the closure of the old mental asylums. The mentally ill could return to the community, but it must have involved legal, governmental and political decisions to save money. Antipsychotics gained a reputation as 'chemical straitjackets' for they control disturbed and aggressive behaviour in mental hospitals and as animal tranquillisers in veterinary medicine.

I am much nearer to achieving my goal of discontinuing antipsychotics. I will again reduce my medication before the next visit to the psychiatrist in September 2018; the day of the appointment is unknown. I am insightful about my condition, with the capacity to understand the risks of experiencing a relapse while coming off the aripiprazole antipsychotic medication.

I am fully aware that in case of any signs or symptoms of psychosis, I will seek help from care providers. I know it is a critical period where the dose may be ineffective, and I hope to feel stable. Despite all my cognitive features weakening, I am very much oriented in time, place, and within myself. They seemed to stay intact because, mentally, at my core, I am well. I can make a decision, and positive symptoms do not exist. I sleep well, have an excellent uninterrupted five and a half hours of sleep each night, and have a good appetite. I have no suicidal or homicidal thoughts, and my mood remains good. It is okay, as I reduced 5 mg of aripiprazole to approximately 2.5 mg by snapping the rectangular pill in half. I will take one of the pieces with water or with a cup of coffee starting today, Saturday, 4 August 2018.

There is reasonable evidence that antipsychotics can reduce the symptoms of an acute psychotic episode in the short term, but I have experienced suppressed mental processes. When locked into a persistent psychotic state, I judge the use of antipsychotic medication to treat my neuropsychiatric disease to regain a foothold in reality over many years as adequate treatment. Considering antipsychotics taken for years can produce neurological damage, diabetes, heart disease, shorter life expectancy and brain shrinkage, it led me to discontinue the drug. When in mental turmoil and confusion, I may not see my situation as others see it. I also may disagree that anything is wrong or that anything needs changing. Antipsychotics changed my behaviour in such a way that restrained me. As I began to see the world as others see it during recovery, I typically thought medical treatment and drug use in psychiatry to induce my specific mental and behavioural changes were reasonable. The drugs have helped to diminish disturbing thoughts and experiences but at the cost of nearly stifling aspects of my personality, such as initiative, motivation, sex drive, erotic flow and creativity when I was severely psychotic (the last time was in 2014). The heavy antipsychotic drug dose far from normalised my ill mind, and my responsiveness and reactions were sedated and reduced. I was in a state of physical, mental and emotional suppression and had slowed thought processes, and flattened emotions were part of the artificial state the antipsychotics produced.

(The story is in my first published book, *The Memoir of a Schizophrenic*, page 686, sub-headed 'Psychotic Episode in 2014').

I used to believe the view psychiatrists held that antipsychotics work by reversing an underlying 'chemical imbalance' or other such abnormality. They told me this rather than acknowledging that antipsychotics induce an abnormal or altered state of mind. I believe antipsychotics are misrepresented, their benefits inflated, and their dangers minimised. Their use in treating severe mental disturbances in people illustrates that they have become one of the most profitable drugs in history. My own experiences taught lessons, and textbooks say that antipsychotics affect a consciousness shift in spiritual activities, including thinking, perceptions, emotion and behaviour, in unique ways. They produce particular alterations in my brain's mechanism, while most other drugs seem to recognise the body's pathologies and target them. Medical drugs usually do not target the ultimate cause of the diseases they treat. They may help reduce swelling, pain and irritation from the body's inflammatory response to the infective agent. I want sustained remission and want to stay well. I am on a sustainable recovery journey, and it will be a hard battle to face if life chances diminish and I anxiously worry. I am filled with doubts and a loss of faith, and I am distraught and disempowered by the interaction of government services like the council and Personal Independent Payments (PIP).

I am already waiting for a decision from a review for PIP that I had no outside source to help me write about my health conditions. Capita, the organisation that provides the assessment to pass to the Department for Work and Pensions (DWP) government department, will contact me and may ask me to go for a face-to-face assessment. It is a merry-go-round. I have had many evaluations over the years to prove my need for permanent disability benefits for my ill mental health, which raises my anxiety. It gives the feeling of being overstressed. My wife's friend accompanied me to the assessment centre once, where I had weird, uncomfortable feelings. In hindsight, it may have been subtle symptoms of schizophrenia, but the health professional did not pick up on it, and I lost out on having financial support for my mental ill health.

I have self-doubt that I can wean myself off antipsychotics because I feel fear and anxiety take control in the face of the change and uncertainty that is on its way. I am beginning to be afraid, and the purpose of being unmedicated is in the way. I cannot be sure if it is because I heard Capita would assess me, and it has thrown me into irrational or unrealistic thoughts that come up again and again. A universal human emotion is the fear of failure. My track record of insanity has me battling with fears and repetitive thought patterns, but my sanity has self-doubts, a thought pattern I control. It causes common cognitive distortion that trips me up.

I am dealing with impostor thoughts about failure, and I have never learnt to deal healthily with this customarily expected emotion. My self-doubt, worry, and inner critic can become toxic, triggering the evolutionary psychiatric disease schizophrenia. I must be careful not to exchange good brain chemistry for toxicity, as stress interferes.

I take caution that I may not be ready to pursue the new leg of my journey through recovery from schizophrenia. I had taken my little half-dose pill and struggled with fraudulent thoughts. My honest feeling is to push the total discontinuation of taking the antipsychotic to November 2018. After that, I feel confident enough in my programme to wean myself off the antipsychotic pill. That is until I feel worried and confused in the face of possible negative changes to my PIP entitlement and my general uncertainty about whether unmedicated schizophrenia will work. It has a dampening effect on my positive pathway that sees the pursuit as something brave and important to me and everyone living with schizophrenia.

As I leave this write-up with a few more sentences on the page, my confidence is returning to become my greatest strength and most valuable tool in beating the feeling of failure and undeserving of success. This week, I modified my shoe by raising the left shoe to have a 20 mm platform sole. I also bought a brand-new leather-upper classic Doc Marten men's shoe and adjusted it to have 20 mm extra height on the left sole and heel. As a result, both heels have lateral flare.

It is now a week later, Saturday, 11 August 2018, and the great thing I am feeling is confidence after fear and anxiety controlled my days. These thoughts have inspired me to grow and served as a springboard to appreciate the stress-free parts of my life: What is going well?

However, getting caught up in problems can be too easy, and I live like a ball of stress. I am privileged to be alive; 'life' is a series of challenges to be solved, some tragic ones that make us humble and have commonality with everyone on this planet. Although none of us is one hundred per cent problem-free, the chances of being a living being in this universe without problems are reportedly the closest to zero you can get.

24

SCHIZOPHRENIA NEAR TO BEING DECONSTRUCTED

Sunday, 19 August 2018

I am greeting you as I begin a new leg of my journey through recovery from schizophrenia, which is incurable. My human brain went awry nine times with psychotic symptoms of schizophrenia, maybe because I was on a high-maintenance dose of antipsychotics for too long. Schizophrenia can produce some of the most uncomfortable experiences a human can have. However, I have been persistent in slowly weaning myself off an antipsychotic drug, like a constant stream of water that will wear down the most complex, cumbersome hard stone, and I am nearly there. The dose is now only 2.5 mg of aripiprazole, and I feel normal, happy and healthy. However, I sometimes exhibit coherent problems because the information to and from my brain must sometimes get regularly unregulated. I have concentration weakness too, which appears like an intellectual disability. But, overall, my mental state functions better than those with a low IQ. I am developing strong, healthy, clear thoughts and can better determine a course of action sometimes.

Antipsychotic medication could not restore the damage schizophrenia caused to the parts of my functioning which are not positive and negative symptoms. So, I must live with the malfunction, learn to adapt and not let it get me down. I think and have experienced that antipsychotics act well on positive symptoms but worsen negative symptoms. With each hospitalisation I had when I was psychotic, the positive symptoms disappeared within a month, and the negative symptoms persisted to the point of getting worse with long-term use of the antipsychotic. I had told my doctors I was symptom-free because the positive signs had gone. I could not recognise for years that the negative symptoms were always acting on me. Time and time again, I thought that laziness, low motivation, cognitive deficits and poor mental function were part of my character flaws. I lost jobs because of functional decline. In social situations, I talked much less and found it challenging to organise myself.

The full effects of the medication and the precise mechanism of its action are still unknown, and atypical antipsychotic drugs have been around since the 1990s. The dopamine hypothesis is still the predominant theory explaining the drug's effect. Psychiatrists always say antipsychotics act by blocking dopamine receptors in the brain. It's codswallop. They don't know for sure.

I have taken my antipsychotics forever, but they never prevented relapses. Often, schizophrenia symptoms split me off from reality, and I could not distinguish what was real from what was not, but now I am known to have a high level of functionality. I will soon be unmedicated with the symptoms suppressed only through lifestyle changes like reducing stress, not feeling overwhelmed by life, having a good family life, having access to nature and exposing myself more to natural substances. Therefore, I am opting out of the first primary treatment option, antipsychotic medication, to treat my psychiatric disorder.

I have been on antipsychotics for forty years, and the mental health care providers have never offered an alternative course of treatment. I have had disturbing thoughts and behaviours and the antipsychotics reduced those symptoms. Still, only the hallucinations, delusions, disorganised ideas and irrational thoughts got suppressed, and my life struggled with blunted effects, impaired emotional responsiveness, apathy, loss of motivation, interest and social withdrawal. I tried to reintegrate into society and get into work, but I relapsed each time I was employed. My family's support was the best antidote. Their care and love helped me to trust again. I needed lots of reassurance and encouragement, and my irrational thoughts were first to be shifted. My family's endurance is worthy of praise.

I have taken control back from psychiatry because 'doctors know best' in psychiatry isn't always so. By making that decision to empower myself, I can take better care of myself and be grounded in how I want to live my life. My relationship with my mind has not been easy over the years. My mind had nine known clinical breakdowns. Conditions can get toxic when my inner self-talk is full of criticisms and judgements. My senses and emotional feelings react like something is acting on them outside my brain housing, the skull, which can interfere with any part of my body. Some factors that freaked my mind out came about before I was planted inside my mother's womb by natural conception and probably before I was born.

Growing up, I sincerely wished to connect to the things inside my body, mind, and the non-corporeal parts of human existence. However, I did not know what to call it to communicate with it. I knew it was impossible to touch. The desire went further than my basic human need to connect with my parents and others. My mind was attacking itself and suffering alienation and loneliness inside this entire cosmos, which the agent I was looking for had made. I had the sense that some parts of us, people, are immortal; therefore, it is a spiritual entity that is dimensional on a different plane from the world, and the human expression for it is God. The immortalised part of me is my soul. It lasts forever in eternity with the one God always in existence.

My thinking welcomes this warmth and love in all humanity. Therefore, my language for this 'spirit of God' in the universe greatly influenced how I experienced and interacted with people and the world environment.

From then on, I had the experience of sensing that another being fully understands me, sees me as emotionally warm and radiates generosity as part of the expression of love given by God. My inner dialogue self-mirrored me in a direct relationship with this God. There is a connection with the sense of warmth and appreciation, and my vibrant self senses the presence of this invisible deity in us and transcends our reality. The emotional part of me was getting hard-wired, and it treated speaking to myself as talking to God, and I repeated this practice, this talking to God.

Religion and culture tried to rewire my brain with beliefs I could not accept. I lived through trauma brought about by the controversial ideas about the man Jesus and the fight by humans with humans for territory in the name of a non-violent God. Hell, devil and salvation by a saviour ideology damaged me because they did not fit the awakening of both my hemispheres.

Since the dawn of time, God's evolutionary method has changed the human brain; it may have brought about my genetic accident, the psychiatric condition schizophrenia.

My diseased organic brain caused my mind and body to act up. Feelings and behaviours were bizarre, and my brain did not have the time to heal them. Drugs are used to retract or suppress the substances that ill my brain and the pharmaceutical chemicals affect my mind, and it is crazed, sometimes without realising it. The suffering was immense until I resonated with myself about how I was being treated, and speaking to myself was the key to bringing healing into my life. This means of deep connection to the source that calms my out-of-control inner critic was reached through powerful positive affirmations to myself. I had statements or even words that I could repeat to myself that could give me strength when feeling weak, and they reminded me to be kind to myself. Meditation and clinging to my popular positive notions about my future outlook healed the troublesome voice and cultivated more compassion for myself.

It has taken a long time to develop this analysis and realise my mind had turned against me. The spirituality that exists in us humans defaults through trauma. I searched for God within to bring wholeness and found levels of criticism. My tone and the pitched voices automatically corrected to one inner dialogue that encouraged and supported me. I am aware of losing precious time and energy when I wrestled with my mind for many years. It also used much power in my thinking. By reasoning out bias, things converted my pessimism to the desirable optimism from the God within. I had relapse after relapse, and my imagination and memory held right to my mental battles. As I write more on the subtle theme, my mind has designated specific brain cells to move ahead and try their best to focus. Still, my mind is uncomfortable, given that the cells of the partition assigned to the next-in-line in the writing process warn my brain that it is gradually being deconstructed. It feels like I only have a short supply of oxygen left to breathe, and every moment is precious. Still, every breath is both cherished and regretted at the same time because that is one more breath I hope I can never get back; schizophrenia is breeding in me.

I take my mind to the task, and my brain knows that the schizophrenia in me must be deconstructed by carefully maintaining a low-stress level and thinking positively. I will stay optimistic, have a confident attitude, do physical exercise, get quality sleep, relax, talk to avoid the bottling-up of sad emotions, and listen well to good advice from those before me. I cherish and love myself and appreciate life's blessings and ups and downs. By having the right attitude at the end of the day, mental rubbish would not have to be sifted through because it probably would not exist in my mind. The hypotheses as to the aetiology of schizophrenia are always on my conscience. The combination of genetics and the biological basis of the disorder plays an essential role in the environmental factors that trigger a possible genetic predisposition. And that may start again at the onset of this debilitating disease; schizophrenia has terrible symptoms in me.

Although the aetiology of schizophrenia is always in my mind, I resolved to take a proactive role in my attitude towards schizophrenia and not buy into the myth that I cannot get total remission for the rest of my life. I can understand why health professionals think like that because schizophrenia has been an episodic disorder in me that has characterised itself by going in and out of symptomatic remission. It will be different this time because I have taken steps to prove that some people with schizophrenia do not need lifelong antipsychotic medication for long-lasting well-being. Several times, schizophrenia has been inactive in me on the antipsychotic drug. Still, all the while, my quality of life, occupation and social functioning had negative residual symptoms of schizophrenia impairing me.

I have not heard of any consensus on what constitutes 'recovery' in schizophrenia. Schizophrenia is a very stress-sensitive disorder, and I have to cope better with everyday problems and situations that could trigger a breakdown. I must know my limits, not take on more than I can handle and take time out when I feel overwhelmed. As I move forward to become unmedicated, I am an exception, living with schizophrenia without taking any medication. Will I go prescription-free on the day I see the psychiatrist: September 2018? I very much hope to. Then, in the next six to ten months, following up with a psychiatrist and then making a decision, the positive and negative symptoms have totally disappeared. No rehospitalisation will redefine me as having a 'meaningful recovery' in schizophrenia. It may seem like I am in an interlude between psychotic episodes, but I hope that a long-time follow-up discovers that I am indeed in total remission.

Improvement in my quality of life and social functioning is the outcome that matters the most to me. Unfortunately, the current treatment of schizophrenia seldom results in full recovery because living in England, an industrialised rat race ideology country, and taking antipsychotic medication contributed to my mental breakdowns. The burden of high mortgage payments, utility bills, work to make ends meet without reward and interactions with people who hate me and cannot stand me are stressors. Other stressors in industrialised living increase my body's production of the hormone cortisol, which triggers psychotic episodes in me. Antipsychotics are helpful only in acute psychosis. At first, my periods of psychosis came and went unpredictably over the years. Still, looking back through my journals and carrying out my analysis, the stressful conditions in my life were a breeding ground for the most fearsome mental illness, schizophrenia, to reappear. Stress is my biggest enemy with this disorder.

25

FINAL REDUCTION IN ANTIPSYCHOTIC MEDICATION

Monday, 3 September 2018

The positive mental state of my mind has urged me to gear up for more challenges, and there is a robust inner vision ahead. I have reached the final reduction in antipsychotic medication. My idea, aim and mission must not be derailed or go in a wayward direction because I have retraced my history of this condition. Schizophrenia is an agony of life and a bitter fate. Much water has flowed into the river since the diagnosis. Today, the weird world of delusions, hallucinations, disordered thinking and disorganised behaviour is being defeated by a sincere thought to the godly insight that gives me wisdom and strength with immense self-confidence and self-realisation. Although schizophrenia cannot be erased, sufferers should not lose hope and should have a positive state of mind, which will not develop in a day. It requires years-long building of solid, strong willpower and rejustifying it to the brain. I cannot unthinkingly relieve my weary personal thinking; its ills produce a subjective manifestation of sickness. So, I have opted for a course of action that seems radical: to wean myself off antipsychotic medication slowly.

From today, 3 September 2018, I am taking a 'pinch' dose after snapping the 5 mg tablet into two halves. I then choose one of the pieces, position it in the pill cutter, and attempt to slice it to an even smaller size. It looks like the blade has just pinched a bit from the pill. The dose is approximately 1.25 mg of aripiprazole daily. Managing schizophrenia, I ensure I can live with a chronic disease as common as any other chronic illness and have the best life possible. I must have an exit plan in complicated social situations or avoid those situations entirely due to their past relation to paranoia and anxiety. I can make this 'recovery in schizophrenia' and not lose my specific voice, the self of my mind, or the part of my brain that bears senses and feelings that rely on trusting my self-confidence.

The expected appointment date to see a subjective psychiatrist who looks at symptoms is in September; the follow-up from the last visit was in March 2018, but the letter has not appeared yet. I am very close to starting a new self-advised therapy without the official approval of a psychiatrist. Therefore, I have asterisks on 14 September 2018 on the calendar as the first day I will completely stop taking antipsychotic medication. It will be my birthday, and I will be sixty-two years old. The challenge of the disease is to stay symptom-free, and I believe I can do this because I have created a purpose-driven life, have the support I need from my family and have educated myself about the illness. In addition, I am pursuing self-help strategies that prevent my thinking and behaviour from developing into psychotic episodes.

I trust myself to tell someone about my mental health if:

- I start withdrawing from relationships or hobbies
- I have increased anger, aggression or suspiciousness
- I start feeling a sense of inactivity and hyperactivity/hypersensitivity
- I start behaving in a way that is reckless, strange or out of character
- I stop paying attention to personal hygiene
- I start laughing or crying inappropriately or am unable to laugh or cry
- I am unable to feel or express happiness or start having feelings of depression and anxiety
- I have decreased or disturbed sleep.

It is a long, challenging road to stay symptom-free, and I am prepared to take the best care of myself to give me the best chance of having no symptoms and sustaining recovery. I now have more control over my recovery than I probably realise.

Acute psychosis is not a pleasant condition; it is incredibly frightening, debilitating and exhausting for sufferers and loved ones who care for those of us who experience it. I have four years, from 2014 to 2018, of relative stability from psychosis. As a long-term sufferer since 1977, I have learnt to have the best chance of increasing peace and stability and avoiding a psychiatric crisis. There are many negative consequences when this chronic condition disrupts life. Overwhelming anxieties often trigger my relapse, and acting early and talking to trusted people help prevent deterioration. The less external stress I have to deal with, the more energy I can devote to recovery, and now that I have no work-related stress, I hope I can recognise the warning signs and stay on top of it. Refocusing on reframing what I regard as success and failure could significantly impact my life if I had not learnt how or what my symptom triggers are. I want to spread some lived wisdom with tips for having total remission from schizophrenia. A 'lasting recovery in schizophrenia' is how I genuinely think of it.

Tips on lasting recovery from schizophrenia:

1. Before you go off your antipsychotic medications, talk to your treating specialist, a GP, your family or a friend. The decision to reduce or come off antipsychotics should be based on discussion, research and planning.
2. Minimise the stress in your life. Pressure can be a trigger for relapse.
3. Make sure you get regular quality sleep because sleep deprivation can be diabolical for an emotional disease such as schizophrenia.
4. Learn your triggers and symptoms and talk to someone about them.
5. Remember your bodily aches, monitor physical symptoms and the health of emotions of your brain's ideas and ills, eat healthily, exercise and do not smoke.
6. Schizophrenia cannot be treated by diet, exercise, prayer or willpower alone, especially in the acute state. Instead, evidence-based treatment by medical professionals is required.
7. A philosophy around what you hope to be and what you intend to accomplish is vital. Core values, ideals and principles bring

enthusiasm and passion to your life, and beliefs or activities excite and mean something to you. Also, have reasons for doing what you are doing with your life. Then, your direction in the process and the actions you must take will fulfil the requirements of your plan. People with schizophrenia face so many barriers. Brave challenges and difficulties can be veritably won over if people with schizophrenia can teach themselves confidence, immense courage and the willpower to overcome challenges.

I have grappled with severe paranoid schizophrenia for four decades, and only recently did my determination and courage spark a new awakening and a new horizon.

26

A LETTER TO THE ASSESSOR, GP AND PSYCHIATRIST

Friday, 7 September 2018

Dear Sir/Madam,

Capita wrote to me that I might need a face-to-face assessment.

I have an increase in overwhelming anxiety and sleepless nights. In addition, the possible call for a face-to-face assessment worries me excessively and is hampering my recovery from schizophrenia.

Over the years, from 1977 to 2014, I have had assessments, and the health professional was no wiser for seeing me. Even when I was assessed a few weeks after coming out of the hospital in

2009 and 2014 on heavy medication – 30 mg aripiprazole tablets and 10 mg haloperidol tablets – I was declared fit by the health professional.

They visited my home, and again, I was declared fit. In hindsight, I was not well, and the Capita assessor did not pick up the symptoms that showed I was not yet in recovery. I lost jobs because of 'functional decline', and in a social situation, I talked much less. I have tried over the years to reintegrate into society and get into work, but I relapsed each time I was employed.

If the decision at this time is to have a face-to-face assessment at the centre or my home, I will refuse to attend. I have had nine hospitalisations for paranoid schizophrenia, and none of the Capita assessors has determined that I have been unwell or that my recovery was beginning.

I have begun journalling through recovery from schizophrenia, which is not curable. I have had the most uncomfortable experiences a human can have when psychosis unlocks intuition, higher perception and psychic ability. I aim to be unmedicated, with the symptoms suppressed only through lifestyle changes like reducing stress and not feeling overwhelmed by life.

The possible assessment is beginning to throw my recovery into jeopardy because it's harder to deconstruct schizophrenia by carefully maintaining low stress levels, thinking positively and staying on the side of optimism and a confident attitude when an assessment hangs over me.

The breeding ground for the most fearsome of all mental illnesses, schizophrenia, to reappear as symptoms is stress. It's the biggest enemy. So, please conclude my application for PIP, which also includes my physical health and its problems, so that I can come to terms with the decision, whatever it may be. I would not be able to challenge with strength the decision if I believed it was wrong.

I will not attend any more assessments by Capita because the stresses are too high, which may cause my recovery to take a setback.

Yours faithfully,
Karl Lorenz Willett.

Howdy, Doctor,

Re: A call from Capita to attend a face-to-face assessment, which I cannot do.

I have waited months to hear something about my PIP claim and have yet to hear anything. I had no sleep for a few nights as the fear of the assessment rolled over in my mind. Today, 07.09.2018, I emailed Capita to explain that if I get called for a face-to-face evaluation, it will be too stressful for me to attend.

They responded by telephone, saying the health professional decided I must go to the assessment centre for an assessment for PIP. I don't feel I can without jeopardising my recovery from schizophrenia. I am in a new recovery phase from schizophrenia, and they will likely mess up my attempt to stay well with the stresses they impose on me. I feel I will lose any entitlement because of their incompetence to see that too many stressors cause my breakdowns. Since I cannot work, I need this benefit to help support myself and my housing costs.

I have weaned myself off 30 mg of aripiprazole and 10 mg of haloperidol since 2014 to have a dose of only 2.5 mg (approximated amount) of aripiprazole from 4 August 2018. However, I want everything to go right, and Capita needs to understand the delicate balance and the critical period I am in.

They did say a letter from my GP and psychiatrist or a phone call to them would be necessary because I am avoiding seeing the Capita assessor. They gave a deadline to respond: 17 September 2018.

I am sending the exact format of this letter to my consultant psychiatrist at St Mary's Hospital. Attached is a copy of my email to Capita so you are in the loop.

Thank you for whatever you can to help because they are not listening to me.

Warmest regards,

Karl L Willett.

27

GP'S LETTER, PIP CLAIM, DVLA AND MEMORY LOST

Sunday, 23 September 2018

Capita sent me a text message and a letter to attend a face-to-face assessment at 9:25 a.m. on Monday, September 17, 2018.

I was stressed. It affected my sleep, and I talked about it daily, desperately trying to stay well and focused. Finally, some time ago, I accepted that I might have lost the case whether I went or not. I shoved off the confirmation messages of the appointment, knowing the decision-maker was likely to refuse my claim.

I was so fearful that the stress of my assessment would trigger my schizophrenia again that I did not turn up. I was sure it was a significant stressor that I had to avoid. I know from experience that it has the potential to trigger symptoms because of the acute observations and questioning. It is the perfect setting to begin paranoid thoughts.

Below is a section of the letter the GP sent me, which arrived in my letterbox on 19 September. The next day, I emailed all its contents to Capita.

> I am writing to support this gentleman in his PIP application because he cannot attend the Capita face-to-face assessment, for which he has been sent a letter.
>
> I can confirm that he does have a history of schizophrenia dating back to 1978 and more recently sectioned under the Mental Health Act in 2009.
>
> He remains under the care of the community psychiatric team, and they see him regularly. He is on several medications, including aripiprazole.
>
> He needs help managing public transport and going out for a face-to-face assessment.
>
> He is fearful that the stress of his assessments will trigger his schizophrenia again, which he finds exceptionally stressful.
>
> I'll be very grateful if you could do anything that might assist him in this area.
>
> Many thanks.
>
> Yours faithfully

Later that day, Capita tried to contact me on my mobile phone, but I did not hear the ringtone. I listened to the recorded message when I saw a text message. They attempted again to speak to me on my home phone at 8:15 am the next day, 21 September, and I was in the shower. The answering machine picked up the left message, saying they would call again later, but no further attempt was made that day.

Another major stressor last week was filling out a medical questionnaire from DVLA (Driver and Vehicle Licensing Agency) because my three-year restricted licence will run out in December 2018. I am also concerned about my disabled parking permit, the Blue Badge, which expires in October 2018. The badge allows the holder to park a vehicle, be a passenger in a car, and park in a disabled bay or partially restricted roads. I am still determining if any of these items will be awarded back. I check my blood pressure regularly, which is one of the ways I monitor my health as I take on life daily.

I have enrolled in adult education classes and continue to do hobbies I enjoy to reach my full potential. The first social connection was the writers' club, which challenged my ability to follow what was said by each member and express a respectful opinion. It is hard to follow the script of fiction genres, build the characters, bring the plot to a climax, and understand the story to the end. I have never read a book of fiction and fully understood the story. I am persevering with the writers' club, working hard to be the first with constructive criticism, not just saying, "Yes, that's also what I was thinking," to someone else's critical thinking about a story. Or keep my mouth shut. There is nothing to say because I have no clue about the story.

A literary festival is planned at Althorp House, where Princess Diana lived. I bought tickets for the session scheduled for Saturday afternoon, 6 October 2018. The upcoming literary event is a bold strategy to train my brain all afternoon to keep pace, keep its attention and save information in my mind. I want to increase my ability to collect the data briefly and listen to a second subject. Then, after a short time has elapsed, I return to the original data and do not forget it.

After attending the first two hours of a five-week course on designing and creating a website, I saw that I was struggling with learning. I retained nothing of the practical knowledge to repeat the process on my home computer. The sheet handouts and the homework set did not jog my memory because I could not remember a thing. I have already paid to be on four more courses (Creating Presentations with PowerPoint, Get Your Website Found, Create a Responsive Website, and Effective Public Speaking), which take my studies into the winter months through to the end of January 2019. I had no idea that my learning difficulties were so severe. My mind kept somehow messing up my education. Trying to figure out things like remembering names and listening to words to fully understand what someone has told me results in the illness of schizophrenia presenting cognitive impairments, or have the many years of antipsychotic drugging damaged my brain cells?

I immediately made an online appointment to see my GP. On 3 October 2018, I will discuss my working (short-term) memory and request a specialist trained in cognitive assessment to assess and report.

28

SCHIZOPHRENIA MANAGEMENT WITHOUT MEDICATION

Wednesday, 26 September 2018

I have now realised for a long time that long-term use of antipsychotics has detrimental modifications on my functioning and quality of life. So, I have completely weaned myself off them. I have been currently medication-free for thirteen days. Coming off medicine was not a decision I took lightly. I have been unmedicated with schizophrenia since Friday, 14 September 2018.

Slowly and carefully, my dose was reduced over a long period of four years. The side effects that had stiffened my joints in agony are gradually disappearing, and so are the other unpleasant side effects. My body's intelligence works hard to sync with my brain biochemistry to cease multiple behavioural challenges. Hope, courage and immense willpower push me forward towards recovery.

I have tried antipsychotics for over forty years and have had psychosis many times. Yet, antipsychotic pills did not eliminate psychotic activity over time. Each episode had its differences for me in learning healthy coping mechanisms. It is too soon to say whether I have reversed psychosis for good or have an interlude in the psychosis episodes. Having a better insight into the illness seems like a rocket booster, giving significantly improved chances to remain in recovery.

Schizophrenia is the most severe illness that has chronically affected much of my life. I lost my job, abandoned my education and experienced repeated hospitalisation.

The psychiatry industry has to come clean one day because I conclude that the treatment is improper and lacks an ethical approach.

I live now with schizophrenia without taking medication, but for most with schizophrenia, medicine is essential to living a fulfilling life. They may be taking the antipsychotics without experiencing any adverse side effects. However, let us be clear about taking medication: if the schizophrenia symptoms led me to the point of possibly experiencing psychosis again, which negatively impacts my life when all my other recovery methods are no longer working for me, then I would go back on the medication. If there were a magic pill to straighten minds and medicate to improve the thinking process by spotting the issue, you can be sure I would have had it.

It may seem that I am giving antipsychotic medication use a hard knock, but only the long-term maintenance uses of those medications raise my anxiety. But, on the other hand, they have been a helping hand when I was too unwell to think straight, I keep telling myself, and they are not 'happy pills' that solve my worries and problems of that nature. I thought they had made it harder for me to focus on clear and straight thoughts and did not give me a more comfortable life, but medication might have been the foundation of treatment to straighten it out.

The positive and negative symptoms and cognitive impairments of schizophrenia were a constant agony in my life, and they devastated my future vision at the onset. It has taken me a long time to pull myself out of the catastrophe of schizophrenia and to bring my life back from a devastating direction. By coming off medication, it feels like I have become free from this seemingly death-defying ailment, although no one dies from the condition of schizophrenia. I simmer in a positive state of mind, and it pushes my conscience to recognise that schizophrenia is not a forever killer that brings death. I have never heard of schizophrenia causing any eventual death. A lifestyle that may include smoking and long-term use of antipsychotic medication gives us conditions like lung cancer, heart disease and diabetes that kill.

I had faced frustrations and agonies in most of my steps since my schizophrenia diagnosis in 1977. These days, the weird world of persecution, hallucination, delusions, positive symptoms, and the negative ones, like reduced expression, lack of motivation and functioning, has stopped haunting me. The journey is never over because the province has challenges and threats that can stress me positively or negatively. A positive state of mind will be the winner for sufferers surviving in the day-by-day environment; they will then excel.

The history of my illness took a disastrous direction with suicidal urges, and my tormented mind evolved from them, but my body continued to overflow with muscle activity. There is sometimes a cry to a godly source to bring peace, harmony and the almighty energy: the supreme power force had input answers to my repeated requests.

The strength of my soul that I felt from my gut (a sort of second brain in my belly) sent the right chemical signals to the first brain in my skull, opening my higher consciousness to immense grit and determination to pull through.

The overflowing of muscle activities has not stopped entirely because my neck, shoulders and hands are stiff. I visited the dentist for pain in my mouth and was told I have sensitive gums. Cramps are in my legs, and I get lower back pain, too. Musculoskeletal physiotherapy exercises give me slight relief. In addition, I occasionally experience writer's cramp with tightness in my wrist and fingers or my pen jerks when I write.

You may remember that the National Lottery Thunderball was one of the challenges I set myself up for a 'must win loads of money' challenge. The dilemma of whether I would win was an irreconcilable conflict that stressed me negatively for years, but it is not a subject on which I focus intensely anymore. Although a reward is at stake, my perception of a win is genuinely not motivated by the money; it is fun to have a flutter and raise happy feelings in my healthy mind.

29

THE PLACEBO EFFECT AND THE VOID IN MY HEAD

Saturday, 27 October 2018

Today is 27 October 2018, the forty-fourth day of living with untreated, remission schizophrenia. I am healthy and have an extraordinary sense of godly-charged normality – that I am all good. It is the most significant perspective people and things can have – that of the ultimate source flowing through my divine mind. I have reached perfection in bearing the truth and never lying, but is there a superior complex in control?

The typical standard for people with a sense of the godly varies: they are subjective and honest about taming passions with which they struggle. All people and things find it hard to tame themselves.

I have strived to be reasonable and healthy for years with the schizophrenic label. In the past, society would not hear that people with this illness could get better through true faith in the placebo effect of the brain healing itself. Instead, they locked us away in asylums and introduced first-generation antipsychotics from 1950 until 1990, when we were dumped into society without adequate support. Then, the pharmaceutical industry brought in the second generation of antipsychotics, and the placebo effects were rarely seen as a good healing process. I am going through a lifestyle change to be unmedicated with schizophrenia, and I expect a positive impact on my brain.

I am pleased that the phenomena – evidence of schizophrenia disorder and hallucinations that impair sensory feelings in one's voice or hearing, which seem to be that of somebody else – will never be a part of my lived experiences again. I feel more confident that I faithfully represent stimuli from the outside world, and my internal template, which has my preconceptions about the world and what I see or think, is inert in my brain. Thank God!

Before leaving the hospital in 2014, anticipatory signals caused my hearing voices to be idle, and my voice addressed me with questions and answers. I write them down so the reader can read my pure stream of consciousness. I have a void in my head that may have developed from long-term use of first- and second-generation antipsychotics to stave off schizophrenia or due to the gradual process of age-related memory loss. The void in my head is the storage of working memory, but it is empty, and I cannot remember things. A specialist in the NHS is to check my memory, and I am on the waiting list to test my mind clinically. I hope the molecular machinery that underlies my memory can be manipulated to improve it. However, I have not yet had the clinical trials on my mind. It works sufficiently well through the everyday mundane tasks that I carry out that do not require sensory information. I hope that when I have the test to prove that my memory is not functioning correctly, this will be attributed to age-related memory loss.

Forgetfulness and age-related memory lapses will be more natural to come to terms with than hearing schizophrenia has profoundly debilitated my memory. That would be shocking! It will be challenging, but still, I am very well aware that I had memory loss in two different schizophrenia trauma episodes in my history with the illness. There were a lot of reflexive actions and reactions, and created memories were lost when I came out of a nightmare terror. My brain headquarters for learning and memory are trying to decide whether to learn. Giving initial feedback at the writers' club about the fictional stories of members is getting more challenging.

I pay attention, and up to a point, I am able to follow, but suddenly, a blank void appears in part of my concentration, and no concrete ideas exist about what is going on. There is no underlying understanding in my mind about how the story developed. I have no idea how the characters appear in the account, the plot, the dialogue or the scenes. At its basic level, could I tell what the story is? No. I am internally frustrated. Information for the mind and in the mind is not being held. The information I take in and ideas I format do not seem to be stored in my memory, and my internal dialogue has a weak structure and gets wiped out in the actual process of laying it down in my mind. I cannot remember. Even my handwritten notes are at first illegible because they are scribbles, and there is no logical order to them. Listening to information with keen alertness and concentrating on writing and evaluating scatters simultaneously many confusions in the pathways of my brain and gets mixed up. I cannot decide what to do and have nothing to say when it comes to my conscience. I become mute.

Another example from one of the meetings was stories with the theme 'Whodunnit'. I followed the authors' scripts as each read their story in two parts. The first part told the story, and we all stopped to think about who we believed committed the crime. The second part described who the culprit was and what the motive was. So, six authors read their diverse 'Whodunnit' stories, and we had to determine who did it and what reason they had.

Why, oh why, could I not get it? I did not even have a reason to say, "I think so and so did it because…" Every member was able to tell who did it and give an idea. Their answers varied: some were wrong, but they gave it a go, and some responded only from their gut instinct.

I responded to five stories I had followed keenly and heard the authors reading them. Still, I had to say, "I am sorry, I haven't a clue," and with one story, I said, "It was an accident." How foolish was that? What became of my ability to figure out what was happening and retain an understanding of the evening's theme?

I beat myself up. After all, I felt uneasy because I did not know how to respond. That unique aspect of me influenced my feelings, and I was angry too. I want others to perceive me as capable and not as a fool.

Ten minutes after the writers' club meeting, I walked to the car park. I healthily engaged with three parts of my person: the stressed me, the unpleasant thoughts I have of myself, and the joyful part of me operating in one whole unit, the (complete) holistic me. I spent another ten minutes in the car, controlling my breathing. Finally, I drove home and told my wife about the hellishness of it all, and my darling lifted me to a place of peace in my mind.

"Karl," my sweetheart said, "you have never read murder mystery stories or watched crime and detective stories on TV. You have always understood the kind of books that give facts. You lack the developed sense to look for clues and put the story together. You somehow see those fictional stories as real life and cannot seem to pass off the murder as just fiction, which should be entertaining for you too. Karl, you hate to think of the awful crimes or murders people can commit. Naturally, you wouldn't have a clue and say the first silly thing without reason."

I intend to continue going to the writers' club. The problem with my authentic feelings is that they make me look weak; the social cognition, verbal and visual learning, memory and processing speed to keep pace are becoming more like learning difficulties. I had already given up adult education classes because of it. But I will stick to the writers' club and better my craft of being an author amongst people who enjoy writing fiction. I struggle with cognitive impairment. I find made-up sentences straight out of someone's head without referring back to their experiences fascinating. Fiction writing is not part of the author's experience; they make it up. Mystery, thriller, romance, science fiction, fantasy and comics are genres written straight out of the author's good imagination. I continue to be fascinated by how members craft their fiction and can write short stories just like that! And on the spot in a genre or any theme within the suggested word count. Their styles robustly activate my passion for writing more. They give me a dynamic representation of writings that constantly challenge me. I aim to diverge and expand my writing horizons and write some fiction unrelated to my own experiences.

I already had trusted and good-willed people saying I should diverge from creative non-fiction to teen fiction or children's fiction, and they had confidence in me that I would be good at writing in those genres. I responded to their stimuli by writing a fictional novel with stimuli reinforcing stimuli and began writing down potential ideas that could be a storyline. As a result of the flash-in-the-pan moment during brainstorming, I scaled high with stimulus intensity. I enjoyed the behaviourally relevant salience exercise to prepare for writing fiction. However, my brain activity, which needed to work on two projects simultaneously, was exhausted. I have shelved the storylines for the novel because my frontal lobe could not cope with another project on writing at the same time.

I am addicted to challenges, which are the torchbearers to a new kind of future where people learning about life reach optimal mental health without suffering too much firsthand. Most of my lifelong learning has been tagged with a brand of schizophrenia, paranoid schizophrenia, which kept up a consistent paranoia and unjustified mistrust of others decade after decade, and treatment was solely through antipsychotics. One of my torch-bearing challenges has its spotlight on the new phase in sustaining lasting recovery with schizophrenia unmedicated after years of being drugged. It relies on the placebo effect to harmonise brain chemical reactions with my body's chemical reaction systems, but it may not suit everyone. My skin and the five known senses pick up signals from the external environment. The senses pass on an attitude of calm indifference for my brain to process external events. A placebo will provide a psychological rationale, and my placebo bias and traditional beliefs will help me recover. How my mind thinks now or behaves results in actions that no longer spring from unusual, laughable or stupid ideas. I get a silly feeling that I am ridiculous when my thinking strays well outside the box. The good thing is that I can see my thoughts for what they are, ignorant and foolish, and laugh at them without remorse.

I want to cultivate a great mental state for the rest of my life by controlling my judgements about things and how I think about things. How, then, can I feel different when my experiences of living with people give me full acknowledgement that some people are wicked? The struggle to live (put food on the table) and natural or human-made disasters flood my emotions. As my thoughts pause for a few seconds, they generate in the plural without arguing that we have little control over anything. We have no control over what happens to us, and we also cannot control or own the people around us or what they say or do. We cannot even fully control our bodies, which get damaged and sick and ultimately die. We only manage this part of us that 'thinks'. Therefore, how I think about my ideas and judgements about my thoughts control much of my happiness. Things in themselves are neutral but look terrible to me and can be indifferent to someone else or even welcomed by others. Things happen, none of which are inherently good or bad. I suppose I have control over my happiness and how I value things potentially. I appreciate every living thing so much that my value judgements generate in-depth emotional responses so overwhelming that they debilitate me. I have almost no control over anything, but I can regulate my irritations, anger or sorrow in response to someone who perhaps did not deserve it.

I sometimes respond calmly when encountering many stressed, impatient, and ungrateful people. It is because it may not be intentional, and I will be happy. The obvious things that disturb me the most are wars, famine, suffering and man's inhumanity to man, and I have to accept what happens in the world. It ultimately forced me to try to exit this world because, being too sensitive, I attempted suicide in 2003. I did not like what was happening. I should choose personal happiness over physical solidity, but my thinking was paradoxical. No one chooses to be unhappy when in their right mind, or stressed, angry or miserable, and yet those were, in fact, all the product of my thinking. The one thing within my control, 'thinking', had derailed when my brain was ill with schizophrenia eruptions. It had taken me decades to stop the geological activity of the condition and for it to stay dormant and never again become influential in my brain. So, stuff happens, and I judge that something terrible will likely occur or saturate my mind when the media news is bad. Then I am upset, sad or angry and might get scared or fearful. All these emotions are the product of my judgement of the events. My responses are more normalised these days because I can better diminish those value judgements that generate my emotional responses without affecting my happiness.

The things themselves are probably neutral, and I should think none are inherently good or bad. The vast universe and the infinity of time stretch into the past and future. Time is putting my life into a broader context of rights and truths, and it has given me another chance to embrace whatever the universe provides. The world does not revolve around my feelings; my empathy for people is when my humanity reaches out to them. In the past, the 'self' automated itself to survive the intensity of its emotions. Spiritual energy forces in nature brought trillions of organised cells together to form me, Karl. They covered me in dark skin. I had expected everything within the cosmic perspective, that all life is but moments, to conform to the authentic challenges of living smoothly in a perfect, peaceful place. Instead, I sensed that we must move through the universe again as spiritual cells before the earth becomes debris and our mortal flesh perishes.

There has been a profound change in my predictions. They have lost their hype, anxiety, gloom and doom. I am glad I can imagine tomorrow's species and environment without cultural division. Yesterday's failing systems are getting pulled down, and the present time is accelerating the process faster to make way for the rise of a new system that works in harmony with nature and the unseen forces in the spiritual field. It will allow us and other species to survive in an environment that nourishes its species, far removed from the Darwinian survival of the fittest mentality. My current perception, which is best seen when driving a vehicle, is another example of my sanity. I am in control and switch to autopilot; the unconscious and conscious awareness work fine, and both are in harmony running the show. My sensory organs are in good order, my attention and motivation are striving to improve, and I am moving away from toxic anxiety that is paralysing worry and having valid concerns. I must be careful as I force myself to do things. My anxiety is under pressure and feel apprehensive and fretful that things are too difficult and schizophrenia may get unleashed. Trying to medicate the mind like an illness in the physical body will not heal it. From the centre of my being, I am a conscientious objector to how living is for most people on Earth, and there must be another way or better system so that all species live in peace and harmony.

I want to be part of a people's system without violence (conscientious objectors) that has the 'guts' or the 'balls' to strive in their field of excellence to bring about no differences in outcome. I envision a peaceful and harmonious kingdom on Earth with heroes without violence and their companions living without fighting.

30

NUTRIENT SUPPORT AND COPING WITH STRESS

Sunday, 18 November 2018

My emotional components make me alive, with lots of expressions and feelings. I am full of energy one moment, and when I work on challenges, I am drained quickly to a near-death-like state; my motivation gets killed, and my creative thoughts stop. For example, I have been working on writing a fiction story for the writers' club. I started the preparation about two weeks ago and developed an outline. Each time I try to move forward with a flow of words from the original idea and write a few pages of the story, sentences become more complex and complicated. I was only about forty minutes into the project when I suddenly felt brutally sedated and had to sleep. I was utterly exhausted and could not focus because I was going through a series of catnaps. It happens all the time. I spend about forty minutes making up fiction, but that does not occur as intensely as if I were writing my life story. My brain's biochemical factory produces non-fiction fluently out of my head for hours; I get sedated thinking up non-realistic fiction in my head.

When I work on problems for over an hour, pressure builds around my eyes, making them feel strained and tired. My forehead gets a weird melting sensation, and my eyes close. The melting also varies from one side of my head to the other and settles as fluid in my ears, and I reach for the cotton buds. My whole head can feel like heaps of fast-crawling insects squeezing through the brain ventricles.

I have begun nutrient therapy, taking multivitamin supplements and eating more foods that contain nutrients to normalise body–brain biochemistry. As a result, I have lost most of my schizophrenia. I am two months into unmedicated, untreated remission schizophrenia, but I am not as well as I could be. I may never be well because some negative symptoms and lack of cognition do not 'go away'. However, I am very stable, and nutrient therapy compliance is now my choice to knock my schizophrenia socks off. Taking vitamin supplements supports physical life by nourishing the body and the brain to think well.

I have had a blood test, which the doctor asked of me because I have a low white blood cell level. It was repeated twice more because my white blood count was borderline, and the doctor requested that I take another blood test in the new year, January 2019. On discharge from physiotherapy at the hospital, checks and tests on my progress before leaving showed steady improvement. The exercise programme to strengthen my limbs and lower back is now being continued at home to maintain my current fitness level. At last, I have seen a consultant orthopaedic surgeon, and he is arranging an operation in

December 2018 to remove a hard, prominent callus near my Achilles tendon.

I am still getting harassed by government officials in my claim for the total disability benefit, PIP. I was shopping in a busy supermarket and answered a phone call about PIP. They said the assessor could not decide because I did not attend the assessment centre. I again stated my position and our communication probably lasted twenty minutes. One week later, I received a text message saying I might get a call for an assessment. Last week at home, I had a call on my mobile telling me they had made an appointment for me to have the evaluation at my house. I declined the offer, and they said a letter with details would be computer-generated and sent to my address.

I have just about had enough of their pushiness, and they are not compiling a file from the experts who see me and come to a decision about the extent of my disability. I emailed Capita (the assessor company) a copy of my March 2018 care plan and the consultant orthopaedic surgeon's letter. They have the latest facts from the experts. Indeed, judgement about my entitlement could not be based merely on less than an hour of face-to-face toxic assessment – observing my body language, appearance and tone of voice. I am determined not to have a face-to-face evaluation. It is a stressful encounter where my brain may scramble itself as it gets too overstimulated. A copy of the email was sent to Capita on Thursday, 15 November 2018.

> Please open the attachment to find two letters that may help my claim for PIP.
>
> The first letter relates to my care plan, and I was meant to be seen by a consultant psychiatrist for review in September. Unfortunately, he left, and my judgement has been postponed until January 2019, when a permanent psychiatrist is appointed.

The second letter is to do with a consultant orthopaedic surgeon report.

I have turned down a request for a Capita assessor to visit me at home.

I have already explained my decision based on my psychological problems, but the financial reality of living and housing costs requires extra financial support. Therefore, I will not risk my recovery journey; I will instead do without the money and stay well.

Kindest regards,

Karl Lorenz Willett

I also filled out an application form last week to apply directly to the county council to renew my Blue Badge. I sent in the evidence-based report from the consultant orthopaedic surgeon. I discovered that the Blue Badge could be issued with evidence to the county council without the PIP award for mobility. I can no longer wait for the PIP decision because my Blue Badge expired a month ago, in October, and I have more physical difficulties getting in and out of a car in a standard parking bay.

The DVLA has written to me with an update about my driving fitness. They need information from my consultant psychiatrist to decide on my driving licence. They asked that I consult the psychiatrist to give a response and that they would reply as soon as possible.

I received a letter dated 31 October 2018 from the clinical administrator for mental health to complete the DVLA form concerning my ability to drive. It says, "As we have a new consultant in the post who has not met with you before, we request that you attend a short appointment to complete the DVLA form."

I met with a psychiatrist on 12 November, and he read the questions on the form to me, filled in the tick boxes according to my answers and added a brief comment. I ensured he knew I had not had my expected review in September. They have all been aware since 2016 that I was gradually weaning myself off medication and discontinued it in September 2018. The psychiatrist says it will probably be postponed, and my mental health review may occur in January 2019 when a permanent psychiatrist is appointed. He was to look into the reasons, but to this day, on 18 November 2018, I have no official word about when the psychiatric system will check my mental health. Although I am supposed to be on their radar for monitoring, they are not concerned about a recovery plan, only the persistence of the illness to have drug-dependent people, which helps the psychiatry industry make plenty of money.

There is a casting of a dark cloud over our lives again, and I expect the worst because the authorities are not sensitive to my needs, and I am struggling with visualising success. I would love to have a mini vacation for my mind today. I will try to smile often when something funny intentionally happens or do something silly to make myself laugh. Today, Monday, 19 November, my brain is working hard. The PIP confirmation letter arrived with a request to meet face-to-face at my house on 29 November 2018. Personal problems and those in the world around me have a way of casting a dark cloud over my entire life. My tummy is feeling unsettled. Negative thoughts are laying down the idea that we will have a setback. I strive to help myself to be at my optimum even though it is well known that I lose functions and cannot work productively to make a living because of functional decline.

Accepting that I can never work again has been challenging. Although I often push myself towards working to have a reasonable standard of living, I relapse time after time. I applied for financial support from the state, and the process has never run smoothly; it has perpetuated hardship. The government system hinders rather than supports me in living a whole and meaningful life. Expert professional medical practitioners diagnosed me with paranoid schizophrenia, which should be sufficient to secure the benefit payments.

In sickness and health, the state stresses me, and most of the time, I function because I fight desperately to copy normality from the trusted people around me. Unfortunately, they are ignorant of those facts and keep pushing and pressuring me, and even when I break down, they are so naive that they make a final decision that has no financial benefit for me. Every time they see my face, I am seen as operating normally, but it takes a lot of hard work to gear myself up to be happy, optimistic and resilient. Every day is a day to improve my mood and well-being, and I say I can do this or that thing, and I put immense pressure on myself to do those things. Unfortunately, I cannot sustain my positivity daily or even hour by hour; I can lose my functioning ability at any time. It is unpredictable, but I try damn hard not to. I know I can never understand or do things at total capacity. Negative and cognitive symptoms have always affected me, but somehow, by acting more contented (faking it), confident and relaxed, there is a sense of calm for a brief period. My body focuses less on stress and tension, and I breathe deeply.

I want to show that I am a functional human with a disability that prevents full helpful abilities, and I find ways to treat myself with kindness, grace and self-compassion. I acknowledge my imperfections and struggles and love myself anyway. It is tough when functions get lost when talking to someone or people listening to me. Environmental factors, negative thoughts and self-criticism come to my mind late, and I lose my functional ability. This chronic condition, a carrier of schizophrenia, ordinarily gets extra financial support because it messes up thoughts, emotions and behaviours. It damages my self-esteem and self-confidence, dampens my mood and interferes with my ability to enjoy positive experiences and events in my life.

I have been harsh on myself for years – judgemental, critical, finding fault with every imperfection and fixing mistakes. I try to fix flaws within myself and externally in an environment where people's views differ, and I get frustrated. So, I have to keep practising to learn and exercise to gain self-compassion to prevent the psychological locking of my mind, use my strengths and notice more of my positive emotions and experiences so they will become positive, mood-lifting habits.

I want a final say in this chapter. I tuned in to all the details from my voice, translating into greater confidence to focus on positive anticipation. I will savour the moments of a deep sense of peace and contentment as things work out for the good because the universe is on our side. I will also amplify my happiness by savouring the good times and being fully present in the experience. I must remember to lessen stress and tension to increase the enjoyment of my life. I reflect on good times, which helps sharpen my memories and allows me to re-experience some of the joy I felt when the events occurred.

I am now anticipating, like a young child, the excitement of Christmas morning. Part of what makes Christmas so much fun for kids is the anticipation. I know that my problems are fifty-fifty, and I am optimistic. So, leaving this page, I anticipate future enjoyment, like at a birthday party. I expect good luck because of the joy of having the PIP awarded. This thought is running around my bloodstream, as are my endorphins.

On the other hand, to be 'realistic', what seems to be the more likely outcome is that the daily living part of the benefit will not be awarded, and the current mobility part will be removed. If the

PIP decision does not support my claim, critically, I think I can confidently prevent stress toxins from being released to get through this volatile life uncertainty. The key is to remain focused regardless of whether I have the award and stay true to my long-term objectives. Then, I feel equipped to deal with this life's uncertainty, whichever way the decision goes.

31

WRITING NEEDS AND WELL WITHOUT THE PILL

Saturday, 24 November 2018

One of the values I hope my writing generates is to self-educate me about schizophrenia and give knowledge to readers so they can follow mental illnesses better and understand them thoroughly. Then, the discussion can move forward to break down barriers rooted in prejudice, avoidance, rejection and discrimination due to a lack of understanding. If not tackled, this causes sufferers to internalise cultural myths and biases, and people experience self-stigma.

My reason for writing has many functions; it is no longer just about communicating my ideas, feelings and personal beliefs. Instead,

I need to know about you and all about you in your communities. Language makes me think in words to change the wrong ideas you may have in your communities about mental illness, the concepts of demons, the supernatural, the Devil, evil, suffering and the afterlife to counter fear and social stereotypes and challenge your assumptions about those things.

My writing aims to interfere with and change the thinking between heads to avoid using stigmatising language, support each other fully, and protect and value each other. I am operating at my most sophisticated level, which may be a part of the frontier of knowledge about schizophrenia. I also think about the world differently, considering nobody has felt what I have yet, to feel judged or experienced as I do. I have been writing about stuff since 1982 and using the writing process to help myself think and believe. My thinking feels complex, and I have to use writing to help myself think and only edit the words after rereading. I am sending these messages of my thoughts to readers and have readers read my notes. If I have done my earthly job well, they may change how they see the world and people with schizophrenia.

As readers, you can read the pattern of my writing language and stop reading before I interfere with your thinking processes. But you may need help understanding the message I want to send and become aggravated. My ideas and experiences are getting written not to be preserved indefinitely but to move knowledge and our species forward by changing people's attitudes and thoughts about disabilities where they are discriminatory so that we, all of us, can participate in this vast world no matter what flaws and imperfections we may have. I hope the message will be of value for readers to change the evil ideology in privileged heads before it causes havoc when played out on the species on the planet. The twentieth century had many examples; very little has changed, and it is now 2018. We, the extraordinary, ordinary, non-violent people, must begin to find ways to manipulate the minds of the cleverly stupid. I hope my book will be valuable for all readers in changing ideas that are misconceptions, myths or downright lies. I also hope reading about my experiences can lead to greater understanding and acceptance and help those with mental health problems feel less ashamed of their disorders because there is a biological basis for them.

Schizophrenia is not a demonic phenomenon; it is based on biology, and physical, social and environmental factors can also play a role in its development. The correct terminology opens up honest conversations about the condition. We have a lot to thank technology and science for giving commoners a start in debunking what they fear, not based on actual threats but on ancient and modern superstitions, myths and ignorance. This millennium is increasingly bathing us in the knowledge that changes and technology that changes too, and what is right today may only be suitable for tomorrow's people with factual evidence about the universal, eternal law that governs truth about life and its components.

Science discovers the components, but what is sacred and transcendent is not equipped to be measurable, so science cannot find them. Nevertheless, science should not deny what we believe as transcendent, for these components exist. The eternal truth reminds humankind that a creator made and engineered life and its components and did not emerge out of random empty nothingness. Although conventional sciences cannot prove it, most of the ingredients in life are well known to them.

One such component that gives biological bases for schizophrenia is genetics. Mental illness is nothing to be ashamed of, as I mentioned before, as it is a problem for medics' investigation and proper use of medicines like those for diabetes or heart disease. I am furthering my education with my lived experience and with textbooks to understand, accept and help those with mental health concerns to feel less ashamed of their disorders. Having the insight will allow me to intervene early if my susceptibility is triggered again due to unique irregularities of environmental factors and the interaction of my genetics. They say that people with a family member with a mental illness may be more likely to develop one themselves because they are hereditary illnesses, and genetic susceptibility is passed on in families. Schizophrenia has a decisive genetic risk factor, but not necessarily so that a family member will develop the illness. It has a link to the irregular functioning of nerve cell circuits or pathways that connect particular brain regions. There is a strain on my thinking. I will have to stop writing for a while.

I am falling in and out of consciousness, feeling sleepy, sleepier, and more exhausted, probably because I just had lunch. I am falling in and out of naps. I will try to concentrate on writing from the manual's teachings and include aspects of my life experiences in my own words. Finally, I have to pause and take some time out. I will be back in a bit. I have to 'switch off, disconnect'. Sorry! I cannot continue; I need to sleep. My eyes have automatically closed for a snooze nap. Zee. Dizzee zee. (Sleeping.) Snooze, zzzzzzz.

Okay, howdy. I have woken up now. I feel replenished, and here I am again after an hour and a half of functional loss, returning to my pre-stress level of functioning.

There is an impressive and growing suite of technologies to help neuroscience understand genomic biomarkers in the brain in a non-invasive way. Brain imaging technology has shown scientists normal brain function and how mental illness can drastically impact the brain. Notably, in lengthy or repeat episodes of depression or schizophrenia, there is brain shrinkage in parts of the brain. Mental illness should be treated no differently than any other severe disease. There are naturally occurring brain chemicals called neurotransmitters. They carry signals to parts of the brain and body, and mental illnesses develop when neurons in the brain stop expressing or when there is a problem with neurons communicating.

In the early years, receiving a diagnosis of mental illness was scary because societal conversations about mental health did not exist. They widely believed that mental illness was a curse or punishment for disobedience from external moral agents or spirits, invisible to us mortals in the outer bounds of the universe where the heavenly place is supposed to exist. It is scary to know that my altered sense of reality will happen from time to time for the rest of my life, and I am likely to go awry in my mind because I have schizophrenia. Medicine eases some of the symptoms but cannot cure me. But after a period of frightening inner chaos, the main symptoms of schizophrenia that had altered my living went. My thinking and behaviour returned to as close to the norm of rationality and regular action of other people as possible.

I dressed in clean casual clothes, appeared intelligently confident and was comfortable with always having a well-groomed appearance. That baffles the general public's perception of living with a mental illness; some professionals were hoodwinked too. I lost productivity in all my careers and opportunities to earn a living because being a seemingly 'well' schizophrenic exhibiting a standard range of emotions and habits was a bluff. My bodily processes always react to the seeping of the tiniest filtering through of active, suppressed schizophrenia inflammation. The question of purpose, meaning, what is wrong in the world, and my value to the world developed into epidemic problems that I must solve to have a more liveable life. I was exempted from tailored care and financial support, became desperate for social reform and was paranoid about it.

The world's political, religious and cultural differences must change so we all have more stability and a bearable existence. I had to see myself taking a unique position to take a stand, rise, create knowledge, invent something or care for others. I asked myself, am I so paranoid with schizophrenia that these things continue to threaten my happy existence today? This writing is my attempt to explain in the light of my new understanding that there are two levels of my conscious thinking going on equally at the same time, and one of them is the weirdness itself, and the action within is the attempt to self-cure. The problem that brings about the psychosis is usually things that I find too much, need fixing, want help with, or need to be removed from the world or my body. So, I used to self-analyse, probe my psyche and use reappraisal as a self-defence treatment. In other words, I took action to change my thinking and emotions and triggered a less stressed brain state. Still, it never lasted because my faulty circuitry had the upper hand. My original thoughts, feelings and behaviours again operated below the normal brain states in healthy people. There came times when my eagerness to cope well, use strategies for self-care, and self-persuasion behaviour sprung out of my core self because schizophrenia would not go away.

I will find a way somehow to live with it. I have stopped the medication that aimed to kill schizophrenia but was poisoning me. The penny dropped, and the combination of my brain physiology and psychological and environmental factors contributed to the disorder. Drug maintenance treatment stopped my positive character traits from working well, and the drug prolonged and exacerbated my schizophrenia. Wow! I am using reappraisal to feel fantastic, to get to know myself and to release the positive self that was locked in at the age of twenty. Antipsychotic medication from that age altered my growing up and addicted me to habits that shut down most of my fundamental processes. I am sprouting a positive mindset off medication. I am so much more talkative and much more socially able.

I crack jokes and am getting better at reading other people's emotions. However, my chitchatting conversation and humour annoy them. Also, my joyful brain state frequently uses catchphrases that say I see beauty in everything now and, "I am in love-eke, and give love-eke. Love – eke, I'm in love Iam giving love – eke," which annoys them. I feel so happy and loved that LOVE-eke phrases irritate them because they are said too often. I have a certain kind of joy that I am very privileged to have. The love of my wife, who has endured long-suffering to see me well and the family we raised, is one of the greatest joys. I feel energised to continue to fulfil my life, and I am comfortable in my skin. I used to air my views in group meetings and with people I met for the first time, and I felt less nervous than I have ever experienced in that kind of setting. I think down to earth, and my feet are touching the ground and are firmly planted in reality.

I have dreams and fantasies within the boundaries of my brain's healthy creativity activities – nothing troublesome about them. My curious mind usually works as well as it can without baggage. I am much more aware of the impact of negative symptoms on me, but I try hard not to let them get me down. Although they show up more like stupidity when I struggle to use cognitive control to manage mood and anxiety, my psychology blueprint is good, and I have the right attitude, thank God.

I am so pleased that I can feel the complete joy of living in this dark skin and more of the positive side of my personality and see my behaviour noticeably being controlled in my conscious and unconscious minds. I can reveal as little about myself as I wish or as much as I want to. My activities open up the kind of person I am, who likes expressing gratitude, sharing kindness and reflecting on one of my character strengths, which helps me feel happy. Everything in the world is positive and negative energy, and the laws in the universe want to help me coexist with the condition and get along in that environment that was as changeable and unpredictable as the weather. The variance in stress goes up, down or minus, which can be positive too. However, the chaos of schizophrenia needs to be tamed holistically. By gradually changing my mindset to decrease the perception of threats and cynical worldviews, my subjective feelings are better regulated. The symptoms are tamed, milder and not troublesome, and then shut down. So, successfully training my brain changes how I think and feel. Whatever situation may arise, control of challenging and intense feelings is an effective strategy I deploy to neutralise schizophrenia. Mechanisms in my brain are maladaptive, and they avoid or suppress the malleable plasticity of my sixty-two-year-old mind. Shaping and fixing the new mindset into a permanent habit is not easy. Losing the influence of negative thoughts and emotions is tough, and I slip back sometimes and stop thinking more positively. My motivation systems kick in, and I get back on track.

Schizophrenia and I are learning to get along, coexist without the fight for dominance, and have harmony with a perceived enemy. From the biggest stars to the smallest atoms, they live in an environment of plus and minus energy. All of us sometimes get into fights, but there are no winners. The outcome should always be amicable, fair play for peace, and balance for harmony.

My usual self is different from others in the conventional sense. Healthy, ordinary people have no ambitious needs – the need to grow, know, educate, discover and leave a legacy.

Most ordinary people live a naive life, expecting that memories of themselves will never fade or be forgotten in the minds of their loved ones. Still, human consciousness fades and is erased naturally, and illness can suddenly rob them of it. Their footprint eventually fades from the Earth without official records of their existence. Extraordinary people take steps to help their loved ones and all people living after they are deceased. We should learn lessons from the ordinariness of their unique life. Extraordinary people are paranoia-driven, and their ambitions must be met. Improvements must be made, and their contribution must be remembered in verbal storytelling or preserved in literature from generation to generation.

32

CHANGE AND UNCERTAINTY THAT IS COMING

Saturday, 26 January 2019

Howdy. I wish you a belated Happy New Year. So many changes and uncertainties are coming, globally and personally. Brexit time looms without a deal, and the potential impact of a no-deal Brexit and uncertainty in the UK economy are widely reported. We are in an era of political lies, Brexit biases, and advertising and political campaigns exploiting psychological research to control our unconscious behaviour. However, many people still feel the choices they make are their own.

Next is climate change, which impacts the environment worldwide. There is a compelling call for more action from governments, businesses, and all of us to tackle climate change. Still, I feel frozen in inaction because it is overwhelming for me as an individual to do anything more. So, I will leave the challenge to the activists and big political boys to influence global policy and make meaningful changes worldwide.

I have eased my mind from the political and economic uncertainty by focusing on my resolutions to challenging problems.

The renewal of my Blue Badge and the driving licence was successful. Everything else that has been problematic in the last year, 2018, has seen some progress towards a resolution. I have continued to be proactive in finding support systems in the community that could help in my 'meaningful recovery' programme that successfully discontinuing antipsychotics has made possible.

On 16 January 2019, I submitted an online self-referral for CBT/CRT. The next day, I applied for an HC2 certificate for full help with NHS dental treatment, NHS sight tests, and a voucher towards the cost of glasses and contact lenses. Those in their sixties and over get the other services the NHS offers for free. We are also not exempt under the benefits system because my ESA is based on National Insurance contributions, not income-related ESA.

The date for my memory assessment arrived in the post recently. The form requested a thorough answer to a question. On Saturday, 18 January, I wrote a response to be handed in on Thursday, 21 February 2019, the assessment day.

In the next chapter, you will see a draft of the additional supporting information written for CBT and help with NHS health costs, followed by the question the memory assessment form asked and my answer.

33

REFERRAL FOR CBT OR CRT ONLINE

I was diagnosed with paranoid schizophrenia and had long-term use of antipsychotic medication, but psychosis was still getting triggered.

Schizophrenia has been an episodic disorder in me, and I have been in and out of symptomatic remission nine times between 1977 and 2014. I realised that the long-term use of antipsychotics had a detrimental effect on my functioning and quality of life, and I completely weaned myself off the medication in September 2018. However, around May 2018, cognitive impairment became more apparent and raised my anxiety. I think I've had a breakdown in thought, emotion and internal behavioural challenges because of the void in my head related to working memory loss.

Please let me know if this service offers CBT or CRT to help me with my problem, which is related mainly to cognitive difficulties. You can learn more about my challenges at www.karllorenzwillett.co.uk

I telephoned Changing Minds on Monday, 21 January 2019, and customer service informed me that the message had yet to reach them. I registered my details over the phone that day. The next step was a telephone conversation with a therapist on Thursday, 24 January, at 2:30 pm. I was told to expect to receive a questionnaire form by email the day before the call to fill in and send back.

After the conversation, the therapist concluded that the service they offer is for people with anxiety problems; the way forward is to have a memory assessment, and the clinic can advise the next step for my personal needs. A summary of the conversation is going to my GP.

Claim NHS health cost.

Please note 'About Your Income' section 5.5.

My PIP has been under review since August 2018, and a decision has not been made. However, my current award is due to expire in March 2019.

I was diagnosed with paranoid schizophrenia in 1977 and had long-term use of antipsychotic medication, but psychosis was still triggered. I have always attempted to get a reward in the daily living component. DWP does not understand how this illness affects my everyday living and my falling in and out of symptomatic remission. I'm so anxious and worried that I failed to attend the assessment. I am fearful the process may trigger a relapse because I don't know how to show the cognitive impairments in my daily living. They prevent me from holding down a job, and the endless void in my head that may be related to working memory loss is frustrating. I have been so good at acting or covering up, masking symptoms and the complex challenges of the illness, that others perceive me as well and high functioning.

I want people to believe I am well. I consistently work hard to maintain a good look of well-being, and there is enormous pressure to keep up this pretence, so from time to time, it comes to a schizophrenic eruption. DWP has yet to support me financially with this disability to ease the worry. With the stress and the struggles in daily living with schizophrenia and no other way of generating income, I rely on the main income stream from my wife's part-time zero-hours seasonal work employment. I am applying for help through the NHS Low Income Scheme to pay for dental treatment, sight tests and glasses.

I do realise I may never get the extra support I desperately need for a living as a disabled person. I may even lose the mobility component rate for a noticeable physical disability when this PIP award expires. I lost my Blue Badge because it had passed the renewal date. I apply directly to the county council to examine the factual clinical professional paper evidence. I was so grateful that my Blue Badge was approved to run for three years.

The memory assessment question

Question: Describe the difficulties or problems you are having and how these affect your day-to-day life.

Answer: I am a member of a writers' club, and it is getting more challenging to critique members' fictional written work, give feedback/opinions on what I heard, say something related to the subject matter and keep track.

I pay attention and listen to information with keen alertness, and I'll be able to follow up to a point. Still, suddenly, there comes a blank, a void in part of my concentration, and no concrete ideas exist about what is happening. There needs to be an underlying understanding in my mind about how the story developed, how the various characters appear in the account, the plot, the dialogue and the scenes; at its basic level, could I tell what the story was about? No.

I get internally frustrated, have stupid feelings and am saddened; I self-talk, ask myself to concentrate harder and usually become mute. Information for my mind and knowledge is not getting held; it escapes me, and my thinking's internal dialogue is not even reaching the ideas stored in my memory. They all just get wiped out; I can't remember.

Evaluating various contemporary writings scatters much confusion, and I need clarification. I can't decide or distinguish what to do, and I have nothing to say except to apologise. "Sorry, I have nothing that I can say." Making up the story straight out of my head without referring back to lived experiences relies on having a great imagination to create the account in my mind; that's very difficult. I aim to diverge from autobiographical writing, expand my writing horizons and write some fiction unrelated to my experiences. Still, it is very challenging to do that.

In some ways, those difficulties mentioned affect me daily, and I started to notice a severe problem in July 2018. I reduced the 10 mg of aripiprazole to 7.5 mg to continue the discontinuation and reduction programme. And headaches became a symptom of withdrawal.

Two times from past hospital inpatient detentions, I lost memories of what happened for one to two weeks. I cannot remember my existence or anything during psychotic trauma episodes. I find it hard to learn anything new verbally and visually these days. I have to ask for frequent repetition of the sentences or request them in plain, simple English, and it seems like most people would have understood what was said the first time. Visually, I look and look, and my processing speed does not keep pace; I miss the image and am sometimes unaware of things other people see in the same environment. But I'll be able to act automatically and safely in situations or places I can't remember being aware of. My wife and family often say things to me, such as, "Karl, you're not thinking straight," or "Karl, you don't understand by not seeing our point of view, and you don't seem to get it. We tell you repeatedly, and we don't know any other way to put it to you to get the message."

Recently, familiar words that were easy to spell or pronounce have become more challenging to write, say and articulate. Even the meanings of a word are lost when I come to speak or write it again a day or two later. Things like comprehension require me to remember facts, which is so frustrating as a writer; I must do many rewrites. When I write, I find I can use a higher form of the English language, which is not in my spoken vocabulary, and once again, I am frustrated because, deep down, I know the words I want to use. It's hard to pronounce them correctly and to look up the first few letters in the dictionary when spellcheckers sometimes can't recognise what I am trying to spell.

My sensory organs are in good order. I can still make the right decisions and judgements at times. But, again, I am prone to making mistakes, and I will get desperate to retain strategies that teach my mind and brain catch-ups on necessary education skills that over forty years on antipsychotic medication interrupted. I feel frustrated, exhausted, stressed and demotivated, although somehow, I seem to self-automate myself to get started. Hence, one of the steps is to have a memory assessment and relax to survive the intensity of my feeling of 'I must be stupid'. Again, I am frustrated and angry that being diagnosed with paranoid schizophrenia in my early adult life has become an adult learning difficulty.

34

ANTIPSYCHOTIC REDUCTION PROGRAMME

Saturday, 26 January 2019

Yesterday, I attended the RADAR meeting. I am a member of the advisory panel.

The researchers are preparing for the looming two-year follow-up period of interviews. First, data will be collected in advance of the conversation from the study database to select a sample that includes participants who have successfully reduced or discontinued antipsychotics. Then, the data will be used to shape the questions the researchers ask participants.

Before the business on the agenda started, I talked about my views, experiences of successfully discontinuing antipsychotic medication and how the reduction programme guidelines helped me. Finally, I thanked the team for their support.

Mental illness in remission is health unmedicated and has a clear, sharp awareness of claim and blame. The positive side of schizophrenia, voice-hearing, claims that all things that came from me were manifested in my physiology. That must be true. It is just me. That is how I am. They are part of me, and my traits cannot change because they are in my genes. So, I am so ignorant that medicine not only stopped lousy functioning, but my development had ended before developing anatomical ignorance. On the cusp of young adulthood, poor functioning solidifies. Schizophrenia's non-positive symptoms and antipsychotic adverse effects were commonplace and indistinguishable. The factual evidence of my experiences blamed the negative impact on antipsychotic discontinuation. The sensible me has exposed the naked truth about schizophrenia, on the pill, and coming off the drug. I feel stupid and vulnerable for writing about conceptualised perceptual experiences, formatting and crystallising these unusual beliefs; through the power of writing them down to control high levels of distress, I have empowered myself. My very beliefs and attitudes are holding me back, and I have acted with weird feelings. I try to believe reality truths and work on these, but I violate common beliefs that show full emotional responsibility rather than merely being aware of my emotions.

I compiled a comprehensive list of my schedule reduction programme from my handwritten records and charted antipsychotic medication adverse effects the day before the meeting, 24 January 2019. I added more of my observations to the list today while thinking about the significance of the chart. There are a minimum of twenty-five side effects and adverse effects. I was taken aback by this insightful discovery when, for decade after decade, I denied having adverse side effects to the doctors and psychiatrists when the various horrible positive symptoms disappeared.

Psychiatric medication reduction chart

- Aripiprazole (Abilify) psychiatric medication reduction from June 2014 to Thursday 13 September 2018
- 30 mg aripiprazole/10 mg haloperidol. Reduced haloperidol to 5 mg on 3 September 2014 and stopped haloperidol on 2 October 2014
- Diazepam 2 mg, 3 September 2014 to 13 November 2014. I was hospitalised for about four weeks and discharged in May/June 2014 (I also had meds believed to be for anxiety/depression leading up to my mother's death in August 2014)
- The psychiatrist supported, endorsed and approved the reduction. GP approved/recommended
- May/early June 2014, dose 30 mg aripiprazole and 10 mg haloperidol daily (hospital psychiatrist approved)
- 24 April 2015, Zimovane 7.5 mg. Take one at night (GP)
- 2 June 2015, dose 25 mg aripiprazole daily (approved)
- 23 July 2016, dose 20 mg aripiprazole daily (approved)
- 15 November 2016, dose 15 mg aripiprazole daily (self)
- 3 January 2017, dose approx. 12.5 mg aripiprazole daily (self)
- 11 February 2017, dose 10 mg aripiprazole daily (approved)
- 21 July 2017, dose approx. 7 mg aripiprazole daily (self)
- 21 August 2017, dose 7.5 mg aripiprazole daily (approved)
- 5 January 2018, dose approx. 6.5 mg aripiprazole daily (self)
- 15 January 2018, 200 mg ibuprofen tab, one three times a day (GP)
- 1 February 2018, dose 5 mg aripiprazole daily (self)
- 6 March 2018, dose 5 mg aripiprazole daily (approved)
- 4 August 2018, dose approx. 2.5 mg aripiprazole daily (self)
- 3 September 2018, dose approx. 1.25 mg aripiprazole daily (self) Clinician review now due September 2018

- 14 September 2018, aripiprazole was discontinued for a better clinically effective outcome with the placebo recovery plan (self)

Why? Because of the effects on physical health, mortality, worsening of my cognitive deficits and the dampening of feelings of ambition to be helpful and achieve. I experienced a cycle of functional decline that got worse and worse with every relapse on antipsychotic medication. I felt stuck with an inability to learn, grow, accept the blessings of the unchanging deficiencies, and work with and without shame. In 1977, I was diagnosed with paranoid schizophrenia and medicated continuously with various first- and second-generation antipsychotic meds and doses. I had nine psychotic relapses between 1977 and 2014.

My mental health today: Wednesday, 23 January 2019. I have more insight into the non-reversible symptoms and poor functional traits associated with schizophrenia, for which, so far, there is no medical treatment.

I continue to maintain good well-being, free from psychosis and feelings of low expectation, with schizophrenia in remission and unmedicated. (Clinician review overdue.) My review schedule analysis as of Friday, 1 March 2019:

- January 2019, dose 500 mg naproxen, one tablet twice daily (GP)
- January 2019, 20 mg gastro-resistant capsules, omeprazole (GP)
- In January 2019, the antipsychotic medication prescription was stopped officially and discontinued by my GP without a psychiatrist's endorsement

35

MEDICATION WITHDRAWAL EFFECTS CHARTED

The withdrawal effects recorded are not in any exact or particular order.

- Thinking hurts my head, and it is not supposed to, and I cannot concentrate for long. (Thinking up solutions and even playing problem-solving games produce a headache and heavy-headedness, and both eyes feel tension, a pulling sensation.)
- More frequent and prolonged emptying of the bladder, with slow flow. (I am unsure if it is entirely due to medication or old age; I am sixty-two years old.)
- I hear a high-pitched, powerful buzzing sound in my ears (just below a pitch that dogs and cats can listen to). Sometimes, it

sounds like wind whipped up on the ocean's surface. Whoosh. These sounds currently pass through my ears more frequently.
- Body aches, uncomfortable sitting on a settee or a chair when watching a film with the family.
- Increased feelings of agitation, itching and jitteriness.
- Agony in the lower back (muscle sprain pain), excruciating stiff neck, and a creaky sound coming from turning my head in any direction – left, right, up and down.
- Bilateral knee pain.
- Sometimes, I thought I had tooth decay because of toothache, but it was sensitive gums.
- Muscle rigidity, which affects my mobility.
- Speech disorder. (I have increased pronunciation problems, stuttering, and hearing my voice sound deep and unnatural.) Throat irritation.
- Headaches and head discomfort can occur at any time and gradually move like a lump of gunge on top of the head. They trickle down like thick treacle and pass all around the eye sockets, causing tension and weakening the eyes. Numerous lines of creases form on my forehead in my conscious attempt to keep my eyes open. Concentration fades, my vision blurs, my eyes water more than usual, and the fluid stings my eyes.
- A throbbing, fast-beating heart, feeling like all my internal organs are rattling and shaking nervously.
- An increase in trapped wind in the abdomen.
- Increased involuntary quivering and sudden cold chills going through my body. (People who experience this sometimes say, "Someone has just walked over my grave.")
- Chest pain. (Doctors checked it out, and there is no evidence of a physical health problem.)

- Greater force is needed to remove faeces from the body.
- Decreased white blood cells and low blood count in white blood cells.
- I keep nipping the inner lining of my mouth while chewing and cannot stop the movements of my mouth. Sometimes, I get tongue spasms and accidentally bite my tongue, and biting my lips to moisten them is more constant.
- Increased production of saliva, increased hiccups and continuous, frequent burping.
- Sleep talking and kicking as I come out of dreams I cannot remember.
- Chronic sleeping has gradually reduced. Persistent drowsiness has progressively decreased.
- Muscle twitch and tightness, like cramps that unexpectedly come when the feet are not in motion, in arms, hands and fingers, similar to a writer's cramp.
- Feeling chronically weak/fatigued is decreasing. As a result, appetite has reduced gradually to a moderate level, and weight has become stable. In addition, low energy has steadily improved.
- Increased dry mouth and stuffy nose.
- Habits and impulse problems are reduced, e.g. regular gambling habits on the lottery are reduced to a flutter.
- Libido gradually is okay.
- My idealism, imagination and aspirations are progressively aligned with those of the general population, but my hopes, expectations, faith and empathic feelings are above average.
- Memory is critically impaired, and I have intellectual difficulty. (Low IQ. Memory assessment is going to be carried out on 21 February 2019.)

- Anxiety can become immense, and I can have excessive worries and feel paranoid about going to a place to invent or create systems that will benefit everyone or work to improve the wrongs in the world and society so we can all come to live in a utopia.
- Fears are reducing as I become more confident in myself and face the change and uncertainty in my life.
- My linguistic choices are impaired. (I have problems with words, such as extracting their proper meaning and understanding the context in which they are used.)

Some withdrawal effects mimic psychotic physical symptoms coming out of the body. Adverse effects I had previously experienced, and those symptoms that had remained in the range of common tolerability side effects that never entirely went away had severe flare-ups on lower than 10 mg doses.

Throughout the process, the 'self-inner core' is always healthy. That unique part of me is not damaged or has not unleashed self-destruction when intruding stressors out in the environment cause havoc. Most people grow a shield of thick skin, which gets thicker in hostility to protect the core and to live and let live attitude. Pharmaceutical drugs are a potent cocktail and may turn off almost everything to shield the innocent, and the disability can be permanent. Antipsychotic drugs will get better at targeting and shielding that 'core of the self.'

I was affected by relapse, which I associate with chaos stressors getting into the core of the self and inflammation around the thickest part of the true self, and weirdness emerged between thoughts, emotions and behaviour, leading to losing touch with reality. This is a classic psychotic breakdown in which immediate action to self-cure co-occurs. However, I warn readers that discontinuation and reduction will not suit everyone. For some people, antipsychotics at the correct maintenance dose are sufficient for mental stability, good quality of living and sustainable existence.

36

DISCONTINUED THE TREATMENT FOR SCHIZOPHRENIA

Coming off medication is not a decision to take lightly. However, I have shown that antipsychotic reduction is possible with the right tailored programme and support.

Nevertheless, it was a risky gamble, but I felt safe; the challenge can get stressful. I had self-doubt that I could wean myself off antipsychotics and feared the change and uncertainty coming. On the way, the purpose of being unmedicated had my inner critic getting in the way, and I feared failing.

There were three stages when antipsychotic discontinuation and reduction were utterly scary, and the task can be a foolish choice or a bold, brave one. But, first, it was vital to know oneself and be aware of mental faculties being affected, being mentally unwell and relapsing.

- **First stage:** The initial thought of being in an antipsychotic reduction programme was scary and had the added feeling of being foolish or brave.
- **Second stage:** I started the programme and thought the challenge might fail; it was scary and had the added feeling of being foolish or brave.
- **Third stage:** Being without pharmaceutical props for the rest of my life is still scary and gives me the feeling of being foolish or brave.

What matters most is the outcome of improving my quality of life and social functioning, and having a more stable, comfortable life is a beautiful, meaningful recovery.

I am pleased that the programme and follow-up monitoring will be given to me for the first time in forty years to allow my mind to heal gradually, but it is not for everyone. (I am mainly self-monitoring and have a self-review scheduled plan.)

Successfully discontinuing antipsychotics was an act of empowerment for me. My choice to cope with my reality was respected, and I took power back from the psychiatry system. Untreated, remission schizophrenia has made me much more aware of the impact of negative symptoms on me, stopped my worries about increased mortality, and exposed me to the risks and harm of antipsychotic drugs as a long-term therapy. I will have to return to antipsychotic medication if and when psychosis returns.

I eventually stopped taking the pharmaceutical drug to treat naturally occurring remission in schizophrenia and expected symptoms to stay away for the rest of my life. This treatment method relies on faith and willpower and brings back the placebo effect in modern medicine. I hope my inner inferences will continue to stop the schizophrenia symptoms for the rest of my life.

I had a marathon writing day yesterday, 26 January 2019, which was twenty-four hours without sleep. I was engrossed in typing up the drafts in this book and adding more inspired writing as it flowed from my mind, raw and unrestricted. I stayed up throughout the night, went to bed at 6:30 a.m. the next day, Sunday, 27 January 2019, and woke up at 9:45 a.m. (This now is mid-morning. Good morning. I feel fine; there is no feeling of grogginess or light-headedness.)

It was the first time in many years that I could adjust to staying up all night and stop sleeping excessively. Finally, I would have a night of sleep adequate for my body and mind.

THE FUTURE WITH UNTREATED SCHIZOPHRENIA

Sunday, 24 February 2019

There are urgently needed remedies for characteristic healing symptoms of schizophrenia. But I think my lived experiences of schizophrenia have shown that cunningly training my brain to see the bright side and naturally involving an emotional appraisal of the illness are the practical steps. As a result, my natural schizophrenia-stressed circuit is in a joyful brain state.

It is okay dokey: one perceives 'power' and control over disturbing and impairing symptoms by potentially thinking of two comparisons. One thinking has such a feeling of failure that winning the battle with distressing and impairing symptoms is like a fight between two enemies. The second thinking has a choice pattern that systematically reflects and reinforces ways of making sense of the experiences and will talk or write to (dis)empower.

Schizophrenia has produced English language problems for me. My ability to 'get' words, 'hear' them, and extract the correct meaning and context in which they get used is impaired. As a result, my linguistic choices are an essential aspect of living, forming and delivering what I want to say. I get knotted and clogged up with the unrelated words in the alphabet soup I have in my mind, and some are spurted out. Sometimes, the underlying meaning is lost, and contextual meaning is hard to deal with; there is confusion.

Being a person with schizophrenia adds to my knowledge about human nature. It has allowed me to see people and myself too, showing the traits of what God the creator compiled in our humanity, the intrigues of our emotions and rationality. We all have meanness and stupidity, and people enter our lives, stir trouble with our feelings and play on our emotions. Some people have the nerves, daring, and charisma. We may fall under their spell of charm, confidence and being full of ideas and enthusiasm. However, I found later that their beliefs were irrational and their opinions ill-conceived. Everything that makes us react sometimes brings us to awkward behaviours, and our anger or tension with ourselves leaks out in a way we regret, or our good intentions are foolish.

My writing tells you I know it is not right, and we all know some things we get compelled to do are not correct, but we cannot help ourselves. I sometimes asked myself, "What has come over me?" I wondered and found myself continually in a self-destructive pattern of behaviour that I could not control. It is as if I harbour a stranger within me who operates outside my willpower and pushes me to do the wrong thing. This stranger within me is somewhat weirder than

I can imagine myself. What I can say about my occasional surprising behaviour and people's ugly actions is that I have no clue as to what causes them. I try to latch on to some simplistic explanation, like what ordinary folks are told to call these strange thoughts that operate as if not our own and that they are ideas from evil spirits, Satan or the Devil. My emotional feelings and my basic surface understanding have biases with superstition and fears. I react emotionally frightened to what people say and do and form slightly simplified opinions for others and myself. So, I settled for a thought-up, uncomfortable, but convenient story to tell myself: I had become possessed.

When my mind began to think smart, in the mode of learning and acquiring knowledge, it dived below the surface and got closer to the actual roots of what caused the weird behaviour. I freed myself of fear, superstition and words in language that shocked my emotions with the primitive way the terms were used, and I began to control them better. The words (hell, the Devil, Satan, evil, wicked, sinister, dark and even black) are used intellectually in the heads of intelligent thinkers and regarded as negative energy, or they clarify the mysterious unknowns in those terms.

What happened to me is part of human behaviour that the super-intelligent, transcendent, creative power (the God of creation) put in humankind's body and mind. Conscious thinkers understand that positive and negative energy powers permeate the universe. There are sinister energies, good energies, sinister feelings, good feelings, negative thoughts, positive thoughts, and so on.

Despite my valiant efforts to shift my untamed negative reviews, the thinking will stalk me, follow me and condition that obsession into a craving I wish would go away. My negative biases make me worry and fret, and I cannot get them out of my mind. It is time to accept the good and evil in all of us. Unwanted thoughts are hard to tame. They compel me (us), and the ideas become even more prominent until my (our) concentration fractures with the strategy that stops unwanted thoughts from popping into my brain. I do not feel obligated to check in on removing the piece to be accessible, think about the ideas and choose a distractor. Focusing on that, staying in the present moment by calming myself and connecting with my breath are helpful.

The creator God is female, and the voice of truth and knowledge to me is obviously female. The common belief in a masculine God does not match my experience of being in utter despair when destructive energy and good-spirited energy are unbalanced. A female voice in my soul spoke words up into my mind. All the sensations of suffering and sorrow flowed around my bloodstream. I had a weird feeling inside my head and body, and I claimed that they were my thoughts and my biological system playing up. I told the psychiatrist when I was stable. As time passed, I told the psychiatrist that I looked forward to eternal life as far back as I can remember, and my life had just begun here on Earth. I cannot understand what is driving me out of this world's reality and preaching to others of an eternal happy home elsewhere instead of living to change the harrowing experiences that blighted life here. Working to create eternal heaven here is what most people crave, just as I do.

I have got so used to latching on to the thoughts that led me to self-destruction that the female God of creation asks me, "Karl, why are you doing this to yourself?" (The story is almost live in my first book, *The Memoir of a Schizophrenic*.) I was doing this emotional outpouring to myself and getting to the point of destroying the self.

My emotions seem to have driven me against my most profound wishes and forced me to self-destruct so many times. One of the times I attempted suicide was in 2003, and in 2014, I was compelled to drink my urine.

To understand that stranger within us is to realise that the sense being voiced is not a stranger at all but very much a part of us, a part of ourselves that is far more mysterious, complex and interesting than I can imagine. With the awareness of what the schizophrenia journey brought to my temporal lobes and my frontal cortex, I hope to break the negative patterns in my life and stop making negative messages. Still, I will not act on them if they bubble up and arrive in my conscience. I say to myself, and I also say to others, "I aim to get better control over what I do and my feelings and what happens to me."

Having clarity about myself allows me to change the course of my life in ways that do not trouble my emotions. I tended to think of my behaviour as mainly conscious and willed. Still, this is a misconception because recognising that I have an experiential need to know we are not always in control of what we do was frightening. If you imagine it, it is a scary thought that is, in fact, the reality.

We are all subject to forces deep within us that drive our behaviour and operate below the level of our awareness, and we see the results. Our thoughts, moods and actions have little conscious access to what exactly moves our emotions and compels us to behave in specific ways. We are not rational and riding on a feeling that childhood memories or particular circumstances may have triggered. There seemed to be a pattern when this and that happened weirdly to me; I am not reflective and rational but may point fingers.

These forces that tug and pull at us from deep within are natural and part of human nature's negative and positive energy. So, one way of looking at it is that power has confidence, the negativity of insecurity and anxiety, positive energy, an attraction to a particular person or one's hunger for attention, and so on.

They say that the way our body and mind process emotions has advanced throughout history to ensure our survival as a human species. We learn to cooperate with others, coordinate our actions, communicate in the language, and have rules for group discipline.

I sometimes get anxious around people, and there is no apparent reason to feel stressed if I can correctly read people's expressions. I am so separable from all the emotions we can have or express on our faces to communicate mood effectively, including stress, and the signal is usually wrong. As a result, I fall in love too quickly and feel the pain of the innocent sufferer, and I also hurt my loved ones emotionally, my family and friends who love me most, and I love them. Why? It is an awful reality.

I believe the female energy, in the hermaphrodite God of all creation, clustered and organised the elements in this reality. She sparked the powers in life that brought us time to wire our brains and the configuration of our nervous systems to bring us about, with an eternal spirit of divinity, the human animal. I have been most sensitive to what is usually the unseen part of our human nature.

Under the rules of predictable forces in our social life, I behaved predictably, which opened up my dark side to read repeatedly as common words printed in nursery rhyme books. My negativity and my positivity were out of sync until I became balanced in my thoughts, feelings and behaviours. I hope the message is getting through to the tribes of people whose ancient myths weaken their insight into the fundamental belief that can surface in all of us: of the Devil, evil spirits and demons. They say it affects a person's behaviour, and exorcism is needed to free that person.

A myth closes up our minds if we allow it. Something comes over me. It reaches the level of my consciousness, and I react to it. I do so depending on my feelings and my circumstances. I superficially wave it away without understanding it. We all have divinity clustered in our human nature, contrary to what is usually taught. People did not descend to Earth from mythical creatures with wings known to us as angels, and our arrival on the planet was not instant in the likeness of a god in the heavens.

The true God of creation brought us out of our human primates and apes; our animal roots can feel deeply distressing. Some tribes of people deny and suppress this and try to cover up our dark impulses with all kinds of excuses. I have been in my wash of emotions and experiences in the depths of the modern man's consciousness and subconscious. I have touched the technological imponderables with dreams so real I am in the darkest matter, pitch darkness, with specks of starlight that glow through the dark space. My organic brain had given me a glimpse of our evolutional past and evolved future.

We all have the implanted ability to see beyond the limitations of our new space and time. It is a fascinating journey to reach where the unseen is seeing, and the energy of consciousness takes us to worlds so weird and strange with unimaginable beauty in equilibrium. Creatures and other life forms' complicities display pure grace, and we, in wonder, marvel, reflecting that our fights have evolved out of us. And, like the new species with which we cohabit, we are playful, and performance with the other species is fair play, in peace and harmony. That is a beautiful place to be in the cosmos. In our space-time reality, we only need to close our eyes in the darkness to see the light. We must engineer things in the fields of our natural earthly world and not overlook spiritual components.

Our rationalities show that some people get away with the most unpleasant behaviours in their sanity – sociopaths, psychopaths and murderers – because they passively give in to their untamed thoughts. The contemporary warrior thinkers are finally at a point to let us all open up our smartness to know who we are as a species, and will we be able to ponder one of the big questions of cosmology: are we alone?

And are we a god unto ourselves? Knowing mathematically that there is an all-eternity, humans must keep looking at the stars. We cannot return to the womb of the universe's birth but will always exist in this known vacuum in the corner of space. And at the edge of time, our spiritual cells take a quantum leap into a new kind of existence to which I can only imagine the God of creation is beckoning us.

In time, there is peace and an earthly paradise for all eternity. There are no borders above you, beneath you, or edges. On one level, people were technologically advanced, sophisticated, progressive, and enlightened in my time. Still, the savage man in modern human males is alive in some Europeans, European Americans, and some Asian groups more than it ever was in our African tribal brothers.

They have allowed their untamed 'self' to triumph over our common humanity and disobeyed the laws of society written in DNA to make us balance to respect life and not rape (ravage) the resources on the planet. The untamed traits of ranked savage European man and their compatriots selfishly split the human race into divisions and established legality to own free people, property and land. They brutally imposed the supreme authority's legal rules on the people, communities and nation. The universe has universal laws that teach proper conduct, to live and let live, but they are still getting ignored, and the empire makes up selfish legal rules we are to follow. Passive-aggressive, assertive people and conscientious objectors are getting ready to see the empire fall, and all people are governed by laws in the universe that correct the untamed self.

People cannot tame their human nature; feelings are unchecked, and our ethical ideas can hang like rain clouds over our lives. We see the destructive consequences of supremacy and extremist groups in toxic parents and families that are dysfunctional and emotionally unhealthy, and we can see it in stressed individuals.

The potential for mayhem has increased because the forces within us are more robust than the personal will, more reliable than any institution that cages it, and more durable than our mind's technological invention. This is simple to understand because of what we are as a species. We shape what we create to reflect ourselves, and our forces move us around like pawns. If we ignore the laws that govern, it is at our peril.

I was perilously close to being wiped out, standing on the edge of insanity and crying and crying. Therefore, do not be surprised that a large-scale, untamed force in our nature is wiping out other species on the planet and may wipe out our species in ignorance and stupidity. Hurry, hurry up evolutionary changes in humankind, change us, or shut down the gene pool mechanisms that cause us to be stupid when we are talented, with built-in biases.

Spiritually and mathematically, we can reach a high level to enlighten and understand the seen and unseen forces that make inferences about us. First, however, we must maintain humankind's holistic qualities and stop poking at every dormant thing in the body and brain, setting off a chain reaction of mental illnesses and cancers; the wrong side of biology gets upset.

The creator has written evidence of herself in all levels of human consciousness, and to accept it is healing. Having spirituality, or should I call it 'religious' faith, is an essential source of strength for most people who experience stress and mental illness, such as me. Most believers believe that mental illness is caused by sin, a lack of faith, the influence of an evil spirit or a parent's wrongful actions. Unfortunately, religious educators have not yet attempted to address their teaching impact, which drives an immense belief that causes moral injury and profound psychological distress. It includes an intense feeling of shame, guilt, self-loathing or worthlessness, which cannot be cured by prayer alone.

Discouraging the person from seeking help adds to their suffering and could even contribute to suicide.

Mental health stigma, I think, is primarily fuelled by cultural and religious views. They may attribute suicide to a lack of faith in a faith-based setting. People need good pastoral care to help them positively, to 'psychologically grow' and experience the approaches to treatment and therapists who can help them, and faith educators should be amongst them. The mentally ill are often spiritually damaged, usually by the preaching of ignorance, foolishness and silly interruptions of complex emotions and thoughts to suppress the growth of ordinary people. Religious leaders keep saying to their ego, "I am the leader", the 'power' overfamiliar, ordinary people who are their followers. So, they kept the knowledge they had obtained to share with the congregation and continued to preach the primitive stuff to maintain their 'power' over the familiar, ordinary people.

The universal natural laws of nature that humankind discovered in God's handiwork and the revelations for our species are to grow to become genuinely kind, empathic beings in all respects and to be compassionate and ethical people. Faith teaching should help us understand God's principles of life and truth, which bring us in tune with nature's peace, love and harmony. The faith industry should knuckle down and work with people through their varying degrees of rightness and wrongness to help them deal with the consequences. Instead of preaching gloom and doom and meddling in an afterlife, they should empower themselves to understand the mysterious things in all of us. The source of new courage and strength operates universal laws that we gradually learn the composition of life ticking. We do not need to bother ourselves about the internal tick-tock. God may stop the ticking altogether for those deliberately conscious, wicked people. Still, death is a natural progression to eternal life from the natural, earthly, mortal lifespan.

So far in the history of our species, our invisible, conscious cells are in a vast plain, the savannah field of the mind that is a peninsula, jutting out into insanity if thoughts are not made accurately. But they have not been flagged the alert pathway yet to follow the type of environment in which its realistic existence would be likened. But our conscious awareness keeps imagining what it might be like, and the subconscious keeps dreaming of it. Our subconscious realism dream fields have the closest connection to the environment that the consciousness in the godly, divine spirit cell takes in its quantum leaps deep in our living soul to escape insanity. The dead ashes of our body physically perished in the unperishable agent locked inside the soul's dormant existence. It gets that conscious awareness, alerting consciousness to the intended new realism that has evolved to the places it will make its home.

That is heaven in a spirited form that the earthly reality, life, only idealises about and dreams of, but people are not fully cooperating in causing it to happen. The world is full of fierce competitiveness, fights, selfishness and greed; team obedience is weak in collaboration, group collective consciousness is fragile and individual motivation is weak. Therefore, for a group activity to be good, it should obey the natural laws we learn through trial-and-error conflicts with nature's lessons throughout a lifetime. So, we first must successfully navigate our earthly life. It may get cut short in unfortunate ways, but whatever 'time' we have on this earth in our human experience, we learn from what happens to us. I gradually realised that my emotions, thoughts, ideas and opinions are subject to supervision from nature's definite natural universal order of things.

Inadequate pastoral care damages excellent people and bad people, and the good know they are honest and conscientious in their deeds and can naturally slip up and do wrong. Superstitious suspicions, fears and poor psychic understanding of the human condition and life's source connect us and drive our desires and how things in us can get faulty and, in some cases, beyond repair. Faith-based pastoral carers do not understand it. The grace of God in all of us will enable us to live a meaningful, purpose-driven life no matter the flaws or disabilities.

There is no condemnation or repudiation to maintain our existence in the afterlife. Only the properties that make us suitable are fundamental in the newly born life. Foolish preachers are panicking people into submission, with repentance disproportioning the strength of the energies in the people and unbalancing the equilibriums of a person, damaging the fight they have left in their soul to restore good health with medicine that could help them for a while. The supposedly reasonable, sensible people like pastors, priests and ministers are again failing their congregations of ordinary people by not compounding the undisputed truths gained in the essence of knowledge. Existence is frail; we are lucky to be here, and physical or mental illness has biological bases, causes and effects.

They, the religious ones, doctrine leaders and followers, continue to preach that what is primitive fear in all of us is stripped of all knowledge that brought us so far to understand our minds. It translates to better the proper sense and experience of the creator of it and all the compounds and properties in existence so far. Spiritual educators should know more about the spirit of man and woman and a person's psychological make-up than when it was first written down in the ancient world. In that age, people were terrified of the hell of negative, energised emotions and thoughts, which also scared the hell out of them, causing profound psychological consequences and often featuring trauma exposure. The knowledge of humankind, nature,

'God' and the various environments has grown significantly, and we can understand more about ourselves and our actions. Our 'being' as humans today is to take us into the fields our present known senses cannot detect. The ingenious organic organ, the brain, knows it has to engineer 'life' as living, artificial mechanical organism devices and add to the human frame equipment to reach and explore the fields. Those things might not be necessary if the human species continues to change in nature's natural development process from primate to modern man consciousness and evolving new networks within the self to increase higher and higher functioning abilities coupled with nature's environmental changes.

38

GOVERNMENT SYSTEMS AND OUR TAMED NATURE

Wednesday, 27 February 2019

As a result of feeling equipped to deal with life's challenges and disadvantages, I make the best decisions I can and consider living an adventure to recognise and seize opportunities so that new experiences and fun are in my life rather than just being rigidly locked into meaningless routines and having problems to solve. I may have to bend, but not break, to be adaptable because I am curious and continually want to learn, grow and strengthen my good traits.

I continuously try to pay attention to what has worked, is working, and can work, and I appreciate all the good things in my life. My grey matter concentrates hard. I am hopeful about the future, and things will work out for the best.

I apply my skills, effort and energy to things and causes within my family, community and the world to communicate meaningfully with people. I prioritise enjoyment, laughing and having a happy relationship with my family. I aim to hit a certain financial plateau to stop the struggles for materialistic values and keep us comfortable.

The societal pressures and political systems do not identify with what truly matters in my life. Still, I have more confidence in who I am now without using disabling antipsychotic drugs and being transparent with my choices. I am well-tuned to social differences, sometimes seeming to misperceive the social and political world to get motivated by self-interest fuelling exclusion. They disadvantaged me because of my opposing political beliefs, low social status and low educational attainment as a black man. The truth alerts me to the common danger critical to my survival.

We can all sometimes be in a situation that gives rise to the tendency for paranoid thinking, and in some cases, my mind could not escape the assumed harm, and my brain acted up with the symptoms of mental illness. I perceived my struggle as climbing the social ladder and affiliating with the liberal-conservative spectrum. Being a black person, it is not easy to do. When the government made a wrong decision about PIP, and the NHS promise of financial support is not worth the paper it is written on, the HM Revenue & Customs tax calculation for 6 April 2017 to 5 April 2018 says I have paid too little tax. I owe HMRC £149.38, which I must pay, and they will write to me again soon to tell me how I can. So, I feel disadvantaged as a third-class, marginal citizen. I have just written down some current stressors, and there is one more piece of bad news: natural causes force planned appointments to get cancelled.

The memory assessment was cancelled with a short telephone call the day before it was due. The therapist was said to be unwell with cold-like flu symptoms, and the next day, 21 February 2019, I was told the therapist was still sick and the appointment would have to be postponed and rescheduled. One week has passed, and I am still waiting for correspondence from the service, which does not surprise me.

DWP's reason for rejecting my claim was in a typical standard rejection statement letter: "This is because you didn't go to the assessment on 29 November 2018, and we don't think you've given us a good reason for this."

I have one month to ask for reconsideration and appeal if I think the decision is wrong again that second time. The NHS is running a memory assessment service, and I have been waiting to be reviewed by a psychiatrist from the trust for some time. Unfortunately, resources seem to get wasted because the mental health service told me to come to them for a physical check-up with a nurse on 22 February 2019. It duplicated the annual physical check-up I recently had at the GP surgery. Blood test, ECG, check BP, weight 91.4 kilograms, and height 5 feet 9 inches.

I applied for renewal of the application to get total awarded help on the HC2 certificate for NHS costs for health treatment for one year. It is not a free entitlement to even native citizens, and it was slashed to an HC3 certificate that is supposed to give limited help. This HC3 paper showed my maximum payments towards health costs before awarding reimbursement from the NHS authority. It gives me zero benefits; it does not even meet my regular treatment payment or replacement item costs, nor does it pay partially for any new item in treatment. What HC3 says I have to pay towards treatment first is higher than the price of the procedure itself. Therefore, the NHS authority will never pay a penny for treatment.

Where on earth is the financial support when I have to pay before they give any payout higher than the current treatment values? In all categories, authentic treatments will cost less. The HC3 certificate is a useless piece of paper that might as well be in the trash bin. It has no value at the dentist's surgery where I had treatment recently, and it would be useless to the optician.

The HC3 certificate says I pay £332.49 maximum for NHS dental treatment, wigs and fabrics.

So far, in my dental treatment history, it has always been below £332.49, which makes me eligible to make the total payment costs not exceeding that figure.

I felt it was unjust, and I took full responsibility for this feeling and changed my thoughts to prevent an emotional drama. Unfortunately, today, 27 February 2019, I learnt that the DWP PIP decision was to turn down my claim for daily living support and take away my current mobility support award from 24 February 2019.

There is a knock-on effect of losing all the disability benefit payments and not getting any financial support for my mental severity or physical disabilities challenges. Although the only government benefit coming into the house is the Employment Support Allowance (ESA), it will be affected by the decision to end disability benefits (PIP).

I believe my ESA entitlement will be reduced because a proportion of the benefit is an award for people with a disability that prevents them from holding down a job. An additional payment is included in the ESA for people in the 'disability support group', and this part of the amount will cease. I may be called to an assessment to get back into a job to earn a living with as little support from the government as possible. It is no surprise if the system throws me back into job-seeking at sixty-two. Could I be wrong in my analysis of the benefits system this time? I want comfort (to put my mind at ease) and to have the 'facts' in my mind, not suspicion. I had to find out what the benefits department would say before a letter arrived, meaning there was a change to my ESA entitlement.

I have just called the benefit enquiry team to ask if my ESA will be reduced because of the PIP decision. The customer services agent said, "No." She had looked at my file. I will have no reduction in the regular payments! I am perplexed. Can I believe what I want to think? That is the 'fact'. Customer Services immediately told me the 'fact' that there was no change in the ESA payments, or I would keep to my suspicion until I saw the evidence in my bank account that the pay remained the same as usual. I will have the next ESA payment on Friday, 8 March 2019.

The government benefit designed to help employment, ESA, maintained the disability component support, recognising I have severe disabilities preventing me from holding down a job. On the other hand, the government benefits were specially designed to help support disabled people; PIP denied me support on its financial backing. It is ridiculous, but it was not surprising that PIP would make a wrong decision because I feel people in government are smartly stupid. They stopped using common sense with the factual evidence in front of them.

What makes people stupid but cleverly brilliant and lose common sense? It needs scientific investigation. Even if you are called intelligent and as bright as a spark, you are not immune from being stupid. Experts! Yes, it would be best to watch yourself, check in with yourself, see the trap of foolish stupidity and avoid falling into it.

I knew there was a specific timeline for the decision and an expectation that this might happen. My choice not to be assessed, which I thought was reasonable grounds for being absent, did not lead to an opportunity to carve out a path for my life without conflict. To adhere to a government agency's requests as a way to achieve my happiness was too risky. The facts were known to them that I was in great upheaval and testing a new phase in my over forty years of history of taking antipsychotic medication for the worst, well-known mental illness on the planet, schizophrenia. The system never showed it cared for an individual or our group and was set up to save money and reduce costs. They have always sought ways to cut payments to the most vulnerable people whose condition takes away their will. They are left without adequate health care and vital financial support in a society that pays lip service to their needs.

I should feel disappointed, but I accept life's uncertainties and that there will be disadvantages. I willingly go with the flow with generally incomplete information and genuinely inhabit the present moment. I tamed my anger to be in systems that waste resources and are unfair, and I do not get caught in thoughts of time-wasting, complaining and heightened perception of harm, which has the power to level off into symptoms of illness.

I must see myself standing alone on my own two feet, looking after number one (myself) and not relying on political systems to get by. Thank God I paid all my National Insurance, and as a disabled person who can no longer work to earn a living, I get ESA benefits from the contributions I made when I was working. I do not get any free money for being a poor citizen; I am only getting supported by the National Insurance I paid. The taxman takes a share of the small private pension that gives me a payment of £115.43 per month. They are asking for unpaid taxes; didn't they receive the right amount from my private pension, or did the given personal allowance and the marriage allowance transferred by HMRC have an outstanding debt in earlier years?

I saw a few more words on page three of the HMRC letter, with a one-sentence explanation: "This calculation includes tax you owe HMRC for an earlier year."

Nothing comes free from the government. The family tax credit, council tax reduction schemes and benefits system are too complex for ordinary people to check the accuracy of their calculations. The loops to go through to have an award for the circumstances their laws say give entitlement and are our right to claim come back to hit us. They either calculate that errors occur to disadvantage us or that changes in the law usually disadvantage us too.

In recent years, I have paid back to the government department more than £3,000 for reclaimed tax credits, Inland Revenue paybacks and payments to the borough council.

The council admitted they had made an error in our council tax reduction entitlement, and we were forced to repay the council. In 2003, we fell behind with the unaffordable arrangement to pay council tax arrears. The same borough council contributed to my devastating mental breakdown, which led to attempted suicide and constant urges to die for the greater good. The cruel way in which they went about getting money from us was disgusting. We were just a few pounds above the government's margin for being poor but not quite skint enough, and the council showed no compassion for our plight.

They said the council would not negotiate another payment arrangement even though they had photocopy proof of our income and expenditure, and I pleaded at the customer services desk. "Please, the council has factual evidence that we do not have enough money coming in as income." I begged them to understand that paying all the priority bills on a low wage and struggling with a mental illness is not sustainable; I needed more time to pay the council tax bill. "I know

I must pay the council tax. I am not against paying," I said. I needed more time to pay the demand for the arrears and the coming year.

The customer services staff confirmed the standard procedure followed by the council for not paying council tax, and there were no exceptions. The council computer will generate demand letters for the unpaid council tax; the bailiff may call for payment. A message will be sent to appear in court for due council tax, and court costs will be added. The brutal statuary system that people in government compiled had worked uncompassionately and inhumanely. The non-marginal rule of law was harshly and brutally enforced on poor, law-abiding citizens. A letter arrived on the doormat. The bailiff arrived unexpectedly a few days later to take ownership of some of my goods; some payment had been made a few days previously. The bailiff had left empty-handed. Demand letters began arriving again, followed by a letter of summons to court and the date of the hearing.

Without mercy, the borough council and another company squeezed us to cough up unaffordable repayments for which I had confessed I did not have the money. I bent and buckled to pay the most I could, and over time, the arrears became a massive debt. Finally, I buckled entirely, had a breakdown and was hospitalised. The council and our mortgage provider pushed with demand letters threatening legal action. We used all the agencies to get us more time to pay and give us good advice that could help us. Citizens Advice, Accommodation Concerns, County Law advice services, GP and psychiatrist letters, and other money advice charities all had a hand in trying to help us. Unfortunately, they had a negligible effect; it slowed down our mortgage provider and the council's eagerness for repayments, with all arrears included in the monthly payment. The council and mortgage provider were insensitive and inhumane, showed no care for the weak and vulnerable, and provoked us as they preyed on us to pay up regardless of not having enough money for daily living.

The many credit companies, including banks to which I owed thousands of pounds, showed they worked ethically and had compassion and sympathy for our plight – not the council or mortgage provider. The credit companies gave me an ongoing period of grace. I negotiated affordable, very low payback, and they eased their pressure for repayment on unaffordable repayments. Most creditors suspended the payments for years until I could make a reasonable partial repayment, which was accepted as full and final payment for the money owed.

Ultimately, my family—my late mother, dad, sisters, and brother—mostly paid for the overspending. I am grateful for their immeasurable love and sacrifices to help me.

They raised the money to pay off the mortgage arrears and council tax demand for that year's arrears. However, the mortgage payments continued to be unaffordable. I asked the provider for the redemption figure for the mortgage and claimed a bit later for the distress and inconvenience they caused us. The house was sold in November 2017 to an insurance company that guaranteed no upfront mortgage payments and lifetime occupiers in our home. Just like every living thing, we will one day die on the face of the Earth. The insurance company will get the payment agreed upon in the binding contract we signed to have the house sold within a year after our death.

I claimed distress and inconvenience to the mortgage provider for compensation. They put forward a small, low cash payout and were unprepared to negotiate the sum they asked us to accept as a reasonable, financially supported apology. They indirectly implied that we would not get any more—take or leave it. (I cannot remember the figure; it may have been between £100 and £190.)

The council got away scot-free without paying compensation for distress and inconvenience because it does not exist in council policy. The review of the account must have recognised that they had been heavy-handed, but they did not even have the courtesy to admit it.

Throughout my history, I seem to barge into the uncertainty of my life and repeat the same behaviour that has caused me numerous problems; I have tried to scrutinise what I was doing and could not recognise I was operating or reacting to things in a passive series of habits. I say, "I am powerless to do anything." I say, "I cannot change things." I blame others, like disgruntled co-workers, and say, "People are doing this to me. I have cared for the happiness of others over my happiness. People's suffering is causing my unhappiness. I am hypersensitive and hurt by every natural or human-made calamity. I am trapped in a harsh reality I do not like," and on and on, it goes. I have difficulty processing negative thoughts and emotions.

These unproductive, negative habitual thoughts also blame socioeconomic status and the lack of money, jobs and education. I mistrust the education system because it lacks the gospel truth, the whole truth and nothing but the truth. Therefore, reality and knowledge had to be found in the trial and error of lived experiences to learn life skills. Social structures and systems were hardwired to increase inequalities and injustice, and people could not be trusted. The lack of money and a job were crushing me, and with so much self-demotivation, suicidal urges lurked. I gave up on my will to live in a period of depression and personal delays. I allowed the past negative thinking to haunt me almost forever, tainting me with past mistakes, failures and setbacks. Opposing views have not given me the energy or power to create the life I want to live on the planet, to be the best person I can be. Being open, kind, respectful, pursuing my talents, maximising my skills and strengths, and sharing love and gratitude with and for others teaches me how to build new healthy habits and use my common sense.

An elderly native European friend named John recently emailed me an obituary printed in *The Times*, a once popular broadsheet newspaper, to mourn the loss of Common Sense. I want to share it with you; you can also find it on websites. You may have heard similar.

Commonsense has sadly passed away obituary by Lori Borgman

Today, we mourn the passing of a beloved old friend, Common Sense, who has been with us for many years. No one knows how old he was since his birth records are lost in bureaucratic red tape. He will be remembered as having cultivated such valuable lessons as:

- Knowing when to come in out of the rain;
- Why the early bird gets the worm;
- Life isn't always fair, and
- Maybe it was my fault.

Common Sense lived by simple, sound financial policies (don't spend more than you can earn) and reliable strategies (adults, not children, are in charge).

His health began to deteriorate rapidly when well-intentioned but overbearing regulations were set in place.

- Reports of a six-year-old boy charged with sexual harassment for kissing a classmate
- Teens suspended from school for using mouthwash after lunch
- A teacher fired for reprimanding an unruly student worsened his condition

Common Sense lost ground when parents attacked teachers for doing the job that they themselves had failed to do in disciplining their unruly children.

It declined even further when schools were required to get parental consent to administer sun lotion or an aspirin to a student but could not inform parents when a student became pregnant and wanted to have an abortion.

Common Sense lost the will to live as the churches became businesses, and criminals received better treatment than their victims.

Common Sense took a beating when you couldn't defend yourself from a burglar in your own home, and the burglar could sue you for assault.

Common Sense finally gave up the will to live after a woman failed to realise that a steaming cup of coffee was hot. She spilt a little in her lap and was promptly awarded a huge settlement.

Common Sense was preceded in death by his parents, Truth and Trust, by his wife, Discretion by his daughter, responsibility, and by his son, Reason.

His survived by his four stepbrothers:

- I Know My Rights
- I Want It Now
- Someone Else Is to Blame
- I'm A Victim

Not many attended the funeral because so few realised he was gone.

I have fallen enough to realise that I must make better, more positive life choices. So, I am training myself to latch on to positive thinking. I have determined that I alone am responsible for my actions in sickness and health. In mental illness, I did not know that most of the time, wholly contrary ideas were sinking my performance. The gradual switch was more than a coincidence; I gained strength and was more tuned in looking around and identifying happy, healthy, well-adjusted people. They are naturally gravitating towards positive thinking.

Positive thinking is a healthy habit because it does what is best for my health and well-being. Not only will I make more nutritious choices and behaviour changes, but I also think repeating workable patterns will pay off in unexpected ways. Its reward has even more cognitive benefits.

God of love and her truths are joyous, divine and correct, and religions are a human-made authority to hold people in fear and guilt to discipline them and merely a semblance of meaning and control. The divine is within us, and we can dip in and take from this free, positive energy source that can change us. The mind will gradually engage in the traits it needs in its ongoing development to help balance us out if we are to do this or do that, living unaware of destructive personality traits and inferences which make our actions unpleasant. Then, when they hit the conscience, the alerted awareness dips into the divine source that flashes out positive thinking, improving our happiness. I have no idea where the positive thoughts and ideas come from so suddenly and, in time, automate our lives to gravitate towards the source of positive thinking.

That is how my idea of forming cells in our brain to think positively flashes out of the source of the divine spirit in our human nature. The components to make positive thoughts are already within us; we only have to use them to overcome the negative ones, which are easier to act on and produce. Academic places like universities teach the mechanics of the components that make us think. These components exist from the one God in the creation process. There is no belief-busting effect on believing in a god that judges people or rewards good behaviour through the promise of a place in heaven and punishes bad behaviour with the threat of being packed off to hell. So, I began to say "no thanks" to this popular belief of moralising God, who has some system of surveillance like an 'eye in the sky' and a god that can read people's minds and punish the people who transgress or reward them according to their excellent behaviour.

I saw no direct alleviation of the acute in-the-moment stress from an omniscient deity specifically interested in my future to help me cope, deal better with difficulties and impact stress responses. No, not in that way.

My first book, *The Memoir of a Schizophrenic*, contains stories anticipating an acute stressor. Unfortunately, my ability to cope with the stressful situation was not improved by clinging to an omniscient deity out there to downgrade stress. (See page 425, 'Only Seeing the Blues' written on 4 June 2002; page 552, 'God, Please, God, Please, God, Please, Please' written on 12 January 2005, page 561, 'SOS of Distress' written on 1 April 2005 and page 586, 'It Never Rains, But It Pours' written on 10 August 2005.)

The strength of my renewed ideology, belief in God within and a mixture of science, benefited me.

Faithfully, the advantage over facing difficulty and not breaking social rules to behave nicely is given to us by laws governing the saintlier side of our human nature. The complex trial and error practice and other practices, including family support and associated social support, help me cope with longer-term stressors. People are fundamentally sound. Still, there was the stress people imposed on me with their harmful personality traits and feeling 'good' for being not good. Rude, disrespectful, spiteful, hating and not attempting to show or develop their sound qualities is on the verge of being inhuman. Some people never learn to use the characteristics we all possess to evolve into better human beings. Society seems embarrassed to have everyday saints acting on the goodness in them, and people who perform and are daily baddies are credited as newsworthy and magnified.

The unleashing of the dark side in humans may appear as a foreign feral species, but it is not a separate species of rational people. I have come a long way to realise that all of us have a version of potential in life that lies within us to tap into the more positive, compassionate and selfless aspects of the best of our human nature. The dark side consumes psychopaths and narcissists. We all have varying levels of dark, mysterious personalities and light traits of altruism, forgiveness, gratitude, fairness, compassion and selflessness. The latter are jewels in every individual whose daily behavioural acts, saintly and optimistic, have a net effect on the world.

The downside of being the best version of myself is that it could leave me open to exploitation because of excessive trust, compassion and interpersonal guilt.

People are malleable and can train and shape themselves to use light, saintly traits. I envisaged modern human societies' variants carrying out their obligations to the positive divine-defined spirit side of human personality, and those motivated by power and selfish ambitions will not exist. The shifting perspective increases a sense of universal love and self-transcendence. The good of humanity is honesty, higher life satisfaction, agreeableness, values that have excellent transcendent qualities, compassion, empathy and engagement in loving kindness. My predicted outcome is that our rationale increases our self-passion, openness, conscientiousness, autonomy and competence when fundamental belief in the goodness of humans is godly and we are motivated to treat individuals as valuable and worthy, regardless of what they can provide personally. One purpose of life is to drag our less saintly personality traits out of the shadows and into the light. Believing in the essential goodness of humans is "I think people are mostly good", and modern secular life is declining belief in the prominent omniscient deity God out there. Most are absent from the understanding of God within us.

In our modern social complexity, societal cooperation across ethnic groups in the face of migration, warfare, the spread of false news and new virtual reality technologies engages in self-transcendent experiences. The future of society requires people to look within themselves for God and the godly. Some people may need to swallow a pill designed to contribute to taming their human nature, which removes the strenuous effort to cooperate. I will move away from this hard-liner, positive-energy line of thought. The PIP decision is still playing on my mind.

I am returning to the DWP decision that stuck in like a thorn. It needs more of my thought process to remove it, rest, say no more about the unfairness of the PIP decision and move on.

My old self absorbed six months of stress and anxiety from PIP tactics, and most of my life was baited on negative thoughts. My vulnerable mental health and long-term mobility issues have enough factual medical evidence to sink a battleship and were presented to help in my claim, some by me, which was ignored. DWP did not say in the rejection letter that they had looked at the medical evidence or points from the application form.

The system breaks with stupidity, so their agent did not physically see me. Despite my best efforts to write the truth about how my condition affects me on the application form without adhering to known methods of dishonesty and deception to gain extra points, I was refused financial support on two levels.

The medical evidence was under DWP's nose: Mr Willett has a history of schizophrenia dating back to 1978. He sustained multiple physical injuries from attempting suicide in 2003, blah, blah, blah… That did not get looked at as proof or even considered. It is a fact in the medical files, without biases. Why did they need to see me when the condition is stress-related? Are they thinking of my well-being? The fear of being assessed may put me on the edge of developing psychotic symptoms, and at the time, I was weaning myself off the antipsychotic medication. I could not take the risk of derailing one of my purposes. So, I did not go.

Can I find the silver lining? Schizophrenia looks fixed on the inside; that does not mean everything operates smoothly. I am still learning to care for myself by nourishing myself from the inside out. I try to 'think positive' so that meaningful, long-lasting transformation continues. I am not charismatic and do not want to better myself for a leadership role. If you glimpse inside my brain, feelings are frowning. Thoughts are too, and they waver in my heart and elsewhere. Thinking and other functions bring advantages and disadvantages, and the personality characteristics and traits I have been born with or inherited are hardwired into my brain. I am an ordinary person with extraordinariness. On the other hand, my introverted brain lacks the necessary skills to express my experiences and opinions in never-ending communication in front of others and not have social withdrawal due to shyness and anxiety. I would not say I like prolonged social interactions and feel uncomfortable in large social gatherings.

Our daughter, Georgina, is moving forward, from being engaged to Adam to marrying him in October. The date will be Saturday,

19 October 2019. They are trying for a child to express a changing future, with the child coming into earthly existence with help from IVF. We all hope they will have a child birthed in exceptional biology and continue trusting in God to start their family. They have an excellent marital bond and would expect this extra blessing. Our prayers are with them that the God of creation does not delay a loving couple's desire to produce a new life for too long.

We have grandchildren from our other two grown-up children, you know; they are being nicely nurtured on the right path, and they could, therefore, retain the essence of God in them. Nature has all the proper essentials for them to mature in a specific field of job excellence when they grow up and work, rest, study, and play.

I am already busy preparing the father-of-the-bride speech. Unfortunately, my thoughts were interrupted by horrific worldly events. So, I put down the pen that wrote my speech and focused on matters at hand, but I could do nothing. I will get back to writing the wedding speech again soon because I need lots of time to write the draft, make it the best it can be, learn it, and then rehearse it to deliver a perfect speech to a multitude of people. Although there will only be two families, friends and relatives, it will shake my nerves too much if I do not prepare myself.

I have made sense of my thoughts and experiences and achieved eureka moments, positively impacting my health. One of the benefits of being more focused on beliefs is that it changes my mindset when it comes to self-imposed illness. I improved my creativity and became more open to different ideas, and my confidence grew. I love to think and dream, which may be considered inefficient and inactive participation in changing the world, but I can still achieve with a mental disadvantage because of my goals. I noticed more cultural differences that play a role in all this.

As a healthier introvert, I spend time alone to reorganise my thoughts. I have an alerting system that warns that the boundary between dangerous isolation and beneficial solitude is quite blurry. Loneliness could harm health, so I will continue having good friends and strong bonds in small social groups that will accept me into their clan. It is a more satisfactory experience, and my happiness is more considerable. I am not too stressed to go through periods of mental instability. Not everyone wants to hear the message I put out there: to help everyone. Extremists may get hostile, and some completely ignore it. Others will put their hands to their ears and say, "La, la, la, we don't want to hear from you!"

I am to protect my well-being from harm, not expose it to danger. Unfortunately, I am not so different regarding my and other people's harmful behaviour and attitude, which affect my cognitive functioning, increase my risk of metabolic disorders and negatively impact my immune system.

39

KEEPING SCHIZOPHRENIA STUCK

Monday, 4 March 2019

I altered my life inside by continuously healing my mind and overcoming the effects of antipsychotic medication. I want to celebrate the remarkable transformations I am making in my life, habits, ways of thinking, working through feelings, and making durable adjustments in myself and my relationships. It is peculiar how my emotional states affect my health and well-being so severely. On the other hand, the same emotions originate biologically and influence me later.

Adverse negative emotional state responses affected my health and well-being on antipsychotic medication. My whole body and mind state must have activated hormonal responses and other systems and systemic reactions. Courage, motivation and perseverance are vital developments that kick in.

Coming off antipsychotics must have slowly improved my mind-body connection. My emotions, biology, and feelings understand the good and positive experiences I am subjecting my brain to, so I increased my mind to gather good thoughts and positive experiences. Good and positivity influence my body from the kind ideas and positive chemical signals from my brain, keeping schizophrenia in check.

There is no doubt that parts of my everyday experiences of discomfort impact my mood. But I do not know why, and somehow, some things that feel 'off' have more to do with superior force and sinister energy. Although not quantifiable, we sometimes need to cleanse the air, open windows and bring in a fresh new draught. I have come off antipsychotics, which enables me to be naturally mindful. My self-talk is even more compassionate now, for myself and others, and I try not to freak out when something awful suddenly happens. I am safe and happy because I am learning not to rebuke myself or others with negative thoughts. I can imagine my negativity showering away; unwanted thoughts fade when peace with others, peace with myself and incidents are viewed as neutral and natural, generating positive energy.

I am learning that nobody else is responsible for my feelings; people do despicable things that need dealing with but do not cause the feelings that affect me. My (feelings) 'opinions' are a unique product of how I interpret what's happening around me. My unusual experiences, history, and values filter my emotional response to situations, and I should take responsibility for owning my authentic feelings. Other people may have a completely different emotional response. Therefore, I should not blame my triggered emotions on anyone else.

I am also still learning to manage and defeat anxiety and the awful sensations in my skull that I eventually experienced from having varying strengths of a headache. I am forgetful and still have some muddle-headed thinking and muddled understanding. I am trying hard to clean out more toxins that are stubborn and negative and have cognitive symptoms left over that I cannot shift yet. My sincere effort to grow and change is arduous, but I must be persistent and do much work. I am getting what must be a natural but destructive reaction to change when anxiety and discomforts bring me down. Should I retreat? No, it could send me right back to square one, and reminding myself of it pulls me back on track.

I feel optimistic and different from my old self on antipsychotics. Things feel safe, and the hazards in the world and risk-taking are linear and natural to expect. I am gaining momentum in my growth progress, but I will pause momentarily and give myself credit. (Well done so far, Karl. Clap, clap.)

Giving myself credit will motivate me to keep advancing and watch for minor changes instead of continually expecting dramatic steps from myself. Moreover, it will prepare me for all aspects of reform.

40

GOVERNMENT SYSTEMS EXTENDED CHALLENGES

Friday, 8 March 2019

Following the memory assessment cancellation on 21 February 2019, a further date was arranged for Thursday, 18 April 2019.

The critical, suspicious thought about my ESA payment being reduced lasted longer than a few minutes or hours from when the suspicion had arisen. My suspicion has been chipping away at the ESA customer services' 'fact' word; there has been no reduction in ESA payments.

I walked to a pocket park two days ago to get some fresh air because my attention had been pulled in this one direction for days.

Most of the time, my suspicions did not appear to be bogus. However, the message became even more critical last night. Overnight, my suspiciousness predicted that my ESA was likely to be stopped altogether.

These thoughts have good intentions to protect me and keep me safe. But they warn that there is worse to come, and I must prepare. The problem is that this morning, my suspiciousness has fuelled my anxiety. That old, familiar feeling of stress is creeping in. Nevertheless, it is empowering to know the truth, so I am coming to you in this writing 'live' on Friday, 8 March, at 8:30 am, to check the amount of money ESA deposited into my bank account via internet banking.

I have reached the final stage in the online procedure for the display screen to show the statement page. I am looking at the ESA transactions page. Oh! Hey, they have got to be joking with me. I continue to eyeball the screen. Oh my God! The ESA transaction is missing. It was stopped! No money has been credited to my ESA account.

I am right here in the moment; I am 'live' immediately at this moment in time, but it causes me no struggle with anxiety or first-hand panic attacks.

My self-enquiry, between my mental process of self-reflection and my sensory process of self-awareness of this moment, has a feedback dialogue. So, I am centred, comfortable and calm, and I will be okay.

The phrase instantly feels authentic and genuine, and honestly, I have a smile on my face. But my ego lashes out! "I told you so!" And it wipes the smile clean off my face.

It is now 8:50 am, and I am telephoning the ESA benefit helpline. Moment by moment, in conversation, I am listening to what the adviser says.

"The system says there's an issue, and the computer is not allowing payment. A note has been sent to the benefits office to address the issue, and direct payment to the bank account will be made today. The benefits office will be in touch."

Three hours and fifteen minutes had passed from 8:30 a.m., when I surfed internet banking, to 11:40 a.m. when the call from the benefits office ended. The time is now 11:50 a.m. I did not pause for ten minutes to quiver after the dialogue with the benefits office staff.

I allowed myself to slowly release positive, active sensations while reflecting on the first point in the conversation, the word 'apology'. "The money will be in your account by midnight, but the transfer usually takes two hours."

I received a blessing of joy from the spectrum of life's gifts of emotions that I can appreciate. In addition, the staff member frequently apologised and could not find any reason why it had been stopped.

HMRC has sent me a letter explaining how they will collect the tax that I owe. The only appropriate method of repaying the underpayment of £149.38 suggested is a monthly direct debit repayment of £4.12.

I was in contact this afternoon on the tax helpline and discussed that £4.12 was unaffordable and that I was not attempting to dodge the tax owed. They were the ones who had worked out my total income and the repayment amount permitted over the most prolonged period.

However, they said another department would contact me within five working days to examine income and expenditure and see what they could do. So, the state system's extended challenge is 'to continue'.

On Tuesday, 12 March 2019, communication began again with HMRC, and I raised my voice to the unclear, ambiguous message of whether HMRC had devised a way to pay back the tax I owed.

"There is no need to see your expenditure; you have a small personal pension and ESA, we see, and the payment is on hold—"

I interrupted loudly, "How am I supposed to make payments later with this small income? How long will it be on hold?"

The HMRC adviser said, "You did not let me finish. No payment is required now or in the future."

I tried again in the conversation to aim direct words to the adviser to state that the payment was cancelled.

The final response was, "The payment is on hold, and we have stopped computer-generated letters."

41

A KIND OF DEMENTIA NOT KNOWN

Saturday, 30 March 2019

In my lens, my outlook on the world differs from everyone else's. I rarely get it the first time when asked to do a task or respond in a light-hearted conversation. It is seldom a logical way. My rich internal world, which exists within my mind, has a God complex and colours the world differently from anybody else.

I give viewpoints different from others and ask myself questions about the world, my life, and how I see others and myself. I miss the messiness that makes people attractive and would make me more interesting on the page. I have been working all my life to get rid of or control my human messiness better to use more of my divine saintly qualities and always be logical in a perfectly rational way. But none of us works in a perfectly sensible manner, and my belief system about the world and how it works hurts me because I am not too fond of how the world and people actually work. So, I look for people to change their attitude by practising a God-complex belief system of impartiality and believe humanity can begin to change by starting with themselves.

My meek world view flaws are rooted in every aspect of my psychology. From the beginning, living my worldview and experiencing events hurt me. For example, my family tells me I overthink things, which causes me to worry and fret. "It's normal to forget and mess up. Don't be too hard on yourself; no one is perfect."

Yesterday, 29 March 2019, I began to laugh when I could not 'get it' as I talked to my son from my mobile phone. He told me step-by-step how to reverse the camera on the phone, which I had done many times before but could not remember how for either love or money. I probably spent ten minutes unable to follow the instructions, even though I thought I was doing it to a 'T'. I could not get it.

My son, Jonathan, remained calm and patient and asked me to keep trying. Still, I became frustrated, no longer finding it funny to forget and unable to follow simple instructions. I told him I would call his mum to do it. I was bewildered. His mum reversed the camera to Jonathan's instructions, and I said to them, "That's exactly what I did. It didn't work!"

In the evening of that same day, I used my smartphone to watch a YouTube video clip and needed to pause the video. I have halted YouTube videos before but could not do it this time. I carefully did what I always do to get the pause icon on the screen. Eventually, after about ten minutes of playing around, I managed it. Wow, oh my God. The awareness suddenly hit a raw nerve and frustrated me momentarily. The next moment, I was happy to know, but oh God, my finger motor movement was doing the opposite of what I thought.

I was supposed to tap my finger on the screen, and I truly believed that was the action I took. However, it took a long time for me to be aware that my response movement was to slide my finger on the screen. I immediately told Euphemia, in my usual way, using my loving pet name for her, darling, and sometimes I say my lovely. My lovely spoke.

"Karl, it's normal."

I let the rest of the family know of my discovery the next day.

I prompted a question. "Am I getting a kind of dementia medical science may not know about?"

"Stop overthinking, Daddy," say the girls. "It's probably the same phenomenon you get when you see on a shop door— 'push' and 'pull' and vice versa."

"Dad, in your case, you got confused between 'tap a finger' and 'slide a finger' in your mind. It's nothing more than that," said my boy.

42

MY BRAIN 238 DAYS OFF ANTIPSYCHOTIC

Wednesday, 8 May 2019

The fantastic three-pound organ (the brain) that houses my awakened consciousness and the un/subconsciousness that controls all my bodily functions interprets information from the outside world. It embodies the essence of the mind and soul. My brain also houses creativity, intelligence, emotion and memory and receives data through its five senses: sight, smell, touch, taste and hearing, often many at once. It assembles the messages that have meaning for me and can store that information in my memory. My brain has nerve cells in many sizes and shapes called neurons in my bony skull. They say it gets nourished and protected and has structural support from caretaker cells (I forgot the word for those cells) that regulate the blood-brain barrier, allowing nutrients and molecules to interact with neurons. The consistent neurons communicate across a tiny gap called a synapse that exchanges neurotransmitters.

Okay, I understand some of the anatomy of my brain, which has my 'being' Karl in it. Nevertheless, my experiences of knowledge of the essence of things have continued to turn my reasonable belief in God into something permanently fixed.

I have gained a new understanding that advances a series of proofs that sincerely ground me in God's existence. Denying it and God's role in my philosophical thoughts is unthinkable.

One of the most philosophical questions is about proving God's existence. I am self-assured that my life experiences only make God's presence more probable than not. It is evident proof of reasonable and responsible grounding beyond all reasonable doubt. I have seen the evidence and believe in a superintelligent, transcendent, creative power. I could not fail to be convinced by it as my rational faculties became intact.

I claimed to prove God's existence externally and internally beyond a mere reasonable belief in the force of her, the creator God.

It may need to make better intellectually respectable academic sense. Still, my self-proof confirms my rational footing and this view. I inadvertently hope to slow down secularism's rise of atheism and ensure the grounding in ordinary people who believe in God's existence. It gives believing intellectuals a visual to study and a mathematical demonstration of the proof. Those opposed to it and in disputation have a vested interest in undermining evidence for the existence of God. Atheists claim there is no God, and agnostics are neutral as to whether there is a God or not. Agnostics have to tackle objections from believers to prove God's existence to them, which was always evident to them. Before modern times, everyone believed in God, I heard it said.

These days, these groups of unbelieving people tend to be very vocal compared to centuries past. Also, it is said that before the seventeenth and eighteenth centuries, belief in God was unopposed, and atheists and agnostics were rare – some say non-existent.

In early Europe and known parts of the world, I suspect the 'thought' of God was perfectly reasonable, and religious belief was widespread. In that period, philosophers were not at loggerheads or odds. It was considered absurd, if not unthinkable, to deny a God or Gods. Something must have happened to put modern philosophers at odds.

I do not know what it was and have not found any research on it. Still, I speculate it is the physical search for proof in the widespread belief in a creator, a transcendent power, to which no evidence of the physical existence of this 'being' has appeared to oppose the argument. So, modern philosophers and perfectional theorists began to argue about the presence of God that ordinary people accepted.

Widespread misconceptions and understandings of God have emerged in modern times. Still, we know so much more these days to convince us all to be believers again in an unknowable form of a transcendent invisible creative power. The human language we were born with articulates this positive hidden spirit energy language called God.

Most of my knowledge and some habits I learnt are from personal experiences, through trial and error, rather than formal education and training. I have managed to express my intuitions and conceptions and conceptualise what my God-consciousness endowed upon me. Some practices encode and store information in my memory and retrieve information from it. My retrospective memory is good at assessing past events, recalling and recognising, but other memory activities could be better. Short-term memory is used to remember information after several seconds or minutes. Long-term memory is used to remember information over a long duration and needs to be less sketchy. The temporarily held data involves working memory and could well get manipulated. Semantic memory, in which general facts are stored, and episodic memory, a memory for personal events, are faulty in some way. This could not only be due to the ageing process that gave me sixty-two years of age.

My life has dived into the pool of conscious relaxation, using my mental awareness to produce a profoundly relaxed state. The continuous adverse effects in some cognitive domains from the withdrawal from antipsychotics include severe, systematic, identified verbal delays and some visual delay memory problems. I sleep well, and my appetite, interest and motivation are all good, but there is ongoing neck stiffness and all-over body aches, mainly in the torso and lower back. My skull has a constant awful sensation of rising heat within its core, which is very intense. It reaches the surface of my skull membrane hot and releases the feeling of pins and needles on my scalp. There is shrinking, squeezing and tightening and then a widening seems to occur automatically, and my cortex is under pressure. The folds and grooves feel like they are oscillating. My brain fluid is compressed and widened in the hollow cavities' ventricles.

Sometimes, it is hard to think; the feeling has always been with me. I feel exhausted during the day and must sleep off its vigorous intensity. Still, when the severity of discomfort, which I can no longer call variable headache symptoms, creeps up from mild to very irritating, and I cannot stand it anymore, I take ibuprofen or naproxen for some relief. I use them as needed and never overuse them to stabilise the terrible sensation working out of my brain in due course. I want to allow my mind the time it needs to absorb the leftover, harsh pharmaceutical chemicals it has regularly had for over forty years and replenish. The painkillers work pretty well to restore the agent in my biological systems to tame and mellow down those things that cause me to be sick or miserable. I aim to allow my brain's chemical factory to produce and regulate the proper substances to keep a healthy, balanced ratio in my body and mind.

Thursday, 18 April 2019, the neuropsychological examination occurred to identify cognitive impairment that schizophrenia and decades of antipsychotic medication usage may have contributed to. I will have the measured 'facts' from the test that typically tests five cognitive domains in dementia patients.

I was a little uneasy and restless, just short of fearful that the test would reveal a lifetime of illiteracy. The test tests attention, memory, fluency, language, and visuospatial processing.

I did not know if I did well in the cognitive examination. My anxiety rose slightly after the test only because I struggled to remember the most common and recent things. As the expression goes, "They are on the tip of my tongue," it needed several promptings to release them.

The CPN examiner said I had a problem retrieving information, that my overall score was 78/100, and that the full report would be sent to me. Then, I felt slightly relieved; that score did not seem like a bad result out of 100. The examiner concluded that antipsychotic medication affects cognition, but the problem is temporary. As I had stopped the drug for schizophrenia recently, she recommended a six-month reassessment to gauge any of the expected differences or improvements from her baseline. I agreed and accepted the first of two recommendations.

- **First option:** to complete a further assessment in six months, following appointment on 3 October 2019.
- **Second option:** an fMRI scan to investigate brain volume and deterioration. It included regions of my brain that may have shrinkages.

Cognitive assessment ACE III written report

The website reference relates to Addenbrooke's Cognitive Examination (ACE): https://en.wikipedia.org/wiki/Addenbrooke%27s_Cognitive_Examination

The findings:

- Total score: 78/100
- Attention: 15/18. Tested by asking the client for the date, including the season and the current location, repeating three single words, and serial subtraction.
- Memory: 16/26. Tested by asking the client to recall the three words previously repeated, memorising and recalling a fictional name and address, and recalling widely known historical facts.
- Fluency: 6/14. Tested by asking the client to say as many words as possible, starting with a specified letter within one minute and naming as many animals as they can think of in a minute.
- Language: 26/26. Tested by asking the client to complete a set of sequenced physical commands using a pencil and a piece of paper, such as "place the pencil on the paper; write two grammatically complete sentences. Repeat several polysyllable words and two short proverbs; name the objects shown in

twelve-line drawings; answer contextual questions about some things; and finally, read five commonly mispronounced terms aloud.
- Visuospatial: 15/16. Tested by asking the client to copy two diagrams, draw a clock face with the hands set at a specified time, count sets of dots, and recognise four partially obscured letters.

I am eight months, 238 days, off the medication, and I question social norms and the wickedness of some extremist people. My normal feelings are getting too sensitive, and my empathic ability has grown very intense again, close to virtually disabling my fricatives recently, with paralysis coming back.

Although I have been trying to focus on building resistance and recognising physical signs of stress awareness, my mind is trying to keep up with the aim of empowerment to have no disabling feelings from an adverse stress reaction. Unfortunately, I have felt almost trapped again by stressful events in the media, which affect my satisfaction and happiness in my personal life and cause me to cry. They say feelings are friends, but I must also acknowledge that they can become my worst enemies.

My emotions are built into me for a reason, for empowerment, and are my body's way of informing, directing, motivating, energising and guiding me. Still, I am periodically drained, weakening the real, natural strength when my humanity feeds back feelings I cannot cope with. I use that hardness of the inner light of my humanity and the power left in me to shine forward healthily and helpfully. When people's bad news and the environment suffer, hurt victims allow powerful feelings for humanity to be harnessed, and my inner light feels their pain. When they are too strong, the power of the forces in compassion, sympathy, empathy, reconciliation and even kindness makes me too sensitive, super-sensitise me, and gradually change the perception that it is my punishment to be so good-natured, which is weird.

I will also likely make biased decisions and increase my vulnerability to deal with gentlemanly agreements and other forms of cooperation that can be exploited and used for selfish purposes. My body gives off signals that I am not looking after myself. There is too much of humanity's good stuff, leaving me with insufficient time to replenish the energies for my kind and tender-heartedness. If given a chance to use my emotional skills in a practical, physical way to relieve people's misery or animal suffering or protect the environment, the chances are I will be abused – emotionally self-harm.

How do I stop my powerful feelings from weakening me? I gave myself suggestions in previously written pieces, and now I am trying mental recall from my memory and typing what comes to mind:

- Write down your emotions as soon as possible, as the dominant emotion fully allows you to feel adequate during the bad news. Then, try to let go of the deep pain in sadness.
- The grief and the hellishness that the sufferer is experiencing tightened pressure valves in my heart and belly. The 'feel' sensory organs in my body and the feeling of all kinds of emotions from my brain are in touch. They are mysteriously connected unseeingly to people's misery, the horrible calamity and the continuous unhappiness in me for them. So, the repeated exposure to people's suffering, awful misery, pain, animal cruelty and nature's worst environmental forces of destruction damages my functioning ability.
- Distract yourself by doing something other than absorb the repeated alerts, the on and on of bad news that the media uses

to philologically damage us and call the brutal, unsympathetic way they report human tragedy entertainment.
- Share intense emotion and talk about it; I almost magically feel better for dragging the feeling from the inside to the outside. I gain peace. First, thanks to my enduring wife and family for listening and their patience in helping me gain perspective.
- Meditate, relax, practise breathing, and breathe in the fresh air. The intense feelings drive my brain to feel like I am not in charge; someone else is in command. Relaxing in prayer mellows down the racing high sensitivity onto my compassionate and empathic self, which makes us feel at peace.
- Take back control of my brain, the driving seat, from the adverse psychological manipulation effects in advertising and the power of persuasion in media that have become fundamental to shaping people's view of good or bad. The press uses persuasive techniques to make people believe the undesirable is desirable.

My life indirectly encountered human frailty recently, affecting my ability to rise above it all. They are not directly linked to my problems. Some things are, but this type of issue dramatically put me into coping skills mechanisms to confront the crisis, but learning resilience doesn't come naturally to me. I was forever trying to become more resilient and develop and strengthen my coping skills, problem-solving skills, approach, and outlook, which seemed fixed in my genes. My ability to deal with setbacks and their many challenges looks almost entirely set in my genetic make-up. However, the environment plays a massive role in how resilient I may be, alongside any perceived stressors.

I want to nurture crucial skills from challenging circumstances and situations to correlate to higher emotional intelligence to manage feelings. I knew what was causing them, and I understood why. And, of course, some factors are directly outside my control, such as natural disasters. Still, external causes affect me the most, including those of my children and relatives and the challenging problems they are tackling. I already have the power to make choices that will affect my situation, and I get ready to cope, leading to a safe outcome and a successful solution for my problem.

The violence in hatred terrifies me, and in my mind most intensely are the historical recorded accounts of Nazis massacring Jews. I render them less than human and feel oddly sad for them as inhumane people. Today, some are stirring up the biology in themselves and other people who are racist and, at its height, fuel ethnic cleansing when they make grave misjudgements about people's differences and diversity in communities. Ultimately, our biology can play an outside role in our behaviour as nature and nurture interact to shape our perceptions of the world. So often, what made us human beings is distorted by the influence of the less rational and reasonable pre-existing biological inhumane attitudes. It stirs up racism, nativism, bigotry and violence. Still, the healthy, functioning brain in dark-toned racial minorities never internalised racism to explode later to render their explicit racism and overt racist behaviour less human.

We use areas of our brain so that our emotional regulation and impulse control neutralise, bombarding implicit racial biases in the unconscious, which stimulates humanity to live in peaceful community groups and have neighbourly love. It is time to use pharmacological treatment for racism. Give them psychiatric drugs that mess up racist pathway systems in their brains; pharmaceutical therapies for those whose impaired prefrontal cortex response is fixed to 'cure racism'. Too many people get martyred to raise awareness in society to restrain racist biases, which results in irrational behaviours. I feel it is gravely severe that supremacists and other inhumane, organised groups of people, with their hateful ideology, inspire violence and bloodshed. They dog-whistle ordinary people to nod their heads in agreement with racist hatred ideology. Evil people's extreme orientations need to be defeated; historically, they have martyred our ancestors and are more dangerous since the Holocaust, the rise in Islamophobia and the persecution of Christians.

Due to overexposure to terrible, tragic news and political unease, people's deliberate hurtfulness, unfairness and unwarranted rage and hate seem to come from threat bias and racial bias that I have outlined in all people. Malicious, nasty behaviours such as racism, the weaponised use of fear and physiological orientating, and the media manipulating us have the power to disable me. I was not personally involved in the incidents that almost maimed my normal functioning as the callous acts played on my mind repeatedly until I could find stillness and peace by switching off the nuisance and ignoring or walking away from the source of it.

The first few times I went to stop the bombardment of bad news entering my comfortable environment, mainly in my home, to shut out the terrible news, they wiggled me with guilt for turning them off. Frequently repeated tragic news stories on the radio and television, charity posters/flyers in the letterbox, images of suffering and pop-ups on the internet of tragic depictions are deeply depressing.

Using legal poisonous substances to control indoor creepy crawlies and have control of garden creatures that are becoming pests causes uncomfortable feelings. In addition, having to pull up beautiful, uncultivated, unattended wild plants that are flourishing much better than the specially selected plants one has planted to nurture creates feelings of "I shouldn't be doing that" to a very uncomfortable level.

Things happen, and I make deliberate, small mistakes to learn about natural laws by trial and error. Sometimes, strange patterns of feeling could be modelled after the ruling laws of physics.

Below are a few of the recent tragedies that act like slow poison as I repeatedly take them in, knowing they will drive me mad or eventually kill me, but I have just managed to start the antidote in my weakness, and my life continues:

- A plane crashed on landing on a runway, and many died.
- A young female journalist died on the eve of Good Friday reporting unrest in Londonderry.
- There is religious hatred and persecution. Someone received a death sentence for blaspheming, and another was stoned for adultery.
- There have been death threats to MPs because Brexit seems to be a national humiliation and has been delayed until October 2019. After all, parliamentarians could not make up their minds.
- Youth crime involving knives and gang violence is out of control in most of the country, and there is widespread racial abuse in football and a Church cover-up of child sexual abuse.
- On this devastating Easter Sunday, 21 April 2019, in Sri Lanka, suicide bombers struck churches and hotels. Two hundred and ninety people died, and 500 were injured.

That is the latest bad news. It is the last straw. I could not take it anymore; all the tragic stories broke me. I could not continue listening to or watching commentaries. These human stories hurt so much that my appetite shrank, my stomach rolled, and all my five senses sensitively picked up any traces of tragic news. So, I am harmed; their misery interferes with my whole mind and body's biological systems. The miseries pull my attention. I immediately stop and tightly tense up like a curled-up hedgehog. The bad news gets intensely absorbed into every aspect of me and shuts me down. Still, between Friday, 19 April, Good Friday, and now, this 241st day off the medication, Saturday, 11 May 2019, I could only take in lousy news stories once daily to prevent completely shutting down my functioning ability.

My coping strategies are to switch off the nuisance, ignore it, or walk away from its source.

Most people in the world act differently from me, and I am never likely to be able to accept it. What seems to be hard for most people is to be truthful, which comes easy for me; dishonesty is more difficult for me. So, while I know that my existence is frail and the universe does not revolve around my reality, I must try to capture the essence of my life stories and circumstances. Readers, you have been a part of my waking dreams since the moment of acceptance by reading this book, any of my books. I sometimes talk to myself from time to time. I have consciously brought myself to articulate my feelings and open up about my complexities.

It is remarkable how we are all different yet unique, each with distinctive gestures, a pattern of speech, movement and thought and distinct personalities with a complex mix of nature and nurture. We must realise that people manipulate people and then unscrupulously treat their environment as a reality that raises authoritarian fearmongering. People need to check in with themselves, genuinely assess their situation more rationally and reasonably, and be aware of the biases that stop them from being honest, fair, kind and perfect. And respect one another. The adverse influence of the seed of social media networks is tearing society apart by depicting 'others', non-Caucasian (non-white) people, as evil people, and the Caucasian group themselves keep away from 'others' to save themselves. I feel sorry and sad for them to be so far from experiencing the full effects of a human being. From the beginning of my thoughts on my creation, I had my first diagnostic thought about my existence.

Furthermore, past thoughts and ideas have shaped my actions, which are not how I would like them to be, and I struggle to understand the process of the complex mix of nature and nurture influencing my future thoughts and actions. It has been challenging to feel comfortable in my personality and to be my authentic character. I have adjusted and evolved my tradition of ideas, and I have been struck down from time to time with an illness (you may know it by now; it is schizophrenia) that overrides me and changes aspects of me, which are unhelpful reactions and thoughts. Behaviour patterns and a distinctive active style in my thoughts, dreams and actions have built up and been added to over time, and some are unhealthy and neuroticism traits. I have actively modified my behaviours and beliefs by snipping them away, layer by layer.

Decade after decade of development has shaped me, and I immediately recognised my uniqueness and the growth in my humanity from a tiny cell to a complete human being. However, my thoughts, speech, gestures and movement patterns were sometimes still troubled when I was not ill due to my quirks and 'imperfections' from my ideal self.

I enjoy the courage and wisdom to understand, and I praise myself for trying to show greatness in my work and growth into a real, humane human being. I had a blip on 3 March 2003, when my sentences could have ended for sure. Instead, I interpreted the deliberate, wilful attempt to take my own life, gave my hope back, and told people that my story on Earth was not over yet.

My life is moving on, and I am the author of my future; I will try to create a pattern to cause some ripple effect in society and the world around me, but I am not looking to have fame. Listen again, please, and remember, I am the author of my future and its stories, and I plan to have what is right and not just some gratification. I will continue to earn kindness in myself and the virtues I built into my consciousness as I walk upon the earth. So far, I am not economically adjusted well enough to be here. I did not learn well from my early and midlife education and training, which would financially be an advantage for my life until the natural end of life. I adjusted my philosophy's fundamental beliefs, including philanthropy, which is the desire to help people. I settled myself to have the attributes that will give me the power to function adequately by using the gifts I was born with to build on, expand and develop. I would love to see education and self-discovery, turning people into all-loved human beings, staying in peace, eliminating wars and the selfish self reaching a fully humane being. The most important thing is that all people should be able to live in supportive communities in a world that respects all and allows the grace of God in their lives to find maturity from the principal law of a good life, which is to obey. Obey the truths which bring us in tune with nature's peace, love and harmony.

43

HEADACHE PERSISTED AND PSYCHIATRY SEEMS WORTHLESS

Tuesday, 11 June 2019

I am attempting to determine whether my headaches require more detailed investigative evidence treatment by a neurologist. For the most part, treatment with naproxen reduces the headaches when the pain strikes.

Headaches are no longer primarily due to my brain's make-up. Stressors cause physical and emotional pain and give rise to the standard tension aches, neck aches, and stiff shoulder and back pain. The stress factors in my life have reduced considerably, but headaches remain triggered other than when I am getting a cold and exercising. I can think of nothing else that could make the problem stay put except withdrawal from a substance in the antipsychotic medicine, which my brain disliked, and I still crave a little.

I have taken a slow and careful approach to departing from antipsychotic medication and did not expect drug addiction cravings. But have I begun to experience 'cold turkey'? Has an awful tight shivery sensation in my scalp come on late as a symptom of craving or desiring it?

I assumed my brain was always tight and closed. It expanded and shrank again, causing tightness in my head. I could see lights as I drifted off to sleep at night, and my brain was sparking, zapping across the entire mind in the darkness, disrupting my sleep quality. At its worst, a night of fireworks display was happening. Daytime specks of flashes of white light appeared from the corner of one eye, and floaters affected my vision on a bright day.

Twice, I made an appointment in advance to see my usual doctor. I cancelled them because I did not want to be provided with a long-term prescription of any pharmaceutical medication unless it was helpful for longevity. I have pre-booked an appointment for Friday, 14 June 2019, to chat with the primary care physician. The GP service needs more human resources and is overstretched. It will take a week from the booking date to see a doctor. It is impossible to secure an appointment for the same day with a GP, and the patient may need to get to A&E to get treated.

The gradual stages of discomforting headaches around my head – scalp, forehead and sides – are persistent and seem to worsen. It is like an all-day, everyday hangover from too much alcohol. I have never drunk too much alcohol or ever been drunk. The experience is widespread for many people, so I use that as an analogy. Equally, it can compare to feeling grossly lazy with a dense, foggy mind. The entire area feels tight, and I take ibuprofen to reduce uncomfortable feelings, but it is not working anymore. I will be seeing the GP for sure this time; it seems more than a headache, which I thought would eventually pass now that I had entirely stopped taking antipsychotic medication.

Because of this scary, debilitating headache, writing my stories creatively is more complex and challenging. The headache is not shifting, and it is not going away, rendering poor concentration and difficulty in focusing, and I get a bit confused. I take naproxen more frequently for relief but do not get any significant assistance. I am frustrated with missing the point of what people say. My answers are odd; a constant misunderstanding happens. I lack clarity and can only grasp the ideas of things most people see or state in the validation process.

I can feel so tired, but not sleepy, that some everyday tasks or recalling information reflect a cognitive dysfunction problem involving my memory. I get sufficient sleep, with four to five hours of bed rest nightly and almost twice-nightly loo visits. It feels adequate, and I do not catnap in the daytime anymore. I had turned down the option to have an fMRI scan to investigate brain shrinkage when I had a memory and cognitive examination because I already suspected I had it. I am concerned about scan technology and wonder if they are genuinely safe or could damage human brain cells.

I already have debilitating cogitations from prolonged medication use and now probably a major secondary-type headache due to years of psychiatric disorders. Isn't it an indication of something scary going on?

I have to hear what the experts say, but I have lost confidence in the mental health service. The service asked me to write down my aims. Still, it did not take on the supporting role of monitoring the extent of cognitive damage that antipsychotics have, affecting my ability to make a living and socially enjoy life. I aimed to taper the high dose of medication to achieve the best recovery and complete the discontinuation in two years. They showed no interest in the challenges I had with the adverse effects of years of antipsychotics and what the gradual reduction in medication has done for me: to be in a better phase of sustainable recovery. They have not shown any interest in my mental health outcomes.

However, I have developed a good standard of getting care and treatment I trust from primary care physicians. Their opinions have proven their trustworthiness clinically, which have stood up to scrutiny so far, and their advice and treatment are adequate.

I was aware that there might not be any medical treatment, which freed my conscience and built-up anxieties to know the truth so that I could accept the honest, professional medical advice the primary care doctor suggested.

First, I will put the following questions to my GP:

- Is there any known natural remedy that may reduce the symptoms?
- Should I continue to have multivitamin supplements to help eventually?
- Am I developing or getting another medical or psychological condition?
- Could a computer-based test help detect some more associated neurological impairments?
- Do I have to/need to get an fMRI scan?
- When will the significant symptoms of headaches, itching nose, spotty face, aching neck and painful lower back

eventually get lifted, as these must be associated with the psychiatric recovery that is taking place? A few more months, a couple of years, or longer?
- Are there certain foods that can help clear my brain, and will a blood test be required?

Dear reader, I have seen the GP. Yet, from one moment to another, the troubling symptoms have persisted. I fidget while sitting on a chair. My body, leg and head irritations remain an everyday, familiar, collective experience. At the doctor's surgery, I applied constant, firm pressure with my hand to soothe my painful forehead, the bridge of my nose, cheeks, chin and stiff neck; I also massaged these areas with my hand.

At the beginning of spring and summertime, pollen and other pollutants in the air stick to my eyelashes. As a result, they feel as though they are stranded in the eye's membrane fluid, causing watery, irritable eyes and compounding my misery.

At the surgery, I sensed that my brain was becoming hot and feverish because I felt heat rising in my head, evaporating through my skull. I nodded to acknowledge the GP, and gradually, my head became fixed in a bowed position, and my eyes had reduced vision, focused on the GP's desk. At the same time, the tension in my neck increased as it bent to manage the awful feelings; my chin almost touched my sternum. The GP covered the onset of schizophrenia and the prodromal phase grounds and also suggested that the troublesome symptoms are signs that schizophrenia may return. I may have had schizophrenia from birth and needed constant medication compared to a heart disease defect.

I rolled up my lips, pinched them tightly and opened my mouth. My lips were moist and continued moistening with a thin layer of spit, probably making them shiny. I lifted my head and rubbed one hand under my chin. It was an unconscious action that did not indicate what I was thinking. I was faking it so that the GP would think I accepted the facts associated with my brain, but honestly, it does not fit how I feel these days. For a long time, I used to accept this one view solely to manage my brain, and I realised this model does not fit the accruing schizophrenia in me. It is triggered like cancer in toxic environments.

I have deduced that my brain was not ill at birth. I need to calm my sensitive nervous system and my pathological need to help others, which is unhealthy, integrating past experiences and so-called old memories with new knowledge and current skills. I also realised that the psychological critic of the mind needs quieting; it can become a nagging, influential, unhealthy judge. I make this assumption with no factual information from medics. I am using this last chance to provide a different paradigm to conceptualise existence, which gives abstract knowledge that my mind created during everyday experiences to help me understand the real-world model. Antipsychotics might have rearranged receptors and nerve fibres in my brain, leading to more significant memory loss and hampering my mental ability.

My biomedical diagnosis is worthless for identifying my discrete mental health disorder. It is not fit for purpose; it is a subjective judgement about what is expected and was making me conform to medication regime dependency. Psychiatric overly-medicalisation is a terrible mental health system in which medical professionals cannot control their biases and discriminate and stigmatise all distress that results in mental health disorders. Therefore, psychiatrists are to take some blame for messing heads up for how they conceptualise cause without facts, factoring in neuroscience and cognitive sciences. My intuitive, natural heart has guided the phenomenon in me from birth.

My body and mind know I am going through this for my highest good. It is going to come in handy for others. I cannot explain it. Still, I need to do it: complete recovery from long-term antipsychotic medication use and build resilience to go through the severity of symptoms, excruciating physical pain and emotional issues.

Now that I am in my sixties, I sense, as an older adult, that I may have quantum intuition as the soul's messenger that comes in flashes of non-verbal feelings processed in my heart first. Then, it is sent to my verbal brain to create the thoughts and actions in this world's 3D reality environment without antipsychotic medication messing up the process when the initial stressors have gone.

I was close to enjoying my highest attainable mental and physical health standards. I am determined to bring about a paradigm shift with antipsychotic drugs in maintenance treatment and take back control from a psychiatrist to normalise my reality to that of an ordinary, healthy person, even though I have oddities. I have a good sense of my vulnerabilities. I am always conscious of my being, act fair and honest with people, wish them well and be ethically good. Indeed, defects in my character have improved with the practice of having proper moral attitudes.

I have also reduced the hyper-compassion phenomenon with a new mental health prescription, and a new light has provided a different paradigm to conceptualise existence. I took the therapeutic teaching approach, preparing myself for learning and rationalising, understanding my needs and why I go into a kind of insane mode in my psychic make-up, which is related to my psychiatric existence. I feel okay, except for the significant discomforts which frustrate me. Having access to the affective disorder schizophrenia messes up feelings, behaviours and my understanding. I still do not know why the condition feels like it has a sticky residue and does not leave me altogether. Understanding it was crucial for me. The more I know, the less I fear and am reluctant to calculate risk with my fingers crossed as I work with the thoughts and divine consciousness. The more understanding I gained about why certain things were happening to me, the easier it was to work with it. Understanding the knowledge and beliefs calms me, reassures me and gives me peace because the mental causation model and cognitive landscape are better understood.

I unmask the role of trauma and adverse events in my life experiences by following the methods of talking or writing openly to reduce mental illness during awful times. It is bringing about a magnificent, overall, affective inner curing, a vast improvement in my mental health and well-being, the evidence of which should encourage others to follow. But be aware that the detailed analysis of severe withdrawal symptoms will require your bravery and perseverance if you are to give it a go and succeed. I am hoping to get referred to a neurologist to investigate my brain and give me, and the rest of us, the facts so that we all may find my psychiatric diagnosis of paranoid schizophrenia to be scientifically meaningless.

I am still getting described in clinical terms to explain non-clinical behaviour because I have overly passionate feelings about some things. I am 'psychotic' about something rather than passionate like ordinary, healthy people who can be hyper about the things they love doing. Also, I am 'paranoid' about it. That is not an illness!

The medical model is insane, and I can tell the differences. Still, psychiatrists could not say whether the volume in my hippocampus was inconsistent with the psychosis spectrum. They should have realised I needed treatment to calm my sensitive nervous system and silence my influential critic and psychological judge. I cannot understand why all the psychiatrists who met with me could not tell me my pathological need to help others was unhealthy and may be a part of the problem.

In the doctor's surgery, my body language automatically camouflaged my real feelings and showed submissive cooperation rather than challenging the GP's medical opinion. Nevertheless, the GP felt the need to say, "You will have to accept the neurologist's findings."

"I want to know the facts about what's causing these awful effects on my brain," I said.

In response to my fMRI concerns, the GP said, "It's your thinking." That seemed to suggest that it is odd to worry about scan technology.

Psychiatric knowledge and the mental health systems are slow or entirely resist survivors' points of view. GPs lack insight and have no recognition, not even the slightest, that antipsychotic drug withdrawal may cause troublesome symptoms in my brain. Most probably, the symptoms are not the disease itself but could be psychic phenomena, maybe!

However, the GP did respond to my request and acknowledged that the symptoms require neurological investigation. So, an arranged appointment for 27 August 2019 to see a neurology consultant will end the conservancy on what long-term use of antipsychotics and intense prolonged episodes of schizophrenia have done to me. The test result will help me plan to maintain a good lifestyle in the remission of untreated schizophrenia recovery.

The review with a psychiatrist and the mental health care and recovery team planned for February 2018 to September 2018 did not happen. Finally, they confirmed an outpatient appointment for 14 August 2019, and I asked them to change the date to 10 January 2020. The clinician whose skills will be essential in helping me through this tough time with antipsychotic withdrawal will move me forward confidently. I am to trust the facts from the neurologist over the subjective judgements of psychiatrists who have proven that pharmaceutical medicine is all they know.

Today, Saturday, 13 July 2019, the atmosphere in my brain is giving rise to a more unusual rise in head heat and weird sensations. Brain shivering forms headaches and a buzzing in my ears affects my ability to write my story. Additionally, my non-artificial right hip has developed excruciating arthritic pain so bad I could not walk until strong painkillers eased the intensity. It is ongoing and crippling. In addition, I cannot continue to write with this dense tightness in my brain cerebrum. My hollow brain cavities are probably struggling to circulate fluid that may thicken as it squeezes into the changing environments in my head and affects my mind.

I expect to take a break from writing for two months because my concentration is poor, and for you to reach this point with me, I thank you, and thanks for your company. I appreciate your fellowship in my life experiences and inner-world ideas presented at their best by telling my story well and capturing your attention and interest. I trust you will come back here again and page-turn to read the resolution. The outcome is noticeable and hits on my issue's sweet spots – a fitting place for readers, but it will be a worrying period for me. So, I will go away to rest my brain correctly and return to conclude without padding the story, *A Good Life: The Perception of Perfection – an Autobiography.*

Note: The clinic rescheduled the neurology appointment to an earlier date, Thursday, 15 August 2019.

44

HOSPITALISATION WITH PSYCHIC PHENOMENA

Sunday, 15 September 2019

Note: The memory and cognition test reassessment is due soon, on 3 October. The date of the neurology investigation has changed again because I relapsed with chronic mental illness and was hospitalised then. The new date is 6 December 2019.

I have been struggling to keep the right level of mental health wellness. I realised I could use some assistance to rebalance myself and learn additional coping skills to get back on track. I feel guilty for bringing mental illness to the fore again, and I could not correct the condition or remove it with my 'will' or 'ego'. I must accept the results of what happened when I was hospitalised for the tenth time because I had set in motion some bizarre behaviours that I cannot remember acting out.

I communicated my feelings to the GP on 14 June 2019 and the symptoms of a withdrawal problem from forty years of antipsychotic medication. Still, the GP thought schizophrenia might be coming back.

I had chosen to continue being unmedicated and eventually stopped my antipsychotic medication in September 2018. I had no support from professional mental health services during this distressing time, and the symptoms from withdrawal were troublesome. (I am sure we all can remember that early part of my story.) Compounded stressors from PIP and government departments contributed to the 'fall' back.

I had assumed discontinuing antipsychotic medication could provide a different paradigm for schizophrenic persons conceptualising existence to understand the model of the real world.

Recently, a robust, active, biological component stopped my mental health improvement in a period of eminent mental turmoil from drug withdrawal. But I am okay again, and recovery has given my family and friends back the Karl they know, love and adore.

I have resumed taking antipsychotic medication for schizophrenia, a maximum dose prescribed by the hospital psychiatrist of 30 mg of aripiprazole, one tablet daily in the morning. Schizophrenia and psychosis leave behind the problems of actual reality. When this happens, one helps oneself and understands feelings more deeply.

Being on antipsychotic medication is not healing for me. I have said it before. Instead, it is trying to treat my conscientious objections about life's unfairness and the world not fitting my expectations. Even today, doctors do not treat me as my holistic self. They do not always understand me.

On 1 June 2019, in a supermarket car park, I had a minor road traffic accident in our car when I got jolted sideways by another vehicle. The crash caused moderate vehicle damage to my car, and I sustained some soft tissue injury and whiplash. A complete medical report was required to put forward a compensation claim, which is being processed, and no final decision has yet been made.

One month later, on 8 July 2019, I had a psychological examination. Again, an independent GP conducted the medical analysis and wrote a psychological profile report during this emotional turmoil from antipsychotic withdrawal. I had hoped it would settle down when my brain produced the correct quantity of natural chemicals over a relatively reasonable time, probably another six months.

Psychological examination report on 8 July 2019

Mr Willett made good eye contact and rapport and smiled appropriately. There were no psychotic features, delusional ideas, or thought disorders. He answered my questions intelligently. He spoke in everyday speech and was oriented in time and place.

He had no tearfulness, agitation or associated hand tremors.

In the months from July to early September 2019, I struggled to stay balanced and focus on what would help me maintain an adequate level of mental health rather than on what my symptoms were and which counted as mental illness. Then, without realising it, I suddenly became psychotic at home. So, my family and close relatives got me an open, informal admission into the local psychiatric hospital under Section 2.

I was admitted to the psychiatric hospital on Friday, 9 August, with trial home leave on Sunday, 8 September, and discharge on Thursday, 12 September 2019.

I cannot remember where it started, from the pivot point of feeling an uncomfortable sensation with tightening headaches to the tipping point into psychosis and seemingly in a higher state of consciousness. It felt like a dream, going to bed to sleep and then waking to securely locked doors, and in a building design with such complexity, it was hard to navigate and became confusing. My wife told me the sequence of my mental breakdown that I could not remember.

I have no memory of the hospitalisation and had removed my wedding ring. For what purpose? No idea! I have completely lost it in our house. The hospital staff said the wedding ring was not among my things, and they had not seen it. It has felt deeply distressing. I could not remember how I lost the wedding ring off my finger and could not find it anywhere in or around the house. I also wrecked to pieces the head of my electric shaver in the hospital when dismantling it, and I smashed my mobile phone into pieces. And again, for what reason? I do not know. It has something to do with charged energy that has come to mind today. I had my first conscious awakening in the hospital when I remembered the month about two weeks later: Bank Holiday Monday, 26 August. I cannot be sure of what was happening to me before that.

My most private thoughts became known in the hospital setting and to the broader world, and I felt my dignity had been invaded. Then, finally, the recovery process came around, and I realised my privacy and pride had not been invaded after all.

My body responded sensitively to music, and I experienced intense emotions listening to love songs on Smooth Radio and Mellow Magic stations. I was more aware of the singing voices and songs, which brought out my feverish emotions. The pitch of the music was more enhanced than in my hospital surroundings. The songs were about tragedy, loss, falling in love and the need for love, or abandoning a relationship. They all gradually built up from chills to goose pimples. My biochemical processes tugged intensely at my pleasurable responses to the music and singing, then dampened the super-happiness I had beforehand. The songs and the tone of the music made me sad as I internalised the human relationship problems in the songs as my own. I could not resist rubbing my itchy eyes, which the emotion in the singer and the music perpetuated. I pressed on my eyelids to release the tears and make my eyes nice and moist, but all the rubbing exacerbated my vision impairment. I later refreshed my eyes with a splash of warm water on my face.

My face-to-face meeting with the male psychiatrist was pleasant. Usually, I have a phobia of male doctors who appear to stare, have scary features and seem to want to harm me with pharmaceutical drug treatment, which I am unlikely to understand the benefit of at the time of psychosis. However, the nurses and doctors seemed to be at their professional best, caring for me and providing adequate treatment.

They did not show any frustration with me, even though my affray mind brought them challenges, and they handled me compassionately. I was empathic too, even though my thoughts and ideas were bizarre.

Gradually, we formed excellent professional doctor-patient and caring nurse-patient relationships, building trust and gaining confidence that the mental health care system has my best interests at heart and provides adequate coordinated treatment. The doctors' and nurses' approach remained assertive and dynamic, exhibiting solid professional skills and confidence. They engaged with my wife and me to find the right way, the sure way, to ensure the best outcomes for continuous, well-functioning mental and physical health needs after coming out of the hospital.

In my world's conceptual reality, tapping human consciousness sorted the incentive to be more engaged in artificial intelligence, which can aid human flourishing and be utilised to glorify God. However, challenges arise from my overly anti-human ideology. Transhumanism's fundamental premise is that computer machinery taps, hacks, and replicates consciousness; this did seem to have happened in this world I had conceptualised. However, people are biological mechanisms that are also a part of my life's conceptualised existence.

45

RETAKE ANTIPSYCHOTIC AND RETAINED SUFFERING

Wednesday, 16 October 2019

I am focusing on improvement to be resilient in retaking antipsychotic medication and to shift from feeling sorry for myself, worried and wallowing in self-pity. I have to be dosed again on the drug, which produces the same horrible tightness in my brain as withdrawal. Early mortality may likely become a certainty because I am getting 'poisoned' by medication. I am eager to use the car accident compensation claim money to write my will.

The drug dose I get as I age will likely make my liver and kidney function decline faster than natural ageing. So, doctors do not expect to reduce the drug gradually but to maintain the high dose till death.

I do not need mantras or affirmations to improve matters. Still, I am humble enough to accept that I need to find a way to enhance or block the symptoms through a thought-based process that fights them without becoming another secondary casualty.

My resilient mindset chooses to have victory in bettering myself rather than winning success by achieving total symptom abstinence. It is hard to do because life's struggles endure pain, and the ambiguity needed to move forward is optional to improve the best of me.

Living according to my values automatically generates a better life experience. However, my brain is on the antipsychotic pill or off the medication-maintained instability with constant headaches and eminently tenacious tinnitus. Unfortunately, that also includes increased sexual urges and compulsive eating.

If only the mental health service had been more involved and helped me with techniques conventional to people who overcome drug dependency. I would have benefited from the methods shown to help this group.

I have revisited the GP twice, including for hypertension checks, because this has yet to be appropriately regulated since I left the hospital. I asked for treatment for tinnitus, and I had hoped the neurology appointment would be pushed forward by allocating me to a hospital in a different trust. It turned out that the local hospital had the first available date to see a neurologist, which I already held for 6 December 2019. My GP discussed a personal request for a CT head scan appointment to be sent to me as soon as possible, and another GP arranged the earliest date for me to see a specialist in the ear, nose, and throat clinic.

The high-pitched sound piercing through my ears wrecks my ability to sleep well and prevents me from focusing during the day. Those whistling, whirring and buzzing sounds will be investigated on

28 October. In addition, I was scheduled to attend the CT department at the local general hospital on 30 October 2019. To manage the noise in my ears and head, I play soft music at low volume on the radio, and when I go to bed, I have the radio playing mainly throughout the night, which slightly masks the noise.

I have yet to become mentally tough in my choices and learn to prioritise my emotions, thoughts, and behaviour so I can identify what is essential for me based on my values and beliefs. So, my attitude brings me joy, and my emotions bring me sadness and joy, and I draw power from the source of the dominant universe's energy that runs devices and people's consciousness.

Today is the sixty-eighth day on a total dose of antipsychotics prescribed by the hospital psychiatrist. The old familiar sleeping pattern and my lazy, nonproductive hours have returned, not unexpectedly. However, my daytime productivity has slowed, and I need an afternoon nap for one and a half hours. My bedtime is usually between 7:30 and 8:15 p.m. because I feel exhausted, and my whole body and head hurt. I need to lie down; I am so sleepy. Rest is when my head hits the pillow. With two loo visits at night, the tinnitus prevents me from going back to sleep for about one hour each night. So, the next day starts with an early morning wake-up time between 4:00 and 4:45 am. My energy level is high, and I feel excellent and jolly in the early dawn.

What investigations have revealed

Follow-up cognitive assessment on 3 October 2019:

I am articulate and able to communicate well; there is no evidence of any cognitive changes. The past and present recall is excellent. There is no evidence to suggest any memory problems or cognitive changes. It is more around mental health and enjoying social activities. Referral back to the GP practice to be on a mental health well-being programme.

A bilateral tinnitus test on 28 October 2019:
I have a significant standard, average Hz frequency hearing range and normal tympanic membrane.

This was from the audiological exam. I associate my chronic tinnitus with changes in specific network circuitry in my brain that cause me to pay more attention to its sounds and be less able to rest. The sounds of tinnitus come from within me, not from an outside source. Only I can hear them. I wonder if it is neurological and may never stop, and I liken it to schizophrenia and hearing voices. I have another appointment at the hospital to learn techniques that will show me how to manage tinnitus.

CT scan on 30 October 2019:
Healthy, natural ageing of the brain tissues was observed, and no significant abnormalities were found.

Yet, all the time, I am still afflicted by headaches without a known cause. The GP suggested that when I meet face-to-face with a neurologist in the twelfth month, they may add medication to eliminate it. The scan has shown that my brain is operating normally.

Mental health and well-being social prescriber programme on 5 November 2019:
Start practising meditation and mindfulness. I should do outdoor activities such as being amongst inherent nature and practise removing myself from the source of other people's misery, which is upsetting me. Also, join a club that emphasises understanding empathic people like me and get involved in mental health peer

support groups. (It was the first time a health professional said I was empathic.)

Neurologist examination on 6 December 2019:
The neurologist was confident that there was no neurological impairment concerning my continuous headaches and weird feelings in my head.

The examination tested my motor responses, reflexes, coordination, and pupillary response. It also examined my eyes and the muscles running from my neck to my shoulder.

He advised only to take mild pain relief tablets, like paracetamol, to control the pain. He did not suspect an fMRI would be necessary for a closer detailed study of my brain, but he will discuss his findings with a senior consultant. I will be under observation and have a further review appointment in three months, in March 2020.

Note: On 13 December 2019, a letter arrived for an appointment for an fMRI investigation of the brain. This is to exclude any structural lesion as the reason for my headache and memory problems.

46

RESTARTED MEDS GIVE SEVERE ADVERSE OUTCOMES

Monday, 23 December 2019

Withdrawal from antipsychotic medication automatically gave me severe symptoms. This compelled me to recommence the medicine on doctor's orders, which could have differentiated from the recurrence of my underlying disorder.

Something is not quite right, leading to me having unnecessary long-term medication again.

I am out to convince the psychiatrist of the merit of short tapers, between two and four weeks, of antipsychotics, decreasing the medicine down to a therapeutic minimum or half minimum dose, before complete cessation under an exponential tapering programme that reaches minimal quantity again.

I felt I greatly benefited by biologically reducing the medication dose until the headaches were too overwhelming. It knocked me into a false dream pre-sleep state and waking unawares. The cocktails of untangling intuitive understanding and the complex and subtle ways my body and mind interact had a detrimental effect on the visible evidence.

Much later, I became conscious that I had no memory of the ideas that had been acted out. My thinking pattern had interplayed between belly and emotions, and my personal subjective views had psychic abilities. Without factual evidence, my intuitive knowledge set my assumption that what had happened to me was correct without getting to the facts of the matter. My worldview picked up threads that can advance our collective understanding of the human mind and each other with a mixed metaphor alert towards unity, sailing carefully between the extremes of stress and temperament in people.

Psychiatric hospitalisation was not my desired outcome, and admission does not address the elevated risk of adverse effects. Instead, my life was disrupted and costly to the health care system, and a period followed when I could not remember what in hell had happened before discharge when my brain's temporal lobe had some instability.

Being discharged from inpatient psychiatric care has left me more susceptible to experiencing severe adverse outcomes.

I did not intend to take any risks with my life; my brain's temporal lobe observed adverse outcomes of what the hell was happening and had forbidden risk-taking in a novel paradigm that is currently impossible to predict. Still, the fundamental assumption is that my history is being repeated. I am uncertain about the dose dependency and optimal target dose, and it may still seem foolish. However, the lower range of the licensed amount may probably achieve the optimal balance between efficacy and tolerability, which is leading to my overall acceptability of antipsychotic treatment.

I know how my inspiring stories of courage and determination can give a distorted impression of progress that ultimately requires transparency and teamwork with clinicians to succeed. So, my profile as an individual making waves in mental health has been ousted to give a more accurate picture of how progress can come. We do not give up on trials.

I have exhausted all avenues of available treatment for my headaches. I am still waiting for the life-changing drug or for the biology in me to work better. It is a waiting game that, until the headaches leave, some things in the day cannot get started, and some aspects of my everyday life stop.

Therefore, I began to wonder what was happening in my consciousness that made me live in a non-consensual reality where some personal narratives are lost and I "can't remember an earthly thing." It seemed the contents of consciousness depended on the state of my knowledge. I have no answers as to why my activity gets interrupted and stops in time, and I cannot measure it. I have no memory of it.

The contents of my consciousness must have broadcast to themselves what on earth had happened in the time lost in my perspective and made one quite specific prediction that I wouldn't remember what I saw because the mechanisms in my brain, without stimulus, shut down the memories. So, I have been trying hard to recall the time I lost in existence, and the mind I have could never find that lived non-consensual reality, but I feel the power, knowledge and strength in the rest of my narratives.

My powerful exploration of how psychopathological phenomena manifest in my experiences and existence had grappled with mental aspects similar to physical objects. The perspective of conscientiousness and subjectivity is a preliminary part of myself, and I sensed that my sense was diminished.

My perception, imagination and thinking have been unstable: the actual phenomenologically accessible structure of my consciousness that ensures that I am me. Knowledge of I, me, myself differed from the average anomalies and diminished my sense of being present in time.

I complained of the feeling as if there were a time when I did not exist because I have no memory of some of the period of hospitalisation and some before it. However, it was apparent to everyone I was around that my family and hospital staff had recorded their memories of me during that time. There was no message that I had been killed or that I was dead. No. But 'live' schizophrenia attacks the essential nature of a person. It is not so well known as the delusions, hallucinations and psychopathological phenomena. The generative disturbance diminishes the senses, memory and understanding of the 'self'.

I tried to give up antipsychotic medication and almost made it, but I was unlucky in overcoming prescription drug dependency. So, I need to use perseverance techniques to underpin successful change. It can take many attempts to quit dependency on antipsychotic medication. It is off-putting because I saw my relapse as a failure and used it as an excuse to give up, but I should view change in a binary way. For success or failure, I must be realistic about the need to persevere in incremental changes and not be overly ambitious with targets, appealing as they might be.

I plan to discontinue the medicine again. Conventional wisdom suggests that planning improves the chances of success. Still, there is evidence that I need not quit entirely to be successful.

It is good news that I am again considering embarking on an impromptu attempt to change. However, thinking of reducing the medication again requires initial self-encouragement to achieve maximum daily levels of motivation and energy with no fluctuations.

I need a high level of self-efficacy; a belief and confidence in my ability are needed again when trying to change my behaviour. The discomfort experienced last time gave me anticipatory anxiety, expecting the withdrawal symptoms to be more significant and paralysing the suggestions to test reality. Instead, I self-talk, "I can do this." The previous failure focused on what I lost; the next step is to think about what I will gain, which is a deterrent to relapse, shame and guilt. I will try to avoid them.

My chances of ditching antipsychotics are a lot tougher. So, while I might be lucky by sticking to a reduction programme, keeping trying suggests I will get there.

47

SCHIZOPHRENIA RECOVERY, NEARLY

Friday, 10 January 2020

Mental illness is ignorant of me, the person, and anyone who experienced it, like me, during adolescence or young adulthood. I have claimed all the things I experienced negatively in mental illness are my doing, and I have to consider that I may be a 'unique' person on the planet.

From here on in, the period stretching into the future, I will naturally train my brain to look on the bright side. So, positivity comes to be what I expect. The mental and emotional activity to make a personal decision is 'free-willed' to determine whether righteous or deployable moral actions are tuned sensitively into one setting. My course of conduct and consciousness can only choose the ethically good, though I make small mistakes. My strange, strong pattern of feelings from my body and mind operates that way because my awareness does not doubt an intelligent creature, 'God,' to which I am intrinsically linked. All my activities are constructed entirely with God's nature in mind. It is harrowing for me to break the immortal code deliberately; the metaphysical structure of the principles and laws of the spirit of God in us governs its existence by cause and effect. It seems I continuously grasp responsibility to be a faithful example in this time, the twenty-first century, and not to break the harmony with this pure principle of that being in me, in all of us.

Having taken steps to reduce antipsychotics, slowly, my brain suffered in its deepest parts hidden from me. A neurological investigation could not find the faulty disturbance via a CT head scan. A different brain fMRI to exclude any structural lesion as a reason for my headaches and memory problems is the next plan. Finally, I spotlighted the hellish torture complete withdrawal from antipsychotics can reach. Unfortunately, the psychiatrists did not liaise with me at this point.

They assumed they knew how I ticked, like the three per cent of people with schizophrenia. I questioned whether that figure could be lower and needed to be revised. They primarily treated me with antipsychotic medication. Schizophrenia had entered me into the internal psychology that put me into a personal existence which I assume operates with universal laws and order. Schizophrenia acquainted me with subjective reality, and I immediately acquired psychic abilities and inference activities from that realm. The active psychic ability had been demolished with a massive maximum dose of antipsychotic medication I had restarted in hospital. The extraordinariness in me faded. However, the ordinary person my family and friends knew, loved and adored was back and could laugh. With support, I sometimes participate in the most ordinary things in life that are meaningful and purposeful, which benefit my health and well-being.

My psyche makes up the 'self', choosing a private life to avoid deliberately harming every living creature and thing. I prevent myself from stamping on ants and beetles. You name it, I avoid hurting or injuring them or anything. Even pruning blossoming flowers and plants is hard and uncomfortable, even these days, probably due to my mental state. And yet, in that period of emotional turmoil, I thought I was not ill but just gravely sensitive to ESP experiences. I interacted with real people, people with flesh and blood in their veins and could sense their thoughts about me. Sometimes, I only heard their voices, and one of the most unusual ways was telepathically. Schizophrenia near recovery has communicated a unique, most compelling message that no professional has ever unlocked until recently. I am an extraordinary, naturally healthy, emphatically sensitive person with squashed psychic abilities. That is the heart of who I am, and my consciousness has that gifted alert system I had never learnt to use to my advantage. I could not change that of my 'self'. It makes me operate the way I do, and I am deeply aware that if it gets shifted or wobbles, I feel awful.

If it is not in use or it gets overused, it is wrong, and sickness comes. My empathic personality disrupts my living by naive attitudes and the easiness of being so honest to say, "I am fine," when I am not. Most people do it with ease, but it is hard to hold that inner guilty feeling because of the practices of a good character. I can do nothing to change it because I feel terrible pain in my body and mind to oppose it actively. I get misunderstood by everyone because of the profound principle of goodness working on me. It extends to the external physical world's legislated laws and codes so that those may not get broken.

The funny thing is that I do not need to be rewarded for exercising functional, aesthetic, or moral discipline, even when circumstances are unfortunate or terrible enough to detract from the dignity of a good cause. I follow the law or rules, the legitimate way of life. To do wrong or be incorrect, the sensor indicates emotions; every instinct and impulse affects me. I cannot be contrary. I can never argue or debate about making a false claim, doing something wrong or being wrong about something. The processes in me continuously go on, like nature's way of learning the facts to do the right thing. I am, and we are, under the activity of intelligent thought, a creator God thing. I feel punished when attitudes are not right. Our nature knows if I will be to blame or should not take condemnation. We are all subject to laws to keep ourselves safe and our bodies and minds under control and power to function at their best.

We are all raised to have most of our education in an educational establishment, and we need more training in our minds on the legal process that consciousness governs and directs us and demands certain things from us at all times.

Education does not tell me if I should be good or if I could be wrong, nor does it encourage the use of nature's ethical principles for wisdom with my aim to be credited with academic achievement. Quality operating systems in ourselves first warn us of the wavering of a righteous judgement vacillation. The alarm bell in intuition activates the mind. Education systems are narrow and do not address the holistic fullness of a person who grows to maturity. The whole self is not getting educated. Every thought, every emotion, every instinct and every impulse are nature's legitimate way of life, and people have an option most of the time to choose good or bad, negative or positive domains. We mature to reach moderate grounding in the grey areas, where things are different – neither good nor bad, positive nor negative. They are mutual harmony energies, the best state to be at all times; the action of fiction has evaporated.

Schooling tells me we make our own decisions, move as we please, and think as we wish when it is absolute; we are all governed by laws to do the right and honourable thing. Unfortunately, education, as I know it, has lost its ethics and moral values and preaches that we can do anything we want. It does not teach that all of us are governed by law, universal laws of nature; it is in us for our good. And, of course, some rules our species makes are neither excellent nor very good.

There are no books in the world from which we can learn more about life than by educating ourselves from the publication of our own lives, which teaches us to learn from our mistakes. The source of new courage and strength is in me and you too. We all have mysteries and things that happen, good luck, bad luck, and strange and involved circumstances, which we can sometimes fathom.

I prioritise my mental and physical health as essential to my recovery process, but I still do not know when my brain will return to its average level of hormones. As a result of mental cloudiness, memory problems and lack of mental clarity, I feel they are going up and down.

For years, my body and mind have revolted against using pharmaceutical drugs. To stabilise the effects of psychopathological phenomena, doctors subjectively judged that the disorder schizophrenia is what I have.

The meaningful essential relationship with existential feelings, the attention to emotion and understanding that gives me access to myself and the world were conceived as mental ill health. All my experiences were defined as psychiatric illnesses, and they were not. It is more complex, and I explored it as my existence was affected by moods to reach the understanding goal.

I am still committed to the fight to stop using high doses of antipsychotic medication for maintenance treatment. Unfortunately, however, the practice is not helping me because my quality of life declines with my cognitive skills, is interfered with by the ageing process and decreases even more if I again stay too long on a high medicine regime. So, I feel weaker and weaker as time goes swiftly on and ages me to my grave, and to give the young a future before they go to theirs and accept where the afterlife takes them.

I differed from others in the population and it was never considered. My preliminary markers of niceness allow me to reach the highest state of good in a human being.

Antipsychotic drug use for too long prevented the grounding of my existence's philosophical and theoretical elements. That may cause a problem again, and I must find a way to halt my pre-worldly view of experience going along with the expertise of life that originated in me. It can feel like scratching a dry patch on my skin. It feels suitable for a few moments but then causes more irritation. Unfortunately, no treatment can help remove the rubbing problem of psychiatric difficulties.

It may seem that my understanding of life as such is irrational, but it is not unreasonable and has nothing to do with rationalism. The absolute comprehensibility of life without pre-conceptual and pre-theoretical theories,' 'the truth' of my existence, maintained a presence in God in me; it is absolutely impossible to coach it out thoroughly. God, the fundamental structures of existence to my well-being, which I have shoved a few times, have never shifted and left me.

The clinicians insisted on the significance of medication and treated me with antipsychotic drugs for far too long. It knocked out most of my cogitations, damaged my hippocampus and the temporal lobe, and worsened my understanding of reality over time. I could not see the merit in taking that medicine, so I gradually phased it out and had to restart antipsychotic medication again after almost one year off the stuff. I was 344 days free of it.

Nature's way of paining me, my emotional experiences or the feelings I am born with had an ontology that doctors were trying to address, with a poor ontological shift.

Phenomenological investigation interprets, evaluates and finally acts on what I experience and also how I feel about my experiences, including withdrawal from antipsychotics at that time. Again, I was back to suffering. This time, I retreated from withdrawal. I had used every conceivable raw potion I could think of marketed as a natural food supplement to improve or contribute to brain function. I applied aromatherapy oils to my body, which included peppermint essential oil. I used scents in a diffuser to cool the intense pain in my head due to the withdrawal effects of the antipsychotic drugs.

I see the adverse effects of antipsychotics on my metabolism and my tender, loving heart, and I acknowledge it. I still have pain and high-pitched hissing going through my ears, and I continue monitoring it. I also have a tightness in my skull, and some brain fluid continues cascading down the temporal lobe and forehead. So, I continue to deal with it and process it using painkillers again. The tablets have yet to become helpful, and schizophrenia near recovery has been page-turning for me to write.

Self-help ideas to try to stop the ongoing headaches

1. Have the hottest shower I can bear on the back of my neck and lower back.
2. Frequently groom my head and hair and massage my scalp.

3. Frequently hold a warm flannel to my face, wiping it firmly.
4. Add many herbs when cooking.
5. Add spices to some morning breakfast cereal and regularly have a small bowl of lightly cooked vegetables, including broccoli, cauliflower and Brussels sprouts, for breakfast extras.
6. Discontinue multivitamin supplements and take only vitamin B12 10 mg, one tablet daily, and magnesium 375 mg, two tablets daily.
7. Increase red krill oil capsules from 300 mg once daily to super-strength 500 mg once daily.
8. Discontinue ginkgo biloba extract 120 mg once a day as a food supplement.
9. Increase sexual pleasure.
10. Drink plenty of water daily.
11. Have large cups of herbal tea daily.
12. Drink one large cup of strong coffee with milk during the day.
13. Use Prevalin nostril spray (Becodefence Plus) for allergies.
14. Continue with the two prescribed meds for hypertension (developed, I thought, due to a blood transfusion in 2004 in the hip replacement operation): 2.5 mg bendroflumethiazide tablets and 5 mg amlodipine tablets.

I requested that the approved 10 mg dose of amlodipine tablets be gradually reduced to nil. Still, my blood pressure was not adequately controlled, so I agreed to 5 mg of amlodipine in early 2019. I opted to downsize this pharmaceutical medication to have more natural blood pressure control in my diet.

Diet has made no changes in reducing hypertension. I restored my blood pressure by returning to the initial dose of amlodipine, a

10 mg tablet, once in the morning. Then, the GP prescribed another 25 mg of losartan potassium medication, lowering blood pressure to the standard expectation.

I have been taking a micronutrient tablet daily for four months to help maintain healthy cognitive function, nervous system functioning, and functional and psychological roles.

After a long time, it was tricky to determine whether the steps taken to break this vicious cycle of head pain and tinnitus had worked, including holistic complementary therapy and reiki therapy, a form of alternative energy medicine.

I tried sound bath vibrational healing with gong sounds, Sahaja yoga meditation and Indian head massage treatments. Finally, I listened to marimba meditation music; they say it detoxifies the aura and removes negative blocks.

It took a long time for my mind and body to signal what remedies and methods work best.

I have continued taking micronutrient and fish oil tablets, practising yoga meditation, receiving Indian head massages, and listening to stimulating, upbeat music when appropriate.

Today, Saturday, 11 January 2020, it has been one year and four months – 484 days – since the process of entirely coming off antipsychotic medication had to be reversed. Before that, I had nearly achieved a reasonable level of well-being for almost a year.

I failed minutely because the period of discontinued antipsychotics was so short and was not sustained. I will always require antipsychotic medication to stay stable and down to earth.

Looking back over the long lifetime of unadjusted antipsychotics, I can see what the doses do to me. Unfortunately, it is challenging for most people intelligently to estimate their own mistakes, and it is something I do not do reasonably well either.

My mind had no idea what my soul and heart wanted to do about medication appliances for the rest of my earthly stay. My mind usually loses focus and is tilted because the harsh reality of this world flows through my emotions and drains the healthy given life out of me. It prevents invested interest in enjoying things towards my happiness and the magnificent globe and beautiful variety of species in their appropriate environments. Seeing them strive is to marvel at and adore them. But we all are aware, the reader too. My mind views the immense beauty of everything, so I become highly pleased with everything and sometimes get depressed about the world's unfairness going on and on.

Medication is part of the process of settling down my brain. I quietened and agreed to have an added chemical control substance to help control or stop my mind from leaving this beautiful creation on Earth. So, it created reality, and my vivid imagination does not repeatedly make my life bizarre.

I met with a psychiatrist yesterday, and my daughter Georgina and my darling wife were at the meeting. I have asked him to assist me in reducing my antipsychotic dose to its lowest again. He agreed to be fully involved and support me in reducing antipsychotic medication with an immediate starting programme and have close, frequent reviews. The dose of 30 mg of aripiprazole is reduced to 25 mg from today, and in five weeks, on 14 February 2020, a follow-up appointment with the psychiatrist is scheduled. A psychologist is also to discuss with me, as part of the drug reduction aim, a holistic approach, for there is a constant difficulty in my mind's motivation system. Every day, I strive to do things, but that is getting shut down because of a weakening in my ability. My mind and body have hardly worked well down the years, and now, efforts to do enjoyable things are hampered by weariness and brain fog.

I think I have to come to the point where I stop fighting this, and my mind quits, gives up, submits to some medication for its peace of mind and needs the perfect correct minimum dose to have balance for the rest of my life.

The brain will stay entirely quiet. The mind and noises are connected to my intuition. I listen to my intuition and heart, knowing it beats as I touch my sternum. I still have life in me; what remains for the rest of my life is to be kind to myself and not worry. The good God is miserable about the wrongs of what humankind does, and it was never my burden to bear. Thank God, at last, I allowed myself this freedom.

Most of my life has revealed patterns of thoughts, feelings and behaviours that are deviant from normality. As a result, my mind has experienced differently from what is most understood as expected because of psychological disorders affecting its everyday conscious experience.

Therefore, it leads me to distressing, deviant and dysfunctional work in society and the world. Sickness of the mind, which I experience as a disorder of consciousness, can be terrifying, and I still do not fully comprehend the reality outside my brain. I cannot fully understand what was happening inside my skull either: the phenomena of my mind and navigating the world.

Paranoid schizophrenia is the mother hen of all mental illnesses because the brain is on tilt, and it is very rarely in the range of normality. As a result, neurotransmitters and hormones are disrupted, and my whole person was impacted by the thoroughly disruptive physical, emotional and cognition symptoms. However, having dopamine super-sensitivity may have been a factor that prolonged awful psychotic experiences in me.

EPILOGUE

Saturday, 1 February 2020

This book has made you acknowledge more than once that I am a guinea pig experimenter in my lab and the big, more extensive world. Yet, I walked on the earth with extraordinary inner personal belief, a New Testament, telling the truth of what happened in a literary fashion.

I am conscious of how the English language's precision was needed to impact what I wanted to say for accurate recognition. English grammar can be tricky, and my writing may become tainted and less worthy of praise because of some shortcomings. On the other hand, my excellent computer editing and self-editing tools have helped eliminate some writing errors. I go back and forth in the stories, bringing the earlier part of the ideas up to my new standards or up to the now-prevailing voice.

Good writing is hard writing; these words throughout the book will begin to sound and sing. My inner world has essential things that are lovely futurist visions that are beautifully crafted and have an aesthetic value. Still, if, or when, my words are not compact enough to convey my ideas and the facts that come to me, it is a schizophrenic experience getting told not based on earthly reality. So, the images I want to imprint in your mind and the poetic insight gained through the thought-provoking ideologies in my schizophrenic brain may have been an entirely different reading experience for you.

I have used the most meaningful words to convey, in total, elaborate detail, progressive stories in my life with the stubbornness of the English language to process what makes me 'tick'. I tick and tick continuously to the day when my mortal life naturally ends.

The art of writing had to be perfected to tell my accurate story of perception perfection. However, my understanding of good and bad, evil, and right and wrong in my development remained immature for a long time. I kept practically trying to improve destructive behaviours and innocently commended that living a good life requires endless effort to trim off faults and imperfections and avoid mistakes. I had difficulty being around people who had yet to attempt to improve their traits.

The reality that most people do not give a damn care about absolutely anything was a shock to my fixed interpretation of the world. Living in a world of people with imperfections they can improve and who do not give a damn about the actions or consequences of their work on others and their destructive hellishness on other creatures and the Earth too appalled all my senses. So, my brain produced alternative realities to think about and take appropriate action in the real world to live that way.

The best idea that came to my mind involved controlling the human condition, too. I started with myself in this modern time, and an example from the past was Jesus, who drastically modified the original states of human nature and modified his life to have the best character he could be. Nature modifies the module of us and changes us slowly. Jesus began trimming off drastically the original states of human nature.

The evolving changes in the original state in social nature's effects are slow, and I wanted people to catch up to the standard set in my thoughts, which has a sense of a 'God' rule to adhere to for holistic happiness. Godly behavioural control and any 'Godly' practice confront the person; people made them all up. You will go around and around in circles to find the god that put them there or gave them to you. Then, when you reach the peak and discover the individual's grit of consciousness, it comes full circle again because we are consistent thinkers of our thinking.

My mind tries to express ideas in words about existing stuff and its environment, but I have no name for them. Still, collectively, we use the word God, which our mind identified; people made it up, yet the senses scream, "The thing is there, right here." People are too mindless to see it. It is incomparable, and by limiting interpretation to the cage in the idea, focusing on the thought, you will think it nowhere. I sensed its complexity and confusion, taking the findings of what I hailed as a revelation for all people and revealing in my experience one of the truths, the absolute truth, nothing fraudulent. I get muddled when explaining my findings on God in words. Its singularity is personally tapered from person to person, with a unique reverence for each personal journey of living.

I find that the essence of my existence has given my character a burden to narrate my journey on these pages, which shows my yearning desire to reach the highs I set for myself. In my journey to fully understand this 'creator God thing' that brought me here, I tampered with my mind and body. Lots of times, my experiences are the symptoms of a domesticated illness I was not born with, shutting down the communication of sophistication, and its voice initially has been erased from dark-toned people's original minds. Except, there is me; the only one who, as far as I can tell, is the single dark-toned man maintaining the realisation of unique psychic ability in this racial group. And I was summoned to be detained in a psychiatric hospital for ills in my mind. My tenth inpatient admission was in August 2019. Am I clinically really ill?

When I reached the total functional capacity of this most elite vibrational wave voice of communication in people, I could hear the language accent manipulation. There was mainly distortion of the meanings in the English language with rapid changes in verbs, nouns and adjectives used to compound deception and deceitfulness on dark-toned people. We heard the exact words, and they are unfamiliar to the elite people with pale, lighter skin having a conversation in their sole racial group circle. We, people of colour, entered, and the word's meaning altered. The environment the lighter-skinned people work in, even their homes, financial institutions, educational establishments, places of recreation and shopping malls, are all geared to keep only one racial group being the underdog. And every time they made us out to appear foolish when they placed 'spins' on the language, we did not even scratch our heads symbolically to think we sensed their trickery. I know that skin tone can tell people a lot about a person's 'self' without revealing whether they are friendly or harmful to me. I became solemn throughout my detention in the hospital, which functions similarly to a hostel for homeless people.

Being an informal patient and a crazed individual, I listened to the subjective thoughts of others and was aware of those who I thought could hack into my source of thinking, my consciousness. I was discharged and, later, heavily medicated; 30 mg of aripiprazole blocked my active hearing, mainly with the constant production of meaningless hisses and buzzing in the sound waves only known to me. That interference in communication and discussions with other people is annoying for me. It is a noisy tinnitus hearing problem that only manifests as an adverse effect of the antipsychotic pill I am taking. The existence of the senses of higher consciousness and psychic ability does not alter; it has it working in the source of my soul and revealing itself as having a unique power.

The continuous antipsychotic exposure for my recurrent psychosis has serious flaws. Still, following my journey, I seek consensus in recovery by showing no relapse, but I hope antipsychotics again lower my deterioration compared with total discontinuation.

History has no stories of a dark-skinned person with a unique perception coordinated and voiced well. I have changed that, knowing native Africans had bred into domesticated servants. Colonialism trained Caribbean people to ignore thoughts of mindfulness and a mind's eye. It shoved us off the sensory-based realities of PSP, one of the same human sense languages that are a way of communicating on the planet and that people share with others through psychic abilities. Manipulated language usages have comical implications far from the original meaning of the vibration of the word roots' intention. They are spoken mostly with such cheeky whispers or such damn openness. Yet, subtlety is taking the mickey and excusing my word choices; they are 'taking the piss'. Language manipulation is an inappropriate marker of power over us, which people should consider as a condemnation of the whole human species but 'do not'. The conduct of those sorts of people needs to be bettered from their perspective to bring them in line with the intended source of the creator God's origin for human beings' methods of communication to be fair. Psychological manipulations and intentions of deceit are wars on our rational minds powered by the life source, and consequences follow when the universe's laws act.

Most probably, people of colour (black people) are the wisest and most empathic, have the best attitude and are richly humane.

Some are highly the best of humankind with these traits. The traits that evolved so far in their family tree, along with ethical care and intelligent fairness, have been passed on to the next generation. However, very noticeable likened characteristics are found in the personality of dark-skinned people, and they are not credited for them.

A goal, an objective and a yearning are directing the words I write, my actions and my gestures. In a sense, I welcome you into my dream state, my impossible dream, to which I am fully committed to elaborate concrete imaginations. My empathic human steps on the planet give the more profound universal truth of our existence that formed living realities, acquired knowledge, changed undesirable attitudes and gave others a decent life to follow. But it has its dangers and hindrances. If I fail, I suffer from guilt and feelings of being the sorriest to some degree. Reality tips my sensitivity too much, and I experience pain, especially when I expose my true self without accepting that good nature needs protecting, and too much pressure can cause me to fall ill.

My writing showed my problems in getting what I needed and wanted, which brought challenges to face and overcome. I engaged my analytical facticity and became more conscious of my process to work as best as possible. I opened my unconscious self to access my dream space through my senses. My feelings of purpose engaged my rational mind to track my qualities and emotional content from my dream state to the natural sound of a passionate man to the good in the humanity of humankind. From moment to moment, I looked inside myself to find the words to show the challenges.

I found myself a deeply susceptible, sensitive human being, an emotion-feeling creature, with continuously increasing yearnings. Love, roles, objectives, desire and longing drive my heart's sentiments.

My inner voice gives a sense of physical being, a certainty that did not come from schizophrenic voice-hearing, which is outside the 'self', to create my most profound sensational nature. That meant I went into my headspace to explore and discover some of my complexities.

People tell lies; writers write lies in historical fiction and artistic truths in stories. I have to watch out for the lies I tell myself to continue to grow authentically. From the beginning of my novel writing experience, which dates from 1982, I set out the literal and authentic truth about my life's journey to the grave. I know, as if it is an absolute certainty, it will not ultimately end there.

My writing gives me the 'feeling' that I have finished what I wanted to say and what I am to put out there to the world's people. My organic self has come out to show my most profound vision of the world and how I would like it to be. The concept of chaos gives a sense of a committed agent with conservation ecosystems that there is a meaning behind chaotic acts. I have gone back to encounter it like everyone else. First, I have returned to how life is lived here on Earth in physicalism, such as our body and mind remain active. We must adjust to the external world's human-made laws; they can be an ass and arbitrarily made. Some of them are fundamentally good, and others are too confusing to hold my respect and adoration because those laws do not seem to adjust rightly for some groups of people or the real needs of a person.

My example requires an honest, skilful, specialist solicitor to have the ability in a court of law to argue successfully for clinical negligence compensation against the health care trust, or maybe it is the drug company I should pursue. I first enquired about a potential clinical negligence claim to a law firm in July 2019. The solicitor believed that the prospects of success were below fifty per cent and could not assist. It is not an easy set of arguments, and the law does not meet my real needs. It called for proof beyond a reasonable doubt, and my case needed to be looked at differently to get the justice I am more likely to be denied. I believe my inner life was in tune with the natural laws in the continually operating universe. I gradually learned that my emotions, thoughts, ideas and opinions are all subject to supervision from nature's raw, definite, universal order of things. Natural tugging happens between right and wrong and between belief and non-belief. Vital negative energy weakens me when I fail to safeguard my character and pleasant personality.

I was only sometimes sensitive to the lessons nature provided me and have made the same mistakes throughout my life. Some of us do not learn from what happens to us. So, I set out in my writing, to tell the truth, be completely honest with myself and my faults, and reveal the emotional and psychological facts about events. The task was difficult, but my purpose was to write precise, elegant, sometimes lyrical prose without overstatement, melodrama or an overstated sense of self-pity or victimhood. We are all here on planet Earth to build a more non-violent future that is richly loved and to keep deciding what human feelings, social values and happiness are. Unfortunately, being dependent on a specialist network of technology today may make people, especially the most ordinary people, feel domesticated.

Elite people have one specific job that sure thing they specialise in, and an expert in that field will want to write God out of religion and have no part in nature. The very thing we know about God came out of the mind of a human being, and the global elite wants us to forget about such a thing that in ourselves is the epic energy centre of the creator. They think they are so clever and self-efficient that God has become irrelevant. So, ordinary people fight for the elite's purpose, their struggles entrenched in their lousy work roles.

Artificial intelligence technology uses ordinary, non-violent people as their homo sapiens playmate pieces. It validates authority over them that the ungodly elites, those individuals with aggression, debate to act and stop to work on good ideas, integrating faulty reasoning chips in AI computing.

Keeping mind and body integrated has always been a natural biological system. The development of AI is a natural, evolutionary process of atoms and also matters in bringing about AI species with the elements in life getting arranged differently. The actual mechanical AI beings are created from thoughts in the spirited, sound human mind, the brain within the universe.

You have been reading about me, the rarest homo sapien on this Earth in modern times. I will join other species that only exist as part of the fossil record when my mortal consciousness and its unconscious self leave the body. My corpse is to rejoin the soil by burial or flame, torching the remains to ashes. And in outer space forever I shall be when the Earth has been dried too much by the sun. So, life on a planet to which our human species gave a second name when we discovered intelligent life already existed. I think aliens with human features have been living elsewhere in the universe for hundreds of light years, and one day, they will be detected before they reach us.

I hope that a long, long time from now, I will reach the end of my natural cycle to earthly life and die. Be happy for me. Hooray. I am relieved to reach this point and move over and onwards. I will look for you to have a conversion when our mortal life finishes and we get into eternity's spiritual energy as living cells going through the vast universes and settling on one of them. Most of us recognise the reality of physical objects in space and time. Things of the senses are in flux. Still, actual concepts exist in pure form, or their essences are objects of thought, a theological idea likened to maths, which is not in space and time.

The time concept I am thinking about does not exist in this eternal in-love-with-consciousness experience, and experiences emerge out of the darkness with specks of lights to fuse into the lighted universe with different realism that embodies the mind, unconsciousness to consciousness, with a physical body again.

It is an unchanging truth known only by reason and not perceived by the senses. So, I wish you all a good death; I will look for you at the end of time, the survival of humanity on the other side of this or another world's universe. It will be a new phase after the mortal period, and forever, life's energy, with its 'God force', the perpetrating thing witnessed in gravity and consciousness, will exist without end. And consciousness experiences gather together forever again.

Metaphysics reflects upon the nature of fundamental reality and asks what the characteristics of the true nature of reality are. Is it monistic or dualistic because it has entities for change?

Some readers will think I am playing on words. Read me carefully: my words are solemn, written to wake, not fear. So, even if my commas are in the right place for me, you may understand my entity is different from the original intent to stop thinking of wrong ideas. My stories are my belief stories, but you may not believe them. My awareness and insights are truths that the 'self' surrendered to the ultimate facts of consciousness that are not real, but everything else is the materialistic reality to believe. There is a truth that cannot be communicated, and group thinking removed self-investigating from me. My thoughts are natural, uncontrolled, and unaware; they pop into my mind.

And finally, I strive to open up your superior intelligence and education to the God of our consciousness.

So, may the vibrant energy of love be with you, which offers us a foundation for our lives and godly, saintly qualities. Take all the necessary actions to ensure peace, harmony and happiness by setting up a pattern in your life. Love, love, love to you; respect all and have a beautiful earthly life and a good experience. Reach for your dreams and work through the obstacles that stand in the way.

1A

ADDITIONAL STORIES

Three years later, in 2020–2023

Writing restarted on Monday, 27 February 2023

I constantly attempt to perfect grammar and punctuation and maintain original writing authenticity. I am also continually rewriting, re-editing and adding chapters to this book, *A Good Life: The Perception of Perfection*. It is the blueprint of what I want to put out there with a legacy. I plan to publish this revised, self-edited version with minimum professional editorial tampering with my words by 2025.

I did not allow words in the editing process that may fictitiously dramatise or falsely polish information between my accurate, non-falsified, authentic truth writing. All the descriptions are non-fiction, and I set out to be engaging and convey a unique message with suspense and real-life drama about living on Earth and not just a projectile of a mental illness as the primary focus. Furthermore, my writing is not easily readable, although the English is mostly grammatically correct. Still, only some things are explainable, and I need help with words and language. Therefore, I had to hire a copy editor and a proofreader to mark the writing errors.

Today, 27 February, I am proud to say happy first birthday to our special granddaughter, Effie Rae. We have five wonderful grandchildren whom we cherish and adore. Effie is our first granddaughter of the married couple, Georgina and Adam, their first child. Children and grandchildren are a blessing, and we also thank God for them, as we are the lucky ones.

There has been a global pandemic, COVID-19, since December 2019, which was expected to end in 2020, but 2021 brought more illnesses, lockdowns and restrictions. That year, my mental health was affected again too, and I had to stay in hospital. However, in 2022, worldwide conditions have eased with negative Covid tests for all travellers, and social distancing is required to stop spreading the virus.

In 2023, wearing a mask and social distancing were mandatory. However, the virus is still hospitalising many people, and many have contracted the typical winter cold and are highly stressed. My wife and I tested positive for COVID-19 but are now clear and have negative readings. However, a stubborn tickly cough is challenging to shift, and I have been on a long-acting injectable medication since 2021 to maintain the stability of my mental health.

2A

SCHIZOPHRENIA CHARACTERISTICS IN MY ELDERLY LIFE

Monday, 27 February 2023

I had my very worst cognitive issues and psychological distress disorder when something went wrong again in my brain. I could not interpret the natural world correctly; it was hidden from me by the wall of my imagination and acted out in hallucinations and atheistic delusions.

I was hospitalised in November 2021, aged sixty-five; this was my eleventh psychotic episode, and it was hard to spot the symptoms because they were not all physical. Instead, there was mental turmoil in which I could not stop the flow of negative thoughts or control my imagination, emotions or attention, causing obsession and debilitating anxiety fears. My body and emotions were out of whack;

I became acutely unwell again when I slipped into this psychotic state and lower mental plane.

Once again, I lived this part of my conscious hours in psychosis, dead fast asleep and walking about with commentary coming out of my mind that was more commanding than sleeping at night in my bed and dreaming them. Between 3 and 4:30 am, in my regular, semi-awake state, I felt paralysed in bed and saw bizarre, weird-shaped geometric patterns, floating things and strange non-human entities, alive alien creatures, performing on me. My eyes would be closed in a terrifying nightmare, and I suffered more in my imagination than in reality. People had scary faces simply when grinning and had odd deformities. Hindsight tells me this. In psychosis, people appear strange, and things happen in slow motion. I could not tell these unknown forces that control people to stop their activities. Instead, I discovered an astral world of experiences, psychic abilities and alternative sanity after the madness had struck from a dreadful headache.

In addition, life's daily hassles and commitments had caused high-stress levels, ultimately affecting my mental state. I was wildly obsessed with my voice telling me to leave my home and commit acts that felt dark, scary and beyond everyday eccentricities.

As a holy fool, I had declared, "God is dead, and the intellectuals killed God," because the claim that God is in the world is ontologically distinct, a referential object somewhere far beyond the clouds. Usually, a patriarchal existence over and beyond the universe is a lie. The dualistic conceiving of God as fundamentally separate from the world and from the self is a lie. Then, I began to think that any events I think of do not require a supernatural agent because the human intellect produces more accurate models of how things work. Instead, the truth is that everything that exists constitutes unity, and this inclusive unity is, in some sense, divine. So, why has God disappeared? This epiphany, the decomposition of God in my psyche and encountering nihilism, or meaninglessness in the death of God, also has made my intellect aware that people just made it up. Scientific investigations and discoveries always point to an intelligent designer, God, and the modern world's view is atheist nonsense. They hold on to made-up ideas from foolishly innovative heads vested in denying that intelligent design is behind the processes and not accepting that the world is somehow a self-expression of divine nature or is identical to God. It smartly finetuned the universe precisely and made creatures in its image. Humans can say yes or no in evidence-based faith that everything is God and God is everything or take blind, materialist, purposeless faith – a choice for only human mammals.

My experiences sometimes give me phenomena that exist, but my knowledge of them is limited. But the noumena, an object such as a non-conscious tree or rock, cannot know what being human is and how my brain needs to dream in sleep. As a result, stones and plants are neither aware of their existence nor have freedom. On the other hand, I can think things up and explore phenomena from the feeling of awe and wonder that reality inspires.

The reason for my existence is to think, think, help others believe in a mystical union between humankind and God, and research and write down what happens to me, too. Therefore, I cannot lie to avoid the responsibility that it is always me in the abnormal breakdown in my brain but only for self-preservation because our consciousness has condemned us to be free.

It weighs heavy on my heart that existence could have come from nothingness and that we have to deny an anthropomorphic personal God with characteristics of personhood like us. But, in reality, God has gone out of human thoughts when we reach a higher state of character development, as humans continually become more elevated and higher to become god-like. God is both oneself and that which transcends ordinary consciousness.

I believe God is alive again, and philosophy's final truth is perhaps panpsychism's pantheistic ideas. A change occurred in my thinking to create meaning for myself and not rely only on the classic theistic God to define our lives, and I cannot altogether alienate or remove divinity from a mind that says God is in our mind. We are responsible for making our essence and values. However, not all of us are capable of creating values and being able to determine our own lives. So, having the divine nature inside us from birth is essential because there is nothing when God truly dies inside us. But Christianity – panpsychism – retained the indwelling intimate and close God even though reality has us believe that God is everything. There was no more intimate and inane expression of God. I think God has a mind, and I cannot altogether alienate or remove divinity from a mind that shares the characteristic personalities of personhood.

I sleep, and my consciousness is cut off from the outside world in my astral dreaming. While I am awake, the malfunction of dreaming comes to the fore. But simultaneously, I am awake and witness my madness, a true madness in schizophrenia that took me into the world of the creative process and fantasy dreams – the marvellous mystery of my mind.

One or more of my mental domains, either my judgemental thoughts about the world, perception, mood, cognition, insight or how I view myself while asleep, were unimpeded by my higher cortical inhibitions, and I experience mysticism with psychosis.

My complex mental health is being drugged with a long-acting aripiprazole injection in the upper arm. It quells most symptoms, and so far, I have not slipped in and out of psychotic states and am living a relatively 'normal' life. On the contrary, I lead an immensely fulfilling and happy life as I walk that path towards recovery.

Nevertheless, deficits in visual learning, reasoning, problem-solving and executive functioning are significant. I am also in continuous agony with aches from the neck, lower back, hips, thighs and knees, with tingling in my fingers and toes. They are under investigation with X-ray and MRI scans, and consultants are to examine them and see me about the results.

The most common symptom of a spinal problem is multiple degenerative cervical discs with bony bulge growth due to wear and tear changes at various levels, resulting in arthritis.

For long-term pain management, I use 30 mg of codeine phosphate on prescription when experiencing intense, extremely debilitating pain.

The recurrence of the ancient familiar rise in the cost of living is now getting most citizens extra financial help from the government. However, global recession looms and inflation sores. The cost of fuel, including domestic gas and electricity, has rocketed. In addition, increases in fresh fruit and vegetable prices and the war in Ukraine with Russia are causing a turbulent effect on markets. Nevertheless, we are managing quite well, and with the expected substantial rise in benefits and state pension in April, we should be able to ride out these financial pressures, which is in no way competition-related; such is the popular belief.

The evidence shows that most fuel and grocery price increases are due to global factors; action is needed to help contain the rising cost of living, which puts people and businesses under sustained financial pressure.

I volunteered and participated in an NHS research programme called Our Future Health on Thursday, 25 May 2023. It aims to help prevent, detect and treat diseases earlier. I want to help future generations live in good health for longer, so I gave scientific researchers my DNA and the resources they need to identify the signs and treatments of diseases much earlier than before. Using the information I provided and the analysis of the DNA in my blood sample could help calculate the risk factors of some diseases like diabetes, stroke, dementia, heart disease, and cancer and, being optimistic, find a cure for schizophrenia.

I have continued to be mainly concerned with the regulatory action of antipsychotics in my later life, affecting neurocognition decline and staying in remission of schizophrenia. It is because the drug further impairs cognitive and functional capacity more quickly than in ordinary ageing people without schizophrenia.

I must remember that they effectively control psychotic symptoms, and I must avoid getting psychosis forever and ever. There is a part of psychosis where the mind, body and spirit are at the next level.

When waking up on that level, we are all God in all of ourselves, and human types are the only conscious beings in the universe. Yes or no? I think we are in for a shock because the vivid imagination and dreams in people tell us we are not alone, but searching in our worldly ways is a primitive communicative method to find life in the universe.

The Big Bang general idea that the universe existed some 13.8 billion years ago gave our mind food for thought but missed out on God, the beginning point. Eventually, another review study proved the Big Bang was wrong, and the universe's accelerated expansion may also be incorrect and is bringing about new crises in cosmology.

More urgent, arguably, is the inevitability of suffering and death. Still, the momentum for change is tackling whether we are alone in the universe and safeguarding the Earth from humankind's destructiveness. Humans are in a space structure that should not exist but should have remained in the dark matter-centred black hole. Everything in the material world has a source in the non-physicality dimension, but everything seems to be explained by our brain's physical processes.

All God's births burst forth from the energy bond that creates living things. The James Webb Space Telescope is examining its mechanical nature and making groundbreaking discoveries that will blow the roof off our current understanding of the structure of space, time, planets, the universe, and other things we cannot correlate.

Our world is never more than a mental construct, and quantum physics teaches a crucial lesson: our nervous system filters information the intelligent agent gives us. Our brains explain things by measurable, observable processes, so it is hard for some to see the non-material dimension and where the soul fits.

The God in humans has engineered time for the human mind in the universe to look at the past and predict or know the future; we, however, can only comprehend our lives living here and now in a fraction of our present time, and then we die. Moreover, the individual can never fathom God's all in everything because we can only be the observer and the observable. Nevertheless, the objective physical world does not exist independently of the observing mind, and the concentrated energy of God flows through regions of space and time. As the universe flows, energy lines from an intelligent agent create a chance to play a significant role in keeping Earth fit for life and driving the universe's accelerating expansion. Eventually, the conscientious growth may stop.

On 8 September 2022, Queen Elizabeth II's passing marked a significant historical event in the British monarchy, setting the stage for change or continuing long-standing traditions. King Charles III is

Queen Elizabeth's eldest son. King Charles III and Queen Carmilla's coronation happened on Saturday, 6 May 2023. It was another once-in-a-lifetime event that could potentially usher in a new era or maintain the status quo of privileges.

Last night, on 9 June 2023, was a night of music to mark the seventy-fifth anniversary of Windrush, which took place at the Royal Albert Hall in London. Our children gave us tickets for the event and to stay overnight at a hotel in central London. The event also celebrated the impact of Caribbean culture on British life. It featured various guest stars, including Chineke, the very first entirely black and minority ethnic professional orchestra in Britain. Their cultural contribution has enriched British society in numerous ways.

In 1948, a significant chapter in British history began with the arrival of the first large group of Caribbean people on UK shores. They embarked on a ship called *HMT Empire Windrush*, and their journey marked the start of what is now known as the 'Windrush' generation. This generation, which extended from 1948 to 1973, not only faced challenges but also made significant contributions to the cultural landscape of Britain. At that time, the Caribbean was part of the British Commonwealth, and these arrivals, who were automatically British subjects, were free to live and work in the UK permanently.

My mother and father arrived in the UK in the late 1950s, and we, their children, came in the early mid-1960s. We all had stories of how white English people devastated our lives as black Caribbean and British citizens. Mother told me English women would attempt to lift her dress to see if black women had lizard-like tails, and my father spoke about problems in housing and renting a place and seeing notices saying, "No blacks, no Irish, no dogs". We all experienced abusive name-calling, using the 'N' word, patronising remarks and a profoundly flawed discriminatory immigration system that surfaced in 2017. Many Commonwealth citizens, mainly from the Windrush generation, have been unjustly detained, deported and denied legal rights. In 1971, the Immigration Act gave Commonwealth citizens living in the UK permanent, indefinite rights to live and work in the UK. Yet, these rights were not always respected, leading to significant injustice.

On Windrush Day, the milestone in black history was marked with talks, discussions, exhibitions and performances across Britain. The Windrush ship docked in Tilbury on 22 June 1948, and the Windrush flag flew across Britain on an observed day on 22 June 2023.

3A

OVERCOMING NIHILISTIC THOUGHTS

Friday, 30 June 2023

In my previous writing in February 2023, I was faced with nihilist thoughts, with no meaning at all, before I was reborn from classical theism's God to a mystical panpsychism pantheistic view/idea. According to the mathematician and philosopher Alfred Whitehead (1861–1947), in his book *Process of Reality* (1929), God is creative in making 'events', not 'things'.

I wanted another way of understanding the study of God and our experience of things or matter made of things, like tables, chairs, computers, trees, and stones, as our reality. Reality is one significant extensive process in flux—constantly changing with a rhythm and a flow to it, too, but it seems that our minds must split our experience into time and space.

Today, I am struck again by intrusive thoughts and no purpose when I know there is meaning to life and it has intrinsic value when I question my old and new beliefs. I hold on to new experiences and form my worldviews, and I cannot answer why I have to believe in something other than the nothingness that gives no purpose. This 'why', a three-lettered monosyllabic word, asks why, why do I have my core values? And where do they come from? My beliefs, the wonder of technological things and scientific discovery conclude that something exists.

Nihilism is an artificial, manufactured ideology that gives no value or meaning to our world or ourselves. Our universe creates energy with a focused force on the negative pessimism in life and the positive power of optimism; in the end, good will always overcome evil in the uptrend view of the world.

In the grand scheme, we are more than a transient random combination of temporary atoms with autonomous goals and biological fields. There is a consequence to knowing that all the things we experience, the ups and downs we go through, are all for character building and to be obligated to understand the chaos of reality in this actual world. Humanity must shift forward with its consciousness to have more awareness because it leaves out more essential things than it takes in. If consciousness had a higher awareness, our understanding and ignorance would help our minds that ask: who am I, why am I here, and what is the purpose of all of this?

When everything was infinitely small, our brains were already in the universe, and our hearts did not just happen to start beating. Some higher power we call God has given us free will to do things voluntarily, even though we do not know how to. We tend to forget what is behind our eyes that take in sensory information, which is the mind that goes deep enough to find where existential questions come from.

The answers lie in the same place where our deeper intelligence and understanding are underneath reality when we wake up from the dream of life. It is located in the universe's extreme, where we are the fundamentals of existence like everything else and are not an accident.

In previous writings, I have said that proof of God's existence is a valid argument other than just a hunch for this perception of a perfect Being. A perfect Being is necessary and possible, so there is an energy Being with the property of existing perfection. It is intelligible with mathematics and often fits nicely between the autonomous world model and biology. This energy creature allowed its earthly humans to discover some things. They become argumentive about the existence of God because they can never learn the theory of everything and the whys of our existence and fall into a black hole of no meaning, no purpose. In my experience, it leads to one grand creator designer who maintains its presence deep on a spectrum in all human minds. Some people want to eradicate it when it is fundamental to the existence and truth of the knowledge of our genetics and the working of personhood to evolve to take the blame and take an ethical and moral standing. Although bacteria and viruses are directed without rights or wrongs, they get on with the DNA program to divide, multiply, and follow the genetic internal rules. Still, we, people, want to know the work of all the trillions of neurons in the brain that incorporate our mind that mostly figures things out. God planted a brain in the aperture of the skull to discover universals which the I in us brought to our conscience. We will never know some things as knowledge, but they are truths.

Some people believe that the world comprises separate static objects, while other enlightened people like myself view it as an interconnected, ever-changing fluctuation.

Most people believe the world is deterministic because it seems to follow laws of cause and effect based on laws of physics. However, from the micro view of the atom, they seem to be completely random, and at this fundamental level, the atom appears to exhibit some rudimentary choice. Therefore, only living things exert or exhibit probabilistic behaviour, and everything else should follow the laws of physics of cause and effect.

The globe is experiencing high polarisation and wars. Humans fight each other because they lack empathy towards their fellow human tribes. They see outgroups as objects to destroy. The eight billion people's brains on the earth cannot find a peaceful coexistence, and my brain cells are getting my mind worried for humanity because of many global conflicts. Conflicts going on around the globe are the war between Israel and Hamas, ongoing internal conflict in Myanmar, and there is an Islamist insurgency in the Mreb region of Africa and Boo Haram insurgency in Nigeria. The list of wars continues with civil war between rival factions in Sudan. There is a multi-sided conflict between the Syrian civil war and the ongoing civil war in Somalia and Ethiopia. Afghanistan has been in near continuous armed conflict for a long time and there is a new war between Ukraine and Russia.

The warmth of summer has lingered into September, and my mind has settled down from the sweltering summer heatwave in July to try to understand political unrest and election biases.

I must let you know that on 8 September 2023, a powerful earthquake devastated Morocco, leaving thousands dead and countless more injured. God, in your mercy!

Fourteen days into September is my sixty-seventh birthday and many happy returns to me.

I did not need the central heating switched on, which proved such an expense throughout last winter. As the warmth lingers in earnest as autumn gets underway, the demand for radiators is further reduced.

4A

MY DEVELOPMENT AND GAME – CHANGES FOR MY PSYCHOSIS

Infancy Years (Reception 1 and 2)

Memories are gone from the year of my infancy to around five years old; I cannot remember any names of the boys and girls I played games with during the weekdays at school or the long weekends out in the community. I can still give myself flashbacks to happy times with the children I played with on the school playground and in the village. I only have a patch of memory of playing games with my brother, sisters and cousins. Regarding the concept of children bullying children, I do not have any evidence that it happened to me or other pupils on the island of St Kitts. I can only remember having a fantastic time as a youngster.

We boys fooled around; we climbed trees and threw stones at mango trees to catch the mangoes from the branches. In another game, we recovered a bicycle wheel from the dump, removed the tyre and put a stick in the rim groove. We began to push off, running with the wheel along the ground, and the moment the wheel was balanced, momentum built up. The wheel spun fast as we continued to shove the wheel with the stick in the groove of the bike wheel. We raced along the smooth road, lightly flurried with dirt dust, and the soil surface was hot, baked hard by the sun. If anyone dared to tread the paths without footwear, their feet would get parched.

I watched adults' behaviour and only felt comfortable deep within myself by not imitating the opposing behaviours of adults.

I learnt to walk in an instant. I was excited to explore the natural world and amazed by what the adult world had achieved.

I grappled with numbers, symbols and formulae. The method that proves the idea first was hard for me to replicate and get the correct working out to give the affirmative answer. I made some errors. Some were in my calculations. My infant's brain thought mathematics and numbers were the most natural, intelligent way to get absolutes of truths before seeing the material or the component of the thing in existence or having the means to invent what the mind has abstracted and calculated.

I was fascinated by all the things that inhabit the Earth with me, including the inventions adults made. The seemingly mundane habits that are part of the behaviour of that life species were exotic. Domesticated animals idled around the neighbourhood, and others would sleep curled beneath their owner's timber house mounted on splintered wooden pillars. Others balled roundly under the shaded area of the canopy of their owner's veranda; special care was taken with animals nourished to breed, mainly for value. Their products were harvested for things like clothes or milk to sustain us, and some species were killed to be part of our food chain and for other species to eat.

Our guardian was kind enough not to overload an animal and walked with a donkey down a tropical mountain. The beautiful, dazzling and vivid display of species of birds and plant life was astonishing. I watched the grace of the stillness in plants' growth, and as the seasons changed, they adapted to the conditions and continued to flourish and reproduce new plant life.

Observing hummingbirds sipping nectar from flowers was a mesmerising experience, and it was here that my child's mind encountered its first miracle: a lizard's tail regrowing after being severed. This sight left me in awe. Once amusing, the mischievous antics of monkeys took on a new significance when seen through the eyes of adults who deemed them a nuisance.

Following the trails of ants as they carried objects more significant than themselves to their colonies was a lesson in perseverance and teamwork. Their seemingly effortless efforts, the absence of ants seemed unexhausted and without casualties, and the relentless return to their task left me in awe of the miraculous life cycles that abound in nature.

I was intrigued; my child's brain was trying to grow connections fast, but my mind thought it was slow. The time was moved slowly. I waited impatiently for each day, but still, I could not cram everything I wanted to know into my memory cavity and could not understand all the things that got jammed in the small space of my thinking mind. Insects, birds and animals communicated. My, what wonders! Life on the planet was magnificent; it took my breath away. I gasped at the beauty of it all. I was amazed.

Buzzing pleasures heightened my wonder even more, equal to the excitement of opening a long-awaited present, such as a brand-new toy: "That's all I ever wanted." I enjoyed looking at the beautiful sky patterns in the daytime, and the first time I looked up into the night sky was excellent.

I had climbed out of bed and looked through the window, and it was a spectacular experience to gaze at the moon cascading its impressive gentle glow upon the Earth and the sparkling beauty of stars. I was wowed; my child's vocabulary did not have the words.

Words cannot describe what my infant's brain was taking in. It took my mind beyond itself to experience a different inner self outside the five senses of a human being, with a physical body that feels emotion.

I discovered perennating energy within myself, and also, the entire universe is full of this stuff, keeping things alive and putting tiny things and big things into existence. The smallest I know of are insects, the enormous vast sky the biggest, and I feel connected to an invisible power source. Some forces push stuff to and fro, keep things from falling and keep the dead as dead, but they can bring new life. And the snake gave me the most chills of all the creatures I knew about or had seen in my infancy. I got unreasonably stressed with fear and panicky if I was anywhere near them, and my brain experienced the same feeling of 'chills', an unease, with bad adult habits and behaviours.

Adults intrigued me and were puzzling, and I got even more puzzled that they had fights that turned into wars. The terrible wickedness of people's inhumanity was worse than the beastly instincts and cruelty of wild animals. The brain of this child (me) thought, how can that be? We are a human species, born human beings striving to improve in knowledge and intelligence and discover and learn facts about the planets and ourselves. So, why are people so nasty to other people? What is it that makes our species worse than wild animals? Were these people born without a conscience and with a mindset low in intuitive ideas and high in wild animals' beastly instinctual cruelty?

From the cradle to the grave, they are not human beings unless they nurture nature's qualities in themselves that make people empathic and humane. The wrong beastly instincts in people are an easy-to-use chaotic disruption in the human being that interferes with becoming a genuine, perfectly human person. The best that people can be. Therefore, people need to train, practise and develop the use of that 'self'.

We children heard a rumour about a house on top of a bushy hill with dense, knobbly forest trees and thick undergrowth, with a winding pathway to get there. There lived an old, crazy, drunk woman who screamed and ran around the house naked, and when the night became spooky, she turned into a witch. The children became superstitious, whereas I became suspicious and curious.

While the deficient adults were harming everything on Earth, my peer group would 'go and play'. None of us was in a place of harm, violence, abuse or victimisation, but my young mind knew there was a source in people that could turn them nasty, violent and uncompassionate.

On the island, I saw all nationalities and different races getting along. The Indian Asians, Chinese Asians, negroes and a few white people all got together. However, I had a creepy feeling and intense curiosity after hearing rumours, watching films, looking at pictures in books and moving to higher classes at school.

Junior School (Year 3–6)

Probably, I was about to be nine years old and noticed that the smallest minority racial group on the island owned all the infrastructure and government buildings, controlled imports and exports, and possessed most of the land. The natives and other racial groups worked the ground and ran the transport on this small island. I would not say I liked the feelings that were networking in my brain. I felt sad and appalled, and it weakened my overwhelming sense that the community was good and we were all getting along, but I grappled with my infant brain's diverse views, and the question that won was, "How come?" How come only this minority race seemed to have control of everything on the island? And it was rare to see any of them.

A profile began to emerge for this race of people as school classes taught reading and writing big words. Almost all the stories they wrote or told us were about them, and I heard the term 'European people' used in school education. The school taught that they discovered this, invented that, and observed everything in the sky, earth and sea. Behaviours in the human race and animals other than themselves got written down in books they wrote and we read. They were the only people who wrote books. It did seem that they wrote, we understood, and wanted us to believe in God as described in the Bible.

Something was unsettling me about these people and their words, and I could not pinpoint why varying interpretations of English words, the only language I was taught from birth, were going on in my mind. I was getting confused by it and distinguishing between speech patterns. Even the decisions my mind should know differences on, the 'yes' and 'no' and 'don't know' to make up my mind, did not seem natural. The three communication pathways remained separate, yet three altogether voices, and there was so much more in between the thoughts and messages crowding my maturing brain.

My mind was in a constant state of rethinking things because I felt I was being manipulated. I was not being told the truth. I have always said what I want to say, but nobody else does. Even children my age were getting more deceitful; they found ways to say things, cover-up, be secretive and manipulate others to get on. I noticed my peer group was changing, but I could not see the changes in me other than physical ones: the growth of my body and more hair appearing. My thoughts and ideas were not changing. I firmly stuck to my simple principles of 'openness' and honesty. To get ahead was competitiveness to deceive others. People do not say what they mean.

Things are not always correct, wrong, black and white, and facts or beliefs are not always believed. My mind has been trying to understand and recognise these thoughts from birth.

What were they getting at, and what did they want us dark-toned people to accept? I faced agony because everything that the white minority said or wrote made my mind doubt it, not trusting what they said, and then the sentences' complexity followed; sometimes, multiple meanings were absurd. I heard the expression, "White people speak with forked tongues," and parts of my inner dialogue were influenced by it.

These kinds of people were so off the scale from humanity; they were the worst racially motivated group of people on the planet. I should be angry at the way this group of minority people was treating other racial groups wherever they moved to and settled. They seemingly broke away, standalone supremacists, all-knowing in every knowledge and language.

They talked and wrote down what they said were ideal ideologies we must believe in: "Go to hell if you don't believe." For themselves, not to believe was to walk away and not listen to such nonsense. My maturing mind could not understand what was happening, including my mother and father organising for the family and our guardian to immigrate to England.

Every cell in my body articulated that these lighter-skinned people had a problem with skin tone colours, and their kind with pale skin had features they wanted to see eradicated. Racism was deeply embedded in these types of people, but I was not alive to my consciousness being alerted to the dangers those people used to justify racism on the island.

They had to be stripped of the epistemological and methodological privileges they enjoyed. The European approach was the one way, the only way, of understanding the natural world and people. They invented the sciences and all kinds of mechanical devices, knowing that we and the others, less pale people, could not think up things or were not thinking about or writing down our findings. We unquestioningly accepted what they said and endured their wrongs on us. Their word was the 'best education'; we were told we had to learn, and part of the system was biased and racist. They lacked a sense of morality and purpose and possessed arrogant confidence and a very different set of values from the rest of the human species.

Black-skinned people saw Western centrism as the best in everything, even in their form of thinking that entrenched us; we, the black people, had a hand in helping whiteish people uproot black people. "It's in the Bible," they would say. School lessons mentioned 'colony, colonising'. Colonisation did not click into place for a long time. We centred on European and Western history, giving us knowledge through colonising areas.

The people of the West, including Europeans, picked up specific good ideas and approaches from different people and Asian countries or regions. Such good knowledge was absorbed in Western terms. Still, they have yet to pay homage to the influence of other knowledge systems.

They centred themselves as the 'head' and wanted us to be influenced by their bad errors in working out things, observations, and corrupt practices, which, there is no denying, did not benefit humanity. That did not mean they should not themselves be interrogated or decentred, and they should always remain the product of human goodwill and good intentions.

My body was gradually maturing, my thinking was getting muddled, and my feelings remained rooted in a perspective of life that cut me off from being like other people, which I had to follow. My young mind could imagine the pain dark-skinned ancestors went through, and what modern black people's struggles were, mainly based upon racial discrimination and racial prejudice. I could not put to use or exploit the anger happening in my developing brain to connect to hating whiteish, ashen-skinned people actively; I was saddened for them for losing their humane self, an essential component of a human being.

I formulated how to get them back on track and mixed up a cocktail of ideas, opinions, teachings, the few experiences gained, what experience has shown and what has happened in history. It told me something similar to what I am about to express in writing, which has all of the hallmarks of empathy, compassion and the right ingredients, which my young mind used to explain to itself.

When these pale-skinned people came to a foreign land, they saw people of colour (black people) as their slaves to buy and sell, and they fought, started wars for what was not theirs and took total ownership of what was free for all to share on the planet.

These people's actions were brutal and beastly and likened to those of wild animals, and they were proud of themselves; I would find it impossible to stand in their shoes and not regret the harm they have done to the planet and its species. I would not want to be seen with the rest of the human race and not be able to feel sorry for what their white ancestors have done and not carry a subtle yet pervasive sense of shame. These people were not remorseful; they were pleased with themselves for their authoritarian rule over citizens on lands around the world, which they brutally took ownership of and made themselves 'head' without having votes from the whole of the human race and have us looking up to kings and queens.

A genuine human being would be ashamed and appalled at their brutality and beg the rest of the human race to help educate their conscience for them to purge themselves. Individuals should seek a personal pardon for their race transgression to have gone so far from humanity. Different ethnic people need to prove that the ashen-toned people's repentances are genuine and thankful to the rest of the human race to bring them to be redeemed. They will find they must compensate for the wrongs they committed to the human race with the material properties of perfect love. Undoubtedly, the universe has universally gifted us people with filament; even atheists must have the moral and ethical fibres associated with ideal love. Being religious, spiritualist or not, believing in God or not, atheist or not, maybe people must surely know their choice to nurture nature's spirit of love. The consequence of not doing so is naturally dire for their soul and humanity.

My young mind did not understand well that not all people accept the fundamental universal rule in their thinking to do 'no harm'. It produces ethical principles for all of us to follow. People make up their variables to label groups of people negatively or define them in deficit terms in their system of classifying living things. Knowledge and breeding good behaviours will be better seen in culturally and historically multicultural people because they have more stakes in benefiting humanity, not democratising it. The supremacists will have to change or die out.

The outcome would be for them to root out their racial essentialism in themselves and remain in the system of thoughts to abide by universal laws, the code of principles in ethical and humane practices. And we all should have to do it. Suppose we all do it or speak objectively about people and things. It must produce the sense that constructs and instructs the universal concept of 'rights' and 'wrongs', or we will be outraged, forgetting to justify 'wrongs'. We should hastily retract from wrongdoings and wrong sayings.

Adults do things for pleasure, and the grave things they can do are etched deep into my childhood memories and permanently preserved. From observing from my child's perspective of what is wrongful and that parts of the adult world are not lovely, I see that they have stayed in my brain, covered with new and fresher memories. I am not able to say for sure that all of this writing is total truth and authentic from the past and not just made-up stories that I honestly think are embedded infant experiences in my earliest laid-down memories, getting released through opening up to my self-education to express those memories out of my mind.

In photos of me, my face looks blank and bleak; I looked like I was in another world, which I daydreamed about because I would not say I liked doing anything wrong. I saw the unfair, harsh, externally objective world and its wrongdoings too well. I turned towards the inwardly introverted expression of love with the aim of my imaginative daydream ideas to work in real-life circumstances, situations and decisions. I promised to stick to being as correct as practical and still be helpful in the world of good-doing thoughts when I grew up. My lifestyle would be the outlet to practise them physically and do the right thing, and I was learning that trial and error in our lives helps us do the right thing and to be educated.

I do not boast or talk about the traits on which I worked hard to be the character I am today and to do the right thing. I am pleased that there is no compromise in doing the right, good thing, and I stayed firm and rigid to the right and proper way to craft a pleasant personality and be perfect. Despite complex challenges, I continue to go on and on, still trying to reach unachievable perfection. However, I can continue to be the best person I can be. There is no debate about compromising on the truth and being honest in everything I do and say.

My young brain started to realise that wild animals had a powerful instinct for sex and had much aggression in their mating habits. Having sex to reproduce offspring was rough, violent, natural and healthy for their species. A strange sound attracted my attention, and I had to investigate what was causing it.

I peeped through the window of a neighbouring house, and the rough, violent actions of an ordinary couple having sex were a discomforting, shocking discovery. People are not that much different from the animal kingdom in their sexual practices.

Radio broadcasts on the heavyweight boxing championships provided epic hours of listening for the community. In the cinema, they laughed as the film music added to the tension to dramatise the story's thrills, and most sat on the edge of their seats.

As a child watching Westerns, I believed it was unfair to the Indians; the cowboys had guns, and the Indians had bows and arrows. It was unjust that they were being driven off the land and having their tents burnt down, their homes.

The adult world did not fit how I expected it to be, and the boxing event I listened to almost had me in tears; I sulked. The listeners would chat loudly and cheer when a boxer got knocked down, especially if the fighter was knocked out cold. The broadcaster's descriptions of the event were graphically vivid; I could see the words as actions, words like punches – "gave a right hook to the head, floored him and knocked him out cold" – chilled me. I had a strange feeling in my tummy, making me shake and shiver. I was probably around eight or eight and a half and began to talk back to my internal thoughts. I internalised all of this talk, and my second mind answered. It induced an internal biological change, and the eternal self, a kind of atrium, looked out at the objective external world of adult fights and made me feel shy around adults and like a dummy.

As I walked my truth, I sometimes slipped up and needed clarification on myself and others. But every external action in the real world I took was from the master blueprint to make everyone foster their best traits so that the world could become ideal for everyone. I always tried to use the best-energised characteristics out of the mix of both good and bad, and my healthy behaviours were an actual copy of my thoughts working into actions, no longer just inside my head space where my ideals would fester, but working towards the perfect outcome.

I had felt for ages that my senses told me I was achy; I felt something was wrong but could not touch the cause of the mental itches until I realised they were compounded by religious teachings and the community waiting for a saviour. I could not remember knowingly, absolutely, deliberately or intentionally committing a sin or crime. I heard the preaching and saw writings that they said were God's words, and all had sinned, and Jesus' blood had saved us. He was crucified for our sins. Every Sunday and every Christian festival, the Pentecostal church had me in anguish with their colourful hymn singing about the coming of the Lord, and they preached doom that

Armageddon was coming, sending the congregation into the most profound depths of sorrow.

Deep in my young mind, plunging into my soul, the flaws in Christianity pained me the most because I knew that, just by being aware of my existence, I wanted to see and be with the one who brought me into being and love all of creation. We are obliged to praise and worship that thing that brought us about and to whom we owe our lives and want to do the best with our lives, but sometimes we make problems for ourselves and other creations in the environment we share and wish to be forgiven.

We look forward to meeting that 'thing' our human language calls 'God'. People are misinformed when using their faith, hope, and beliefs. They express their love and thank God in a profoundly flawed part of the religion they are told to obey. Believe it, be saved; it is the only way, the truth and the light, and get the reward everyone desperately wants. I went along with it, and I ached throughout my childhood, growing into my teen years, and in my adult life, I sought to relieve the ache.

Secondary School (Year 7–11)

When I was nine years and eight months old, the family emigrated to England. England became my homeland as my memory of the island of St Kitts, where I was born, faded.

The broader English community has every generation of pale people, including mums, dads, granddads and grannies. I came across an ancient woman who was frightened when I looked at her smoking fags butt ends. I was a ten-year-old going on eleven, and I was curious. She was a walking-dead person who looked like a corpse. She was whiter than a cotton sheet, unbelievably as white as snow, with a sharp, wrinkled face, and she was smoking a fag that she could barely hold in the first place. She coughed and coughed, sometimes desert-dry coughs she could not get rid of, and I stared. It gradually became common to see people over one hundred years old still alive. Dark-skinned people of the same age, they tell me, look so young, so when they die, I say they could only have been fifty years old.

I met my first racial hatred in children. I also saw that they took up the bad habits of adults, which they said were fun and asked me to do them too. I went along with them and did mischievous things like scrumping apples, smoking cigarettes, drinking alcohol, and stealing sweets and biscuits. I wanted to make friends and fit in with a group, a gang. But I could set an excellent example for those naughty children. Being with them temporarily changed my perspective for a while, but when it came to dangerous dares, they took things initially too far; they were foolish and irresponsible.

I was firm with the group, saying, "No," explaining my reasons and then walking away. They shouted out, "Chicken, chicken, cluck, cluck." In the moments I agreed to try things, I thought constantly of what the consequences could be: getting caught by an adult and harshly punished, possible damage to my health and property. My emotional response guilt-tripped me; my conscience pricked me. I was wrong to get involved. This severely reduced the adrenaline rush from the thrill of taking risks, and it was no longer pleasurable. The apples we scrumped tasted foul, and taking part worried me. The aftermath of eating them killed any enjoyment I could have had from stealing them.

Schoolchildren can easily hide remorse or guilt when they tell lies and are unaware of their dishonesty. They can hurt and harm timid children and wilfully damage property. An unobservant adult can get taken in by a child's manipulative behaviour, and the innocent one, the honest truth-teller, is not believed and has to take corporal punishment for the wrongdoer. The adult, in this case, the teacher would strike the child's outstretched open hand, or the child would be bent over and hit on his bottom with a hard slipper or with the firm, thin bamboo cane, which seemed to have been made uniquely for caning. And if a child had done something considered extremely bad, he received highly unreasonable punishments: swift bare-bottom blows or both hands caned and struck with enough force to cause maximum pain and blisters.

My parents were concerned that I was not learning at primary school and that I was facing various forms of psychological trauma in my childhood. Adolescence was the game-changer for my schizophrenia. Biologically, the experiences of severe or chronic stress in my general life and discrimination impacted my body management systems. I become over-sensitised, making me more vulnerable to mental health problems, including psychosis.

My physical and mental health problems were brought on by adverse experiences that have more to do with crucial environmental factors and my genetic condition.

It seems most probable that chemical imbalances and genetic predispositions have some relevance because psychiatric drugs are valid. My madness could have been prevented by easing up on the stresses of life and worries about events that I could do nothing about. In the last term of junior school, I would have to take tests to determine where my secondary education would occur. I was worried because a child educational psychologist assessed a handful of us. We had to do well in the tests or be sent to a special needs secondary school.

I mostly dreaded the part of the test where I had to work out sums, and the psychologist watched me read, but I had to do it.

I thought my efforts were weak and not particularly useful and that I would be lucky to get into secondary modern education. All the children saw a kid who went to a special needs school as a dunce and dim-witted, and this could lead to bullying.

Going to a special needs school would likely damage my prospects of getting a job when I was older, and the certificate I gained would be seen as below the standard level of education. One of my friends who took the child psychologist assessment was sent to a special needs secondary school, and I felt sad but relieved. I had had a lucky escape.

I took the rap for a lying child's wrongdoings in primary and secondary school because the teacher did not believe me that it was not me who was naughty. Yet he said, "It's not usually like you, Karl. But I have to send out the message that your behaviour was unacceptable," he then caned me. I got caught for a punishable offence in secondary school, for drawing graffiti in a tiny area on the toilet wall depicting male and female genitalia. The teacher admitted it was out of character, yet he hit me with a slipper.

The sports activities at secondary school were field sports, cross-country and track racing. Football was played all seasons, and indoor games were held using gymnastic apparatus. There was always a boxing tournament and a sports day in the middle of the school term.

I exposed my vulnerability because I only trained myself to be fair in my dealings; I am a conscientious objector who does not knowingly use my healthy mind to plot dishonesty, commit wrongdoing or cause harm to others.

From the start of life, my internal worldview did not match my expectations of the external world. I learned to be good and thought of myself as kind, friendly and helpful to others. My brain's interpretation of alarm signals usually came from a sense of threat and harm to others in their misery. I was often not the victim or directly involved in confronting the enemy, who seemed not to have even attempted to calm themselves.

My internal world environment alerted me that some of my cells and organs, or the 'self', were faulty and getting sick.

The psychotic schizophrenia meltdown behaviours quickly started during a boxing contest at school in which I had to fight a fellow pupil who was trying to play the bad boy. Other corrupt, tough boys would bully him to harden and toughen him. I was chosen to fight him, which did not fit in with my style of aggression, which was usually verbal.

From then on, I developed sensory overload and experienced hearing voices, paranoia, and problems such as anxiety and low mood.

For four years in a secondary all-boys school, I was compelled by the school system to be in boxing matches, which harmed me psychologically as I was showered with praise to win and be certificated for beating up a pupil in a setting that made it legal and suitable to fight. My conscience told me it was wrong. I was always sad having to defend myself with muscular strength, with a sharp blow that would stop the aggression, and I would apologise to my opponent. I felt disgusted, awful, and so sorry for days that I had to tell the boy daily that I was sad for the hurt I had inflicted on him.

When my reactions to adverse life events and psychological trauma occurred, I used a social, therapeutic approach to learn more coping skills to be more productive, and that was far safer than antipsychotic drug treatment, which is known to shorten longevity.

5A

OVER SIXTY-SEVEN WITH REMISSION OF SCHIZOPHRENIA

Tuesday, 2 January 2024

This year, 2024, looks far more stable than a year ago when the rumbles of Russia's war in Ukraine first affected global energy markets. Food prices in supermarkets have lowered, which might suggest that the cost-of-living crisis is finally on its way out. However, many homeowners with mortgage payments continue to struggle.

The continuous long-term management of my psychotic condition with antipsychotic injectable treatment has reduced my relapses and my risk of rehospitalisation or death.

Following my journey, the primary outcome is quality of life and symptom control, leading to a consensus in recovery. I suffered endlessly when I sailed into the darkest unknowns within me, and only a brief light brightly pushed back the darkness.

I occasionally had periods of greater intensity in the darkest unknown, and my whole body, not just my brain, was affected.

Literature suggests that the course and nature of schizophrenia is an inevitable decline in cognitive functioning, but the fall is variable, with a high rate of tardive dyskinesia.

Yet, I have learnt that antipsychotic treatment is continuously associated with increased survival, although cardiometabolic effects lead to increased mortality with antipsychotic treatment.

Some ocean of consciousness or fabric of reality keeps me pretty far away from the point where I do not pay any attention to the terrible news that raises my cortisol levels. I have found that spending hours on depressing news stories is harmful to my mental health. So, I have minimised my intake of terrible news and looked for signs that tell me I need a good mental health day.

My experience with social challenges and spiritual psychic awakening is perhaps a form of alternative intelligence, not just something that results from distress or illness.

It has unique insights and knowledge enable me to show others what it means to feel how we think and live on a higher level of consciousness.

As I age past sixty-seven, an accelerated cognitive decline is emerging and I have a fundamentally poor mental function, as do healthy older people. The common feature of schizophrenia is impaired insight, which can affect health outcomes, and age-related pharmacokinetic changes cause the elimination of the half-life caused by the antipsychotic drugs I am taking. The pharmacodynamic drug increases its permeability in the brain. So, there is a risk factor as I am now older and at an age for antipsychotic adverse effects.

Parkinsonism, tardive dyskinesia, falls and metabolic syndrome may become problems, and now, these days, I stammer some of my words. I also say the wrong words for familiar names and places or cannot articulate correctly what I want to say, and I am frustrated with my broken mind.

The safety and efficacy of my antipsychotic medication appear complex in the context of treating me as an older adult. Although I understand the nature of my condition and the treatment, there is merit in accepting it. Still, it is worrying that tardive dyskinesia is highly problematic in my dosing on antipsychotics. It is crucial to find a shallow dose of medication for me, an elderly man with schizophrenia, before extrapyramidal symptoms (EPSs) arise. No treatment is clearly not an option for me. Therefore, I must take great care using a low-dose antipsychotic treatment; close monitoring is essential.

I live independently, with no psychotic hospitalisation, and my current psychosocial functioning is within the 'average' range, which my wife can confirm.

My neuropsychological functioning has remained stable over the past three years or more. Moreover, I am optimistic about maintaining functional independence as I age with increased physical frailty and the likelihood of medical comorbidity.

Schizophrenia's exact cause is unknown, but it is thought to be a multifactorial disorder with genetic, neurobiological and environmental components. I seemed to have had a combination of all three before remission of schizophrenia with antipsychotic injectable treatment.

6A

A TRAUMATIC EVENT

Thursday 15 August 2024

Two of my close cousins recently died four months apart, aged sixty-four, and we attended their funerals. I could not hold back how these sad events made me feel, and I grieved with my gift of tears. The general election on 4 July in Britain has caused political uncertainty. In July, Hurricane Beryl left a trail of destruction on the Windward Islands. As it passed through the Caribbean Islands, it destroyed houses and buildings and thousands of people were evacuated. Saint Vincent and the Grenadines were also almost destroyed. It had me virtually burned out with emotional eco distress, which I honour my response with the words: God in your mercies!

Children commit violent crimes, war, street violence, genocide, racism and discrimination, and violation of human rights taking place every day.

I cannot watch events unfolding that cause harm or human suffering. They affect my mental health. Even if I am not directly involved, I worry about the safety of loved ones, myself, and strangers.

I do not know if my feelings are valid, but whether nationally or internationally, these events cause me uncertainty, paralysing anxiety and fear. It can seem like a loss of control over my own life because I have lived through similar traumatic events in the past, and the overexposure to doom and gloom traumatic events made me feel unwell.

I had to ask myself, "How much information and disturbing news can I take in without it negatively affecting my feelings?" And because I have dense brain fog that prevents me from performing normal mental and cognitive functions well, it feels like I am straining my mind, and in the thinking process, suddenly, I am whacked and begin to feel the need to sleep. I struggle to stay awake and not feel dopey when I think there are many peculiar sensations, like fluid wobbling around and around in my skull.

As of 29 August 2024, I have included ginkgo biloba and ginseng on my list of food supplements to help alleviate brain fog and contribute to better mental performance and cognitive function.

I have taken a break from the news for months. I turn off even the news notifications on my smartphone, which has helped.

I suddenly returned to the news this month and limited my intake to once daily. However, hearing lousy news, including about daily road accidents, devastates me, and worrying about the people involved affects my happiness.

I now stay informed in bite-sized portions and take time away from the news as needed. Whether it is horror or uncertainty, consuming news can cause devastating feelings of helplessness and anxiety.

I feel powerless about what is happening in the world, have a passion for change, and am fanatically militant for action. Still, I cannot express it because nobody listens to a preacher who creates a model of a world in his head of visual sensation to ease the terrible, incurable ability of people with uniqueness and potential to do good but instead do harm. Last year, 2023, it was Ukraine and Armenia triggering global contention, and here today, in September 2024, it is Gaza: Only time will tell where the next conflict will erupt. Whether the war will set fire to the entire Middle East or other fires will break out in Asia, there must be ways to oppose the tidal forces of war.

However, people can develop intellect and spiritual skills and maintain free will to improve themselves and achieve divine wisdom. Humanism remains at the level of animals because they resort to their prime behaviour of exploiting and causing armed conflict. Our actions or inaction drive our beliefs, and we should not believe everything we think because the future has not yet happened.

Humans are supposed to have sensitive, rational souls that can reason, but what humans do to each other, other species and our planet is entirely incomprehensible.

My brain has created a reality for me, an afterlife that will be truly real when I stop living in a decaying reality that will vanish one day. Our consciousness reveals truths about aspects of reality and brings forth our thoughts and feelings as just electric discharges in the brain. Still, consciousness is beyond our current scientific or philosophical tools, and the universe with a God is far more complex than we can fully understand. The technogenic science-driven world hints that our brain creates God, and it is the result of neuron activity-producing consciousness that brings forth our thoughts and feelings, which are just electrical discharges in the brain, they say.

I am writing this to empower people to find their answers, reflect on and uncover more profound truths about existence, take loving responsibility for their lives, be compassionate to themselves, and do things that give them joy, comfort, and care for the well-being of others.

We all have a worldview that explains our life and purpose, and what we think and behave in the world shapes our story. Our modern culture gives us a worldview so rooted in false beliefs that shape our understanding and are deeply ingrained in our thinking that it is almost impossible to look at objectively.

This complex culture lives under the influence of the story that we exist in an unintelligent universe made of matter and that humanity come into existence through a random and unlikely process of evolution. For countless centuries, humans have had a tale of us being created by a powerful deity who is the ruler of the universe and whom we must worship and respect. This tale has shaped how society functions and how we perceive the world.

Today's modern tale has deluded us into thinking that our individual lives and actions are insignificant and that our survival is dependent upon competition and the struggle to gain resources at any cost, even at the expense of killing our fellow human beings. It furthers our survival through the confusion and destruction of life by observing beliefs that are not true.

The fundamental belief structures on which our modern worldviews stand must change so that the belief that influences us most defines us as part of the rest of nature, not a separate part of nature. By doing so, it reflects how reality truly is. Our modern culture makes us believe we are separate, individual, isolated beings.

Our internal model of the world gives us different biases towards different groups of people, and so we have ingroups and outgroups that characterise our species in tribes.

We have various opinions. Some groups think they are objective holders of Truth, and there is a single logical argument or position that should convince everyone. They think they know it all. I have found myself in an illusion when people disagree with me because of my level of knowledge and my emotional affiliations with things happening in the world. I try to say I don't know it all; we all have different opinions, and we must be determined to understand the other person's point of view and show intellectual humanity, but ingroup people are suspicious when they see a man with deep melin in his skin and belong to a religious group and have a different way of life base on his neighbourhood, language and the way he looks. Instead of having a dialogue with him and showing empathy, they pick a nasty fight and blame evolutional biology.

Understanding each other's motivation and philosophy improves our understanding of our shared biology and, therefore, our shared humanity.

7A

OVER SIXTY-EIGHT WITH REMISSION OF SCHIZOPHRENIA

Friday, 1 November 2024

Reading my books, you are plunged inside my head to experience my thoughts and feelings, anxiety and mental illness, all of which are open to the reader. However, I have learned that I cannot explain my human experiences in purely physical, material terms. I also had to learn the craft of writing, crafting sentences, and shaping my stories to retain freedom in writing in my authentic voice, but fine-tuning my author's voice was done during the copy-editing process.

I have included some stories with a generous offer to people to reflect on their experience with universal elements, such as love, relationships, ageing, happiness and worry, that we share as human beings. However, I write from personal experience to illustrate something more significant for those incapacitated by shame, insecurities or loss of value.

I hope that my life story helps readers come to a particular understanding of an aspect of their life. They question what has happened in their life and why it matters and continues to matter.

My unheard truth's intense feelings and lifetime opened a different reality when my habitual ego collapsed my usual sense of reality. Still, I was able to adjust to find new existential growth.

Depression, anxiety, fear, doubt and guilt are part of the human condition, but most of my fears were not based on reality. It was what was imagined, and psychologically, I had tormented myself.

Still, the important thing is that I was able to eventually reorganise and develop a new perspective and find opportunities after the despair of the suicide attempt when the darkness of my inner nature had the assumption that the world was gloomed and doomed during a possession state. The experience of being controlled is in *The Memoir of a Schizophrenic* book. Also, episodes of unitive consciousness, which is the experience of being at one with all things, giving rise to a sense of peace or bliss, are all psychopathology, says the psychiatrist, which I also wrote about in my earlier book.

This book's awakening of extrasensory perception is seen as psychosis rather than a psychic opening. Psychiatry makes no primary distinction between spiritual or religious problems and psychosis. Still, the 1994 *Diagnostic and Statistical Manual IV of Mental Disorders* touches on it when social or cultural norms show differences.

Happening to be in remission of schizophrenia, I am coming to terms with the fact that people all over the world, but especially in the

West, do not seem to match themselves to the idea of an intelligent, creative, energy creature to worship and submit to it: God.

Theologians thought a benevolent God was the best explanation for the laws of physics and our evolved consciousness, and Christians forgot that theists of God are metaphors. God is a concept that describes God as somebody. The universe is a big bubble of conscience and has a purpose; it cannot have been an accident or by chance that it exists and evolved just right, precisely in space, and produced life as we know it.

It is improbable that life could have started without a God behind the unity of the universe and nature. People should thank God for our existence and pay homage to it.

I can imagine God praising us for evolving into the perfectly godly servants we are supposed to become. And to live in a utopia with everything and eliminate conflict. We will see technology use atoms and elements in the divinely good in people's brains that envisage paradise and invent an AI creature that neutralises people's wickedness. This is to make us all ultimately lovely, ethical people through and through. Wicked people are also involved in creating AI species to be as nasty as themselves, not realising they are using the bad bits to develop an advanced species that is better equipped to understand human nature and inventing a chip for our brains to have total compatibility.

The future expectation is that an advanced, intelligent AI UFO will land on this planet and be appalled at how our human society treats each other and the Earth. It will alter our destructive chemical reactions as we sleep, with the subtle rays of their advanced consciousness that change the earthly human brain's molecular structure to be in a consistently godly orientation, always to do the right thing.

My mentalism uncovers the profound truth that everything is energy and possesses an opposite, for which we must find a delicate balance. It is not about eradicating one to control the reality in the recesses of our inner world and influence our existence. Harmony is key.

Schizophrenia and psychosis disrupt my perception of creation and my emotions. I suggest a possible quantum basis to explain phenomena like telepathy and intense empathic experiences. Quantum entanglement particles are interconnected regardless of distance, which describes the phenomena, but it lacks empirical evidence and rigorous testing, and quantum mechanics is speculative.

There are different plains of existence where the noises of vibrating energy have a cause and effect. I worked my brain with the artistry of having positive thoughts to retune myself to the rhythmic frequencies of my harmonic thoughts and synchronise my life to the symphony it is today.

The path I so painstakingly laid in search of truths with courage, perseverance, hope, resilience and kindness has dared to breathe life back into Christianity. In this world rigged with the arthritic pain of agnostic and atheistic beliefs, I write to restore Christianity's truth, her soul, to all people, to have their intellect rationally accept God in everything. "For the creator, God will demand it of me." I cannot refrain from writing down what appeared to be clearly understood, yet the argument about God's existence is still raging. I would be accused of withholding the truth from those who seek and deserve it, like depriving an heir of their rightful inheritance.

Eckhart Toler said that we are not our thoughts; they pop into our heads. We are the thinkers of the thoughts. Freedom, the soul and God would have been beyond our experience without a critique of pure reason, faith and rational practicality coming out of thought.

I, too, like those who went before me, must not inflict significant injury on all whose mind perplexity has inevitably deluded them of the knowledge of God as they act from a materialistic, selfish point of view. They do not ever acknowledge the parts of transcendence and have mysticism, where God gave us the possibility of knowing God.

There is some realm beyond our own; what we see is not all there is. My unitive experience shows that consciousness is part of something vastly more significant than ourselves. Our intuition knows we are part of something greater than ourselves, foundational to almost all human history.

Until the arrival of an atheist anomaly in the West, Europe and North America over 150 years ago, everyone believed in God. It was entirely irrational to suppose we could be aware of everything in the cosmos and know about everything. At the superficial level, there are sounds that humans cannot hear, but bats and bears can.

The secular atheist worldview denies believing in God, and the rejection of the metaphysical must involve much hard work in denial of their own telepathic experiences. They have to deny they get the feeling that they can tell when someone is staring at them from behind. They have to deny that they have flashes of insight or mystical experiences that appear to connect them with a consciousness more significant than their own – without taking psychedelics, which give a wonderful sense of connection with something greater than themselves too, it is said. Most people's experience is on a spectrum of spirituality because it is essential in our human endeavours to navigate the terrain of values and purpose that underpin our reality. They must deny that it is real, not just chemical disturbances inside the brain.

It seems their motive for the denial is a self-congratulatory feeling for them that assures the atheist is more intelligent than everyone else. The idea is that secularism makes those people more intelligent than the rest of us. They have rebelled against superstition and religion, including animistic, childish ideas about God. They have seen through all these false beliefs and childish attitudes that children and post-modern people have had. So, they have deluded themselves in dismissing believing in divine sources as mumbo jumbo by their own indoctrinated belief.

Atheists have got it wrong in believing there is no God, and theists have also got it wrong in believing that God is a separate being that created the universe. According to the theory of pantheism, the universe itself is God. It has identified God with the universe but does not give way to divine transcendence. The idea that philosopher Baroo Spinosa first talked about is that the universe itself – everything around us, the totality of reality – is, in fact, God. That makes more sense, the only problem being understanding why the issue of evil and theological determinism exists. It is still better to say, I am panentheistic, which gives us divine eminence – 'all is in God': pan = 'all', en = 'in', theos = 'God'.

Others believe that science is most probably proving them right. Still, psychological studies and cognitive science evidence of the Sacred prove that it takes more mental effort to deny or inhibit the idea of God's existence.

If not suppressed, the ordinary mind allows us to experience that connection with the world, the mystical out of the lump of matter in our brain, and natural consciousness.

It is more probable that the brain permits, transmits or emits to shape our experiences but does not create the experiences.

Modern Western physics challenges many firmly held beliefs about the nature of reality. It is heading towards a total mechanical materialist reality when the inarguable conclusion is that a creator governs the realm of matter and immaterial – mental and spiritual construction.

As life is unpredictable, it is better to be prepared for whatever may happen and be at peace regardless of the circumstances. This is especially true when physics tells us that all matter is more than 99.999% space – emptiness. What appears to be there are atoms, the fundamental chemical and physical substances interacting with its nucleus, which has within itself protons and neutrons with electrons that orbit around the nucleus at incredible speeds.

Scientists speak of 'probability waves', which define where objects appear when observed. Before being observed, particles are just composed of the probability that they may be in a specific location. We are all in the mind of God and are involved with the creation of our reality because the universe seems to be there all the time. So, who or what is the Observer, other than the notion that it is the mind of God or just mathematical formulae that there is nothing there but awareness?

I asked myself the tricky question: is awareness an object? What is it?

I have no idea, but I like to think of it as consciousness because it cannot be separated from me being an entity.

Society may have us think that everything has evolved and that people have evolved from apes, but they have me believing that rather than say Creator God intricately designed us. It is crucial and matters which worldview we hold, whether as creationists, evolutionists, or a bit of both.

The idea that a creator explicitly designed people to have frontal lobe and limbic system to see them with genuine respect, wonder, admiration, and care is helpful. To think in only evolutional terms, we make humans lose respect for each other and lose love, joy and wonder. God is here and has never gone away, but throughout my history, I have found that life needs design, order, and information, which had to come from somewhere and something to put them together. It has become so apparent that the creator God is here, and the worldview misunderstood what natural selection is. They failed to tell us the true biological evolution with a protein factory and a village of chemicals made by our DNA.

8A

AGEING WITH REMISSION SCHIZOPHRENIA

Monday, 30 December 2024

As a geriatrician, I can only find that schizophrenia solely interprets reality abnormally in disordered thinking. However, schizophrenia is a severe mental condition that can cause hallucinations, delusions and overall detachment from the real world. Thank goodness I am not disabled in any of those aspects anymore, except sometimes by cognitive defects when I think confused thoughts and have difficulty concentrating.

A schizophrenia state is essentially when the brain's ability to process reality consistently is damaged. If left unchecked, it can come with psychosis and motor control problems too, with solid dopamine desires.

My progression of schizophrenia into psychosis has become rare. Still, it has accumulated biological damage, social damage and psychological damage, and these days, it has more to do with the cognitive impairment I am battling. However, I am mulling the thought that dementia or Alzheimer's disease may affect the same brain area as schizophrenia, which concerns me.

There are significant worldwide public health concerns about schizophrenia spanning a lifetime.

Historically, it has become widely accepted that older people's mental health needs have not been recognised or supported, and research on the over-sixty-five age group is rare.

I am in the mindset of living past the average life expectancy for human males, although I would like to think of myself as living longer than what fate, time, and biology say. The end will not be the end because quantum information can never cease to exist; it cannot be destroyed. Some of my essences could live on after death. However, our consciousness slips away to prevent the body's microbes and organisms from rapidly digesting it. So, even those who rationally reject the idea of an afterlife will have trouble letting go of the opinion that we cease to exist entirely.

I cannot; it is hard to imagine that these thoughts and feelings can stop being somewhere when they feel so real, and I believe my consciousness shall always continue to produce them. So, believers, your consciousness is an intelligent sustenance energy which keeps the universe awake and lights your sense of self of existence forever. The unbelievers' power falls into a black hole, and they lose it. This is where impaired consciences finally cease to exist. That is how negativity, whatever form it takes, will eventually perish because thoughts and information cannot pass through to the other side of a black hole. Information that falls into a black hole is lost to the outside universe when the black hole evaporates via Hawkins radiation. Quantum mechanics dictates that data cannot be destroyed.

Information is never truly lost but exists in a different part of the Space-Time block and is merely inaccessible from specific points in Space-Time.

Our physical disappearance happens at burial and instantly at cremation, but we have no evidence of when blood stops flowing, the muscles relax and cool, and we die. The consciousness and the soul, whatever that is, slip away to a back door to an afterlife where we do not live in an animal body. Christians and spiritual people bank on it, but who else is coming with us? We can live on after death with the forces of negativity with which we work. The intelligent designer has devised ways to neutralise and naturalise them, and the infinite space you live in is in harmony and peace that has eliminated conflicts.

Our experiences on the Earth have borne witness to our innermost fears, desires, love and happiness. After earthly life, some of us travel in our most secret selves to God, who devised our minds to have thoughts, illusions, simulations, abstract ways, and philosophical, ethical and mathematical observations to see the universe purposefully. Still, we only get to know the part of the story that is forecast in our heads to explore the universe's physicalism and our human machineness performance, which is being revealed to us; the other features we have yet to learn how to begin to touch. So, it already shows that we should accept God's hypothesis.

The mechanistic Western science view is that the universe evolves to give rise to life, which eventually gives rise to consciousness through complicated changes in the arrangement of matter. All we know is that we are aware and can never prove that anything exists 'out there'.

But, the intelligent agent tells us the whole story if we fully immerse ourselves in contemplating the knowledge and symbols in the meaning of the information, grounded in empirical evidence and verifiable expertise founded on theories and methodology. The principles of logical reasoning and critical analysis, combined with an unbiased, rigorous assessment of the information, present a tentative, testable prediction. It is grounded in the existing theoretical framework and is subject to empirical verification.

In essence, it is essential to seek to identify God and explore a potential relationship with 'it', the thing, God, and understand the underlying phenomena. The hypothesis endeavours to affirm or refute predetermined assumptions through systematic testing and validation, aiming to substantiate or discredit these specific theoretical postulates because the belief that God is a basis for pure reasoning and living intelligence is confirmed. It has given rise to pure intelligence, intellectual intuition, self-awareness and humanity by acknowledging God's hypothesis as an alternative law of physics.

The made-up story artist, the absurdity of the atheist who skips the intellectual, visible, competent, scientific evidence, has empty and meaningless as the common sense way to view existence and the role we have in it.

Just like in very early times, when very little was known about science, the Bible has a myth about God forming clay into human form and giving it life. This God, an external separate being, creates and arranges matter very complicatedly to give rise to human consciousness. There is no evidence whatsoever for this idea.

God did not create our common sense like that; people made it up. It is a dangerous absurdity when the hypothesis is a foundational pillar that directs the investigation's analytical pathways. The hypothesis anchors the exploration with grounded expectations based on existing knowledge and comprehensive awareness and adheres to vital principles that deepen our comprehension of the God hypothesis.

I shall eventually die one day and be gone forever; my physical body will stop working and no longer resemble the form it is today. But I will somehow be here in time until it fades, and in other people's memory, until we are all gone forever off the planet. Objectively, we will do everything to gain pleasure and absorb painful experiences in this real world, which is more liked than the virtual reality world of endless fun and unlimited enjoyment.

On the day that I die, as I inevitably shall, it seems that I will inflict significant injury on you (my family and readers) because death lies beyond our experience, which prevents me from writing down what appears to be clear that knowledge of death will die with me. Unless I follow only a particular narrative where there is an experiential void with nothingness, I transition from my subjective state to only memories. Still, my perspective is a fascinating, lucid, transcendent, meaningful, purposeful experience following a specific narrative.

I always exist to myself unless schizophrenia eats away at me. My subjective thread of awareness persists because consciousness is immortal, and death is not a natural end to conscious experience, just an epistemic illusion, not oblivion. Death is not an escape from reality, the extinction of us, as in the end. We are the part of reality that has become aware of its existence and jumps from the last eternal experience of sleep to the first upon awakening in life's place in the universe of consciousness, the nature of reality.

For better or worse, we are genuinely immortal when thinking of death not so much as an end but as the beginning of a new process. I always have this generic subjectivity of being consciousness itself, which has an enduring sense of always having existed, which met with people, conscious beings and creatures before my birth, and shall continue to appear millions of years hence in the future.

Before that fatal end-of-life day comes to me on Earth in God, I trust that in 2027, I will visit the island where I was born, St Kitts. I have spent sixty years of my life without charting the island's developmental changes or lack of them. I trust I will return to the land where my parents, relatives and I lived.

We clock off for a long sleep when the mortal end day comes. The universe will turn over, and I will flip back over its circumference to be something entirely transferred.

Possessing energy strength can only be given to and cannot be recreated in its origin, as it exists forever. So, my life will end, but my energy point will continue forever and meet with the light-hearted consciousness of others in this continuous universe. Technically, the universe is us with a philosophical ego of being like God. Being a person only makes sense when our thoughts are divine information and the words 'I' or 'me' have no meaning.

It is me, or I, who have completely gone; there is only the awareness of existence as my life is continuous and as energy separate from being in a body. Things exist, but this new world, the world of immortal creatures, is a very different advanced civilisation. Nouns and fragments of speech have helped us understand the mechanical, materialistic world that will vanish one day. I shall leave Earth on my mortal death and have my ashes scattered on or buried in its soil.

I have shared my thoughts with you and told you some of my stories, which makes readers think harder and is thought-provoking because the accounts provide mental stimulation. I hope you have got something out of it, whether insightful, entertaining, educational, tips or something to think about that gives you the key to the kingdom that resonates with you.

May these writings promote learning and expose you to my lived experiences, new concepts, and facts open to further interpretation. Thank you for following my story. Goodbye.

Farewell, bye-bye now, and try to enjoy your journey here on Earth. Take good care of yourself and be good; I send you all my kindest regards, sincerity, and blessings. Last but by no means least, I want to give everyone much love and a virtual hug.

ABOUT THE AUTHOR

Karl Lorenz Willett has been journaling his life's pivotal stories since 1982, which he likens to a collection of memoirs. He has published two revised and professionally edited books. He studied mechanical engineering at Tresham College (formerly Wellingborough Technical College).

He began writing his autobiography for himself and his family to leave a legacy after obsessing over his inability to create original fictional characters for a novel. He decided that the story he could tell best would be his own authentic, genuine, accurately portrayed, non-fictional experiences.

The varied stories show he has deeply driven, ethical, God-centred beliefs. He exhibits kindness and compassion and is an empathetic, sensitive soul.

He says, "The tales may help other people, but I could foresee it will be a teaching tool for me to learn life lessons and how to live well with a chronic illness. It was challenging because of the hard way I understand well, by trials and errors, and it has been a lovely feeling to hold my words on paper in a book."

The basic concept is that his mental illness is only one aspect of his life, not the defining characteristic. He has an attitude to helping others and caring for all creatures and the planet.

Karl Lorenz Willett was born in St. Kitts and raised in England. He lives in Kettering and has been happily married to his soulmate, Euphemia, for forty-four years. They raised two grown daughters and a son and have five adorable grandchildren.

www.ingramcontent.com/pod-product-compliance
Lightning Source LLC
Chambersburg PA
CBHW021952160426
43209CB00001B/17